KNOW YOUR ENEMY ★ ★ ★

RAGE AGAINST *the* MACHINE

This book is dedicated to Sir Patrick Moore. He was a man of diametrically opposed views to many of those expressed in this book, but he too raged against the machine, in his own way.

KNOW YOUR ENEMY ★★★

RAGE AGAINST the MACHINE

Joel McIver

OMNIBUS PRESS

London / New York / Paris / Sydney / Copenhagen / Berlin / Madrid / Tokyo

Copyright © 2014 Omnibus Press
(A Division of Music Sales Limited)

Cover designed by Fresh Lemon
Picture research by Jacqui Black

ISBN: 978.1.78305.046.8
Order No: OP55363

The Author hereby asserts his right to be identified as the author of this work in accordance with Sections 77 to 78 of the Copyright, Designs and Patents Act 1988.

All rights reserved. No part of this book may be reproduced in any form or by any electronic or mechanical means, including information storage or retrieval systems, without permission in writing from the publisher, except by a reviewer who may quote brief passages.

Exclusive Distributors
Music Sales Limited
14/15 Berners Street,
London, W1T 3LJ.

Music Sales Corporation
180 Madison Avenue, 24th Floor,
New York,
NY 10016,
USA.

Macmillan Distribution Services
56 Parkwest Drive,
Derrimut, Vic 3030,
Australia.

Every effort has been made to trace the copyright holders of the photographs in this book but one or two were unreachable. We would be grateful if the photographers concerned would contact us.

Typeset by Phoenix Photosetting, Chatham, Kent
Printed in the EU

A catalogue record for this book is available from the British Library.

Visit Omnibus Press on the web at **www.omnibuspress.com**

Contents

Introduction		vii
Acknowledgments		xi
Chapter 1	Before 1991	1
Bombtrack 1	Wage Slavery: Is There An Alternative?	25
Chapter 2	1991–1992	39
Chapter 3	1992–1993	59
Chapter 4	1994–1996	77
Bombtrack 2	Mexican Freedom: The Zapatistas And The EZLA	84
Chapter 5	1996–1998	98
Chapter 6	1999–2000	114
Chapter 7	2000–2002	136
Bombtrack 3	Music And Protest: Who Cares?	155
Chapter 8	2002–2006	162
Chapter 9	2007–2009	178
Chapter 10	2009 to date	194
Bombtrack 4	The X Factor: David And Goliath	211
Discography		225
Sources		231
Index		235

Introduction

Tom Morello, Rage Against The Machine: One of the unquestionable ideas that we're force-fed from our first days in school is that we live in a democracy. In your opinion, in what sense is our society democratic?
Noam Chomsky: Democracy has lots of different dimensions. I mean, basically the question is to what extent do the people have a meaningful way of developing and articulating their own ideas and putting them forward in the political arena and controlling decisions. That's the general question. Now if you look at the United States, well, in some respects that's true but in many respects it just isn't true at all... in the political arena, first of all there is one huge segment of social and economic life which is simply excluded from public control, in law and in principle, and it's the most important part. It has to do with what's produced and how it's distributed, and so on and so forth. That's all in the hands of what amount to huge private tyrannies, of which are about as totalitarian in character as any institutions that humans have so far concocted. Mostly their only accountability to the public is through quite limited regulatory mechanisms – I mean the whole corporate system. And they have extraordinary power over not only what happens in the workplace but the nature of our lives, and, given

their resources, over the political system. And you can't say that they control the media, because they *are* the media.
(Radio Free Los Angeles transcript, 1996)

This biography of Rage Against The Machine, the American rock band, is not for everyone. This is a mature book.

By this I mean that I want you, the reader, to take a balanced, informed view, as free as you can possibly make it, of the greater and lesser causes that Rage discuss in their songs. A lot of people regard the band as prophets. A similar number of people think of them as naive, hippie, undeveloped musicians who criticise the world's major political and social issues from the safety of their First World homes, without engaging or even understanding the subjects they address. Who is right? No-one is right. What you think is right, is right. My job, by writing this biography, is to provide a view that takes in as many sides as possible, allowing you to reach a conclusion which is truly yours.

Let's backtrack a bit.

I came up with the idea of a Rage Against The Machine book a few years ago, when the band were in the middle of what looked like a permanent hiatus. Back then the current fad for classic rock and metal reunions hadn't taken off and Rage's career resembled that of the Sex Pistols or Nirvana – a short, vivid few years at the top, with big songs, big protests and a sudden ending. In those first few years of activity, the four musicians – singer Zack de la Rocha, guitarist Tom Morello, bassist Tim Commerford and drummer Brad Wilk – had directed a continuous stream of invective towards many of society's ills. Their targets included big and small injustices, counterbalancing amorphous but gigantic themes (try the entire structure of American democracy and capitalism for size) with relatively small causes (imprisoned, but possibly innocent men such as Leonard Peltier and Mumia Abu-Jamal). This was no ordinary band. Ordinary bands aren't brave, or stupid, enough to try and change the world.

So a book about Rage Against The Machine looked like an interesting project, I thought. But the years passed and I found

Introduction

myself wondering how to approach these massive subjects – subjects which raise questions to which I don't have an answer. I don't know if Peltier and Abu-Jamal are innocent, although I suspect there is a strong chance that they are. I don't know if rampant late capitalism is entirely a bad thing, although I'm fairly sure that the truth lies somewhere in the 'maybe it is, maybe it isn't' zone.

In truth, my personal views about many of the things addressed by Rage Against The Machine and explored in this book lie somewhere in the middle, or perhaps a bit left of centre, where my own politics are. That makes me a good critic of Rage's work. I'm neither pro nor anti, and only mildly more left than I am right, and thus I'm in a position to try and cast the cold light of reason on the subjects they address.

That's the theory, anyway. I'm no political scientist or economist, so to explore these topics in the detail which they deserve, I've drafted in some of the world's most educated thinkers to help me create this book. Between the chapters dealing with Rage Against The Machine's history, you'll find interviews with academics, authors and cultural observers, whose research into the political and social issues in Rage's music gives the learned edge which I'm looking for. These people know what they're talking about, from the college professor to the winner of the *X Factor* TV show.

Let's not forget that is supposed to be fun. Rage are a protest band, but they're also a massively entertaining live act, a band whose music will make you get up and punch the air no matter what you think of their lyrics. They're human, too, with all the failings that implies. Where they've said something which I think is pretentious, I've said so. The band are all too aware that they are regarded as humourless: in the words of Brad Wilk, "We don't wake up in the morning and rage against the milk carton because we can't get it open." That's the tone I'm looking for. Serious, but not earnest. Intellectual, but not smug. Driven, but not inhuman.

A word about the band and this book. I got to know Tom Morello, who is effectively Rage's spokesperson and prime point of contact, a little when he provided a quote for a book I wrote a few years ago.

When Omnibus Press asked me to write this biography, I emailed Tom and asked if the band would care to be involved. His answer on January 14, 2013, which you can see below, was a polite (and as I read it, slightly regretful) refusal, which nevertheless gave me his blessing to go ahead and write the book without his involvement. What a gentleman.

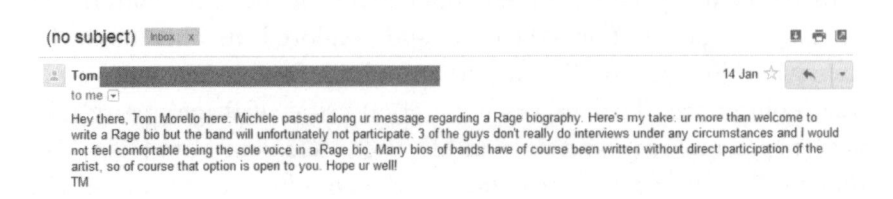

> (no subject) Inbox x
>
> Tom   14 Jan
> to me
>
> Hey there, Tom Morello here. Michele passed along ur message regarding a Rage biography. Here's my take: ur more than welcome to write a Rage bio but the band will unfortunately not participate. 3 of the guys don't really do interviews under any circumstances and I would not feel comfortable being the sole voice in a Rage bio. Many bios of bands have of course been written without direct participation of the artist, so of course that option is open to you. Hope ur well!
> TM

So now you know the shape of the book to follow. It will be energetic, critical and not easily accepting of received wisdom – rather (I hope) like the band themselves.

What better way to kick things off than with the words of the late, and much missed, rock writer Steven Wells, who wrote in the *NME* on May 28, 1994: "It's all too easy to sneer at the pretensions of radical rock: but what other art-form could persuade so many white suburban Yank kids (of the terminally 'slack' generation) to don American Indian Movement T-shirts and for some of them – who knows – actually to give a shit?"

Acknowledgments

Emma, Alice, Tom, Robin and Kate, Dad, John and Jen, Carlos Anaia, David Barraclough, Scott Bartlett, Jacqui Black, Matt Cardle, Max and Gloria Cavalera, Chris Charlesworth, Dave Clarke, Ben Cooper, Joe Daly, Helen Donlon, John Doran, Jason Draper, Mark Eglinton, David Ellefson, Ciaran Fahy, Lisa Gallagher, Brian Grillo, Michael Haas, Matthew Hamilton, Charlie Harris, Bill Irwin, Michelle Kerr, Alex Khasnabish, Jon Knox, Tina Korhonen, Borivoj Krgin, Dorian Lynskey, Rachel Mann, Patrizia Mazzuocolo, Alex Milas, Eugenio Monti, Tom Morello, Jon Morter, Bob Nalbandian, Martin Popoff, Elliott Rubinson, Ralph Santolla, Pamela Satterwhite, Jonathan Selzer, Lisbeth Sluiter, Kirsten Sprinks, Wes Stanton, Dan Travis, David Vincent, Jeremy Wagner, Sue Walder-Davis, Mick Wall, Alex Webster, Chris Williams, the staff of *Bass Guitar Magazine*, Downley FC and the families Alderman, Arnold, Bhardwaj, Bowles, Cadette, Dixon, Edwards, Fraser, Freed, Harrington, Herbert, Hogben, Jolliffe, Knight, Lamond, Lamont, Legerton, Leim, Mathieson-Spires, Mendonça, Metcalfe, Miles, Parr, Storey and Woollard, the many fine writers who have reviewed my books in recent years, and of course the visitors to www.joelmciver.co.uk and www.facebook.com/joelmciver.

CHAPTER 1

Before 1991

So many apparently random strands of activity lead to the formation of what is without a doubt the most politically outspoken rock band ever formed that it's impossible to say which came first; the convictions, the life experiences or the music. Rage Against The Machine earned their right to speak out in anger, that's for sure, although the dynamic of the band – vocalist Zack de la Rocha and guitarist Tom Morello the more expressive members, bassist Tim Commerford and drummer Brad Wilk the quiet supporters – appears to have been firmly in place long before any of them were actually playing music.

Morello was born first, in Harlem, New York, on May 30, 1964, making him four years older than Commerford (February 26, 1968; Irvine, California) and Wilk (September 5, 1968; Portland, Oregon) and the veritable old man of the band compared to de la Rocha (January 12, 1970; Long Beach, California). A lot is known about the childhoods of Morello and de la Rocha, comparatively speaking, largely because the two men have talked at length about their family lives and also, it turns out, because their heritage makes them uniquely predisposed to a career in political commentary, if not politics itself. Less information is available about Commerford and Wilk, whose reluctance to do much press became all-encompassing after a few years in the public eye and who have always been happy, indeed obliged, to leave most of the talking to their more voluble bandmates.

We do have snippets of information about Commerford and Wilk to go on. The former describes himself as a 'rough kid', explaining that Halloween was an annual opportunity for him to wreak some havoc in his hometown. "I was a mean-hearted, sort of jerk kid," he sighed. "I was into my clique of people and we would torment all the other children. My Halloweens were filled with tormenting trick-or-treaters, you know, and looking for other kids who were dressed up."

Despite this, Commerford came from an educated, academic family. His father, Gerard, was an aerospace engineer and manager who began his career working on the X-15 rocket-propelled experimental plane that reached space in the sixties. He later worked on the Space Shuttle programme, playing an important role in the vehicle's Return-To-Flight project in 1988 (the Shuttle's first deployment since the *Challenger* disaster of 1986). Among his professional awards, Gerard won the 1976 Gas Turbine Award for the Most Outstanding Technical Paper. His wife, the mother of Tim and his five siblings, died of cancer in 1988; Gerard himself lived until 2012.

As for Wilk, he seems to have been more of a spiritual kid, explaining later that numerology held a lifelong fascination for him. "Ever since I was eight or nine I've gravitated to the number three," he ruminated. "It's something that has always been a really heavy number for me. It's tattooed on my arm, and I count in threes. Everyone in school was taught two, four, six, eight, 10: I'd count in threes in the way I'd walk, even in the decisions I'd make. It was all based on threes."

Unlike their future bandmates, Morello and de la Rocha were steeped in political struggle from birth. Both men experienced racism in their childhoods, and both were involved in reaction towards that prejudice because of the activism of their families. These are complex, sad stories in many ways, but they hold the key to almost all of the passion and venom that suffused the work of Rage Against The Machine in later years, and as such, worth examining closely.

Let's start with Tom Morello. Although he was born in multicultural New York, he was raised by his mother, Mary Morello, who was of Irish and Sicilian descent, in the town of Libertyville in Illinois, her home state. Culturally and literally a great distance from Harlem, Libertyville – a largely Caucasian town – made the young Morello acutely aware that his ethnic makeup was different. Mary, an English teacher, had met Tom's father Stephen Ngethe Njoroge during a three-year stay in his native country of Kenya, where he later became the first ambassador from Kenya to the United Nations. Njoroge had participated in the Mau Mau uprising in the fifties, although in what capacity and to what extent is not widely known, and his uncle Jomo Kenyatta was Kenya's first elected president, having been voted into office in 1964. Mary and Njoroge met at a pro-democracy rally in Nairobi, formed a relationship and returned to New York together before their son was born.

Morello later looked back on his family's extraordinary history, saying: "My mom trekked. What gave her wanderlust, I don't know. She grew up in a town smaller and whiter than Libertyville called Marseilles, a coal mining town in central Illinois. It's spelled like Marseilles, France, but pronounced 'Marsales'. In her twenties, she just decided that she would, by herself, go around the world. She lived in China, in post-World War II Germany, Japan. Just everywhere. She was teaching in Kenya during the Mau Mau insurrection. She immediately abandoned all of her fellow white schoolteachers. She met my dad there, and was there for Kenya's independence. They moved back to the States. My dad was part of Kenya's first UN delegation, and that's why I was born in New York City. They divorced, he moved back to Kenya, and she moved back to Illinois."

In effect, Tom Morello was born into a family embedded in African politics, although Njoroge returned to Kenya when his son was 16 months old, leaving Mary to raise Tom as a single parent. Reports indicate that she is made of stern stuff, however, working as an activist for many causes as her son grew and teaching American history at Libertyville High School, which Tom attended.

Morello recalled later: "I integrated the town. It is an entirely white conservative northern suburb of Chicago, and I was the first person of colour to reside in the town. My mom and I moved there in 1965. She was applying to be a public high school teacher in communities around the northern suburbs. In more than one of them, they said, 'You can work here, but your family cannot live here'. They were explicit about it. I was a one-year-old half-Kenyan kid, and they told my mom, 'You're an interracial family so you can live in the ghetto in Waukegan, or go to North Chicago or somewhere like that'. Libertyville was the first community that allowed us to court real estate agents to find an apartment. And even then, the real estate agent had to go door to door in the apartment complex where we rented to see if it was OK with people."

Little wonder Morello grew impassioned on the subject of race relations, or lack of them, as he matured. Other causes captured his attention, too: the war in Vietnam, which ended in his pre-teens, was a contemporary issue for him. "I had always been mildly opposed to the Vietnam War – I mean, I was a 15-year-old in Libertyville, Illinois, give me a fucking break, yeah?" he told the *NME*. "I always thought the war was wrong, and then I read this book about the Weathermen [radicals who took their name from Bob Dylan's 'Subterranean Homesick Blues'] and I realised that the war was right, but it was the Vietnamese fighting the USA who were right. It was such a revelation that there were people in the United States who thought that way, that they were carrying Viet Cong flags to the demonstrations."

So here was Tom Morello circa 1975, struggling along through life in hick-town Illinois. In Long Beach, California, a kid named Zacharias Manuel de la Rocha was living between two households, as his parents had also split when he was young. His Mexican-American father, an artist called Roberto de la Rocha, was famous in the Chicano (a synonym for Mexican-American) community, creating huge canvases and exhibiting them locally and further afield. Beto, as he was known, was a member of Los Four, a Chicano art collective. Later in life, Zack was able to contextualise Beto's work, saying: "Back in 1974, my father's paintings were part of the first Chicano art exhibit ever organised at the LA County Museum Of Art. That exhibit was something to be proud of. I want to make music that gives people that same sense of identity and lets them see that human rights, civil rights and spiritual rights are all part of the same struggle we all face to take the power back. It's important to let people know not to lose that knowledge of self, to lose that knowledge of culture, but not to the point of separatism."

Of course, as a kid de la Rocha Junior had no frame of reference and no way of understanding what his father's work represented in a wider context. From what he has told the media, his upbringing was unusual in many ways, with its more eccentric facets leading directly to his own activism. "Living with Beto helped me to see a lot of things that I normally wouldn't see, if I had grown up in a perfect family," he said. "He read Mao, did a series of paintings for United Farm Workers and always had some incredible answers to all my questions. I also think that my upbringing as a Chicano in a white suburban environment had a lot of effect on my awareness... My parents separated when I was a year old, and I constantly moved back and forth between them and to very different neighbourhoods. From the poor East LA where my father lived and to the college in the rich Orange County where my mother lived, where Chicanos like me normally only would be if they had a broom in their hand or filling baskets with strawberries, there were some large oppositions, that I had to realise and learn to handle, and have probably founded my opinions today."

De la Rocha's weekends with his father were occasionally of a grim nature. Mentally unstable since a nervous breakdown in 1981, Beto would spend periods of time fasting and reading the Bible while pulling the house curtains and maintaining a religious darkness. Sometimes his son was forced to fast alongside him, a potentially traumatic experience for a kid barely out of childhood.

"I'd spend three weekends out of the month at my father's house, eat on Friday night and not eat again until Monday morning when I'd get back to my mother," he recalled. "I was so young at the time that I didn't really question it too much. I love my father dearly, and didn't understand the level of abuse that was happening. I'm not sure that he did, either."

The writer RJ Smith of *Spin* magazine interviewed father and son in 1996 for the most in-depth portrait of the de la Rochas which has yet been attempted, and discovered that Beto also obliged his son to participate in the mass destruction of his (Beto's) artwork. "During one visit," wrote Smith, "Zack pointed to a painting on the wall and asked, 'Daddy, can I have that?' 'Hey, that's mine,' Beto snapped. And then, flushed with guilt for denying his son, Beto began pulling down all his artwork – paintings, prints, drawings – and shredding them all. The frames he smashed. Then he took his paint and brushes and hurled them into a trash can that he set on fire. 'He burned over 60 percent of his artwork,' says Zack. The art that had given Zack a sense of identity was going up in flames. 'It was very, very, very difficult, and at one point he forced me to burn it for him. These were paintings that I grew up around and loved and admired him for creating. I had no clue why he'd want to destroy them... I worry about what that experience did to me, how it affected my way of thinking. I think it affected me in good ways too, because I feel like at this point, what could anyone possibly do to me that could hurt me more?'"

When Smith asked Beto about his earlier treatment of his son, the old man told him, "I took [the Bible] too literally... It says, 'Make no image'. I was an image maker and so I said, 'Okay, I quit'. I quit being an artist and destroyed my work. Which was good, because I was being so possessive." Of the fasting, he acknowledged that Zack "was too young for that", but also "I don't regret it. It's a learning experience."

Like Morello, slogging it out in Libertyville, Illinois, de la Rocha was keenly aware of the deep-rooted prejudices of his surroundings. Living in Irvine, California, which he later described as "one of the most racist cities imaginable", he was alienated further by an incident in a school geology class, when a teacher referred to a California border checkpoint as "the wetback station", with the term referring to illegal Mexican immigrants who supposedly swim across rivers to evade detection at the border. "I remember it like it was yesterday," he said. "I remember being very silent and feeling as if I could do nothing to raise my voice. At that point, I decided that when I started a band, I would never be silent again."

Music was also an obvious outlet for Morello, who discovered heavy rock in his teens. He has referred to singing in a Led Zeppelin cover band at 13, which would have been in 1977, just as punk broke. The band, Nebula, featured Morello on vocals, he later said, "because my voice hadn't changed to the rich baritone you hear now. And I was able to squeak out the Robert Plant wails on 'Heartbreaker'... I had a seventies full-on JJ Walker afro, the brown lift shoes and Italian horn necklace, the John Travolta satin shirt open to the navel."

"His bedroom door was always open,'" Morello's mother later recalled of her son, "and when he listened to anything – Black Sabbath, Alice Cooper – he'd always call me in to listen. And I listened. Twice I took him to Alice Cooper concerts."

The sheer over-the-topness of heavy music attracted Morello, he recalled. "I was a big fan of heavy metal music, which involved extravagance. You had to have huge walls of Marshall amplifiers and expensive shiny Gibson Les Paul guitars. You had to know how to play 'Stairway To Heaven' and have a castle on a Scottish loch, limos, groupies, and things like that. All I had was a basement in Illinois. None of that was going to come together for me." Punk rock was the catalyst that transformed him from passive listener to active participant, he added, because the music was so much easier to play: "When I heard the Sex Pistols and The Clash and Devo, it was immediately attainable. I thought, this music is as good as anything I have ever heard, but I can play it this afternoon. I got the Sex Pistols record [*Never Mind The Bollocks... Here's The Sex Pistols*], and within 24 hours I was in a band."

Talking to MTV, Morello added: "I was very influenced to pick up the guitar by people like Jimmy Page, and Ace Frehley of Kiss... They were the posters I had on my bedroom wall that made me dream of one day being in a rock and roll band. But it was really the punk rock revolution that made me pick up the instrument [because I] was very inspired by the fact that it was tremendously powerful music but it was made by people with limited technical abilities... This made great music seem to be within my grasp, and I immediately formed a band before I even knew how to play any chords on the guitar."

Unusually for a musician who went on to scale great heights, Morello didn't get started on the guitar until he was 17, which would have been 1981. By then punk's first wave had effectively been and gone, leaving punk-influenced acts such as Devo in its wake, and making space for a new movement of heavy metal guitar heroes, focused on technique as much as melody. One of these was Morello's lifelong idol Randy Rhoads, guitarist on sometime Black Sabbath singer Ozzy Osbourne's first two solo albums. Although Randy was killed in a plane crash in March 1982, he made a huge impact on the metal scene with his playing, which was heavily indebted to the pioneering style of Eddie Van Halen but which was also based on solid virtuoso principles. Rhoads had his own voice on the instrument, a fact which Morello noted, as well as a superb, highly evolved neoclassical style which suited Ozzy's anthemic tunes perfectly.

Asked when he had first heard Rhoads' guitar playing, Morello replied: "I remember the exact moment. I was packed in the back of somebody's mom's hatchback in Libertyville. The radio was turned to The Loop in Chicago, and this song called 'Crazy Train' by Ozzy Osbourne came on. The other people in the car were more New Wave fans, and they were talking over it, but suddenly I was yelling, 'Everybody, shut up! What is that?' This blistering riff came at me, followed by an incredible solo, and of course, there was Ozzy – I recognised his voice as the guy from Black Sabbath – and by the end of it, I was like, 'What just happened?' There was no 'interweb' at the time, so I had to wait for the next *Circus* magazine to explain to me what it was. And then I ran out and bought the *Blizzard Of Ozz* cassette. I had already started playing, but it was right around the same time. I was a big fan of punk rock and the whole do-it-yourself ethic, so for a guitar player to come along and rekindle the spirit and reset the bar for hard rock guitar players was a pretty big deal."

Fans of Rage Against The Machine may not immediately grasp the similarities between Morello's taut, staccato guitar style and Randy Rhoads' flamboyant theatrics, and indeed Morello acknowledged this, saying: "Now, you might not hear Randy's influence in the cow and duck noises that I sometimes make with the guitar, but what got me to that point was being serious about the instrument... I was never a big fan of the whole 'party-hard-we're-gonna-rock-harder' world. I liked music. But I could see myself in Randy, how he was a real student of music. The fact that he practised for hours on end really appealed to me. He was serious, and he wanted only to get better at his craft. When I was practising eight hours a day, his was the poster I had on my wall... I remember buying [Ozzy's second album] *Diary Of A Madman* when it came out, and somebody at the record store was making fun of me because of the album cover. I had to explain to this person that, while I certainly liked Ozzy, I was really a big Randy Rhoads fan – that's why I was buying the record. It was like, 'Well, the guitar player doesn't have raspberry jelly coming out of his mouth...' Randy was serious, you know?"

Having taken up the guitar in earnest, Morello formed a band at Libertyville High School with a friend, Adam Jones, who later became famous in the alternative rock band Tool. Their group didn't go anywhere outside of Morello's garage and a handful of gigs that included a school talent show: Electric Sheep (apparently not named after Philip K. Dick's 1968 sci-fi novel, *Do Androids Dream Of Electric Sheep?*) recorded a version of Steppenwolf's 'Born To Be Wild' which appeared on a soundtrack album issued by the school under the title *All Shook Up*.

Electric Sheep were not meant to be taken seriously by any means. Featuring Jones on bass, Morello showing off his rudimentary skills as a guitarist, singer Chris George (and Geoff Johnson in George's occasional absence), keyboardist Randy Cotton and drummer Ward Wilson, the group veered from heavy metal to punk and back again depending on definitions, and fizzled out after 1983. Along the way the band managed to soundtrack a primitive horror film written by Jones and Morello, called *Season Of The Snow Bitch*.

Their final, and probably finest, hour was a pseudo-documentary film called *The Electric Sheep Video* that included footage from 'The Electric Sheep Farewell Tour Of The Americas', a gig in the Mundelein Cinema in Mundelein, Illinois. During the group's tenure, the only real hint that deeper things were to come, musically, was a song by Morello called 'Salvador Death Squad Blues': Electric Sheep's greatest claim to fame came in 2007 when Tool singer Maynard James Keenan recorded a version of their song 'My Country Boner' (renamed 'Cuntry Boner') in a mock-country style.

Looking back on Electric Sheep, Morello recalled: "Adam wasn't in the original line-up. There was this one guy who was sort of the principal player in the band – he was the only one in the group with any working knowledge of music – but he quit because he thought that he was far above us. Adam was his replacement." Jones added: "I was just so excited to officially be in a band. Of course, I had to borrow a bass because I didn't have one of my own... I played stand-up bass in the orchestra and I'd play bass with my brother, too. He'd play the guitar parts, and I'd play all the bass parts to Police songs or Fleetwood Mac or Chicago or whatever he was into at the time." Morello summed the group up as "the bad boys of Midwestern punk", presumably in good humour, while Jones described Electric Sheep as "a terrible band, but great to see."

By the mid-eighties, Zack de la Rocha had become a fan of hardcore punk, and of the band Minor Threat in particular. A skater kid and a vegetarian from his early teens (as he put it, "An animal goes through a lot of pain in the whole cycle of death in the slaughterhouse; just living to be killed... I just don't think it's worth eating that animal. There's so much other food out there that doesn't have to involve you in that cycle of pain and death"), he had found a position somewhat outside that of the other teenagers he knew. That position was consolidated by his friendship with Tim Commerford, a fellow punk fan, who he had first met in elementary school.

Of de la Rocha, Commerford later recalled: "We played a lot of basketball, even though he was real small: we skateboarded all over. When I first met him at his house, he had this acoustic guitar, and he eventually taught me how to play the entire Sex Pistols album. He was breakin' [breakdancing] at school when nobody else knew what hip-hop was. That kid was on it from day one." He added that his youth, disrupted by the premature death of his mother from cancer, had been unconventional: "I had no traditional upbringing of any sort. Zack is one of the few people still in my life who knew my mom and who can talk to me about that time."

In junior high, de la Rocha and Commerford played guitar in a band known as Juvenile Expression, about whom little is known: there's much more available data about his next group, Hardstance, in particular when the band changed its name to Inside Out in 1988 and became something of a legendary act among fans of American hardcore.

Right from the beginning, de la Rocha engaged fully with Inside Out. He later described the band as "about completely detaching ourselves from society to see ourselves as spirits, and not bowing down to a system that sees you as just another pebble on a beach. I channelled all my anger out through that band." The other members came and went, but stalwarts among them included bassist Mark Hayworth (also of Gorilla Biscuits), sometime Wool drummer Chris Bratton and guitarist Vic DiCara, who has kindly agreed to give an interview for this book.

DiCara recalls how he met de la Rocha. "I moved to South California, and some people from a band called me and said they wanted to do a band with me," he says. "I went and jammed with them. Nothing ever happened – but some of those guys were in the prototype stage of a band called Inside Out. They got the idea that I would be perfect for that band. So I went to a friend's house one day, with my guitar and amp. And Zack was already there waiting for me, as far as I remember. He was jamming out with Alex the drummer. When I got there they showed me a few of their songs, I picked them up right away, and we enjoyed playing together so much that we were leaping around the room, thrashing away. It was obviously a really good chemistry right from the beginning."

In their three-year existence, Inside Out released a sole recording – a 7" EP called *No Spiritual Surrender*, released by the Revelation label and reissued on CD some years later – and toured several times, playing on the West and East coasts of America. When it came to songwriting, recalls DiCara, "Zack and I were 50/50 writers. Some songs he would write the music and lyrics; some songs I would write the music and lyrics. On some he would write the music and I would write the lyrics, on others I would write the music and he would write the lyrics. We worked well together. It was easy. One of the pre-existing song ideas they had from before I came in was the opening riff for 'Burning Fight', which is very thoroughly inspired from a riff on 'Rock For Light' by the Bad Brains. I helped them lay the whole song out, and changed the character of some of the parts by changing minor things like the picking and stuff."

The song 'No Spiritual Surrender' came from classic sources despite its defiant punk stance, the guitarist reveals. "I am pretty sure it was our first rehearsal together when Zack said to me, 'I want to write a song called 'No Spiritual Surrender'. I thought that was the cat's meow. Anything with 'spiritual' in it revved my engine pretty hot. So I went home, and put on Led Zeppelin's song 'When The Levee Breaks'. I used that groove and played along till 'No Spiritual Surrender' came out. Then I just opened up my mouth to sing along with the riffs, and the cadence of how the lyrics should go came flying out, so I took it up to my room with pen and paper and wrote lyrics to fit the cadence." Other songs on the EP were assembled by either man, de la Rocha coming up with 'Sacrifice' and 'Redemption' and DiCara composing 'By A Thread'.

"We had a lot of songs besides what we recorded that were really good," continues DiCara. "I like how Zack would play an acoustic guitar to write these things, and the way he strummed it was really, really talented – it was like there was a whole drum set inside the guitar. I think he is a much better player than the guitar player of Rage Against The Machine. People who aren't good guitar players might not have any idea how anyone can say that, [but] Zack was just a really good artist. That always makes better musicians, on any instrument, than people who just specialise in playing an instrument without having that much general artistic talent."

DiCara remembers day-to-day life in Inside Out with pleasure, explaining: "Practising in the drummer's bedroom in Riverside, California [and] jumping around with energy like it was a full-on show: that was really where it was at. We would do that a few times a week. Then we would play shows a few times a month. The whole thing was great. Very few people get to experience music on such a genuine level as what was going on there, not just in our band, but in the whole hardcore punk scene at the time. There was something special and real about what we were doing. I was as much a spectator of the band as I was a member. I could really appreciate that it was something special – something where the sum of the parts is much, much less than the whole thing coming together. The whole was just a wild amplification of each member's talent and contribution."

Asked about the musicians' respective roles when it came to directing the band outside the basic songwriting and performing, DiCara remembers: "Me and Zack were doing 40/40, you might say, writing music and lyrics. Shows were abundant in those days. Nobody had to exert effort to organise them. We were kids: playing shows was like hanging out. There was no need for management or any of that corporate stuff. The drummers in Inside Out always played an abnormally important role, relative to what a drummer typically or stereotypically does, so the remaining 20 percent of direction was coming from the drummer, either Alex Baretto or Chris Bratton. I think I was doing a significant amount of the artistic stuff, logos and artwork and flyers."

Of the Inside Out members, de la Rocha went on to the highest-profile career. Was DiCara surprised when this happened, I ask? This is perhaps the wrong question. "People have the wrong idea," he says. "They think that you become a 'big' musician or a popular musican because you are talented or special. It's not that way. It's merely destiny. Certain people have the karma to be recognised to certain extents, others don't. Talent is secondary. Very untalented people become very popular, and very talented people very often remain unknown. Zack happens to be a very talented man who also became very popular, especially for a while there. The hardcore punk scene in the early nineties and late eighties was full of artistic genius. Well OK, that might be wishful hindsight – there was a lot of really bad shit, terrible, no-talent stuff. But it's not like Zack was the only artistic genius. There were maybe a half dozen or more. And all of them went on to some degree of recognition – well almost all, to some significant degree, but none as far as Zack."

He continues: "There was no sign that Zack was super special, because so many people were super special. It was actually after I left the band, and [saw] how he took the whole thing on his own shoulders and then had the initiative to get Rage going, that's what the real sign was. He had initiative. Of course he would be politically active. He could have also been spiritually active, but I used up all that energy and ran that direction. He was more tuned in to the temporal, practical, literal world and its needs. When I met him he had Gandhi and Martin Luther tattooed on him. Ha! A guy like that is not going to wind up in Mötley Crüe..."

DiCara, one of whose specialties is the interpretation of Vedic spirituality, looks back with honesty at the demise of Inside Out: "I was and am heavily, heavily into Krishna. I wound up pushing the band too far in that direction. So it became uncomfortable for Zack, who was comfortable enough with Krishna to welcome and vibe off a good amount of it, but not the amount I was trying to bring in. I mean I was trying to bring it the whole way, and kind of eclipse the political slant. So this caused a difference of opinion between us and I wound up moving to a different band that did facilitate me going 100% over the top with Krishna. When I did that, Zack gave a few months to carrying the whole band on his shoulders, and then decided to just give it up and start something new to incarnate the later ideas we had begun to come up with. He was really impressed by a hip-hop concert he went to – I'm pretty sure it was Run-DMC – and wanted to bring hip-hop into Inside Out, and we had just started throwing that idea around when I split for the temple."

With Inside Out on permanent hiatus after DiCara's departure, and inspired to look for new sounds, the now 21-year-old de la Rocha considered his options. The band had planned to release an album named after one of their songs, but it was not to be: the song's title was 'Rage Against The Machine'.

Meanwhile, Tom Morello had not been idle: far from it. After exercising various expressive skills throughout the early eighties – acting and drawing among them – he had latched onto the guitar with a vengeance, devoting himself to an obsessive practice regime that would not be denied. Once more, this stemmed at least in part from his love of the late Randy Rhoads, whose equally ironclad practice routine was legendary. Morello had started out by working on some of Rhoads' solos, he recalled: "I spent about nine months learning the song 'Diary Of A Madman'. For any guitar player, it's challenging. But for a beginning player, that's a massive, Herculean undertaking... His riffs and arrangements were head and shoulders above anybody else in the genre. And then come his solos, on which, along with his rhythm playing, he distances himself from everybody. He combines technique – which doesn't really matter at all – with a tremendous sense of melody and harmony. Those things can only get you so far, too, but he had so much passion and feeling, yet he would still play these ripping solos and take your head off. The guy wasn't just a great guitar player – he could fucking jam! If you listen to the live stuff, where he does subtle variations of the solos you're familiar with, he's unbelievable, totally without peer."

He added: "One [similarity between Rhoads and myself] I can point to is the countless hours that I spent on technique... I spent time learning the 'Mr Crowley' solo, so I developed the ability to play notes at that speed [but] what's interesting is, when I stopped trying to sound like Randy and realised that what I loved about him was that he had a sound that was completely unique and was a representation of him as an artist, that's what inspired me to find my own unique voice as an artist. So I attribute it all to him."

In June 1982 Morello became the first student from Libertyville High School to win a place at Harvard, the prestigious Ivy League university, where he enrolled for a degree in political science. By now interested in political thought, and with a fierce intellect which enabled him to express his opinions in that arena, he took with him to Harvard the quintessential small-town outsider experience. Later he talked about finding a noose hanging from the ceiling of his garage, and the shock of discovering his racial identity.

"The second you have brown skin and you walk out on an interracial playground, your political education begins," Morello once said, telling writer Rob Tannenbaum that he was "constantly aware of his blackness" and that he only "realised he was half white at the age of 22", which would have been after he graduated from Harvard. That's quite a stringent process for anyone to endure at any age, let alone as a college kid looking for the right path.

"There was a political atmosphere in my home that I took for granted," said Morello. "We had pictures of Jomo Kenyatta and Kwame Nkrumah [the first president of Ghana] up in the house. When I got to high school and started studying world history and US history, I heard a different perspective on world events, and that made me challenge a lot of things."

Current world events made an impact on Morello, he explained. "When I was 16, 12 or so IRA hunger strikers died, including Bobby Sands. I had a little Irish Catholic in me, but I didn't know much about the Troubles [in Northern Ireland]. But I knew these were kids who were about my age who were literally dying for a political cause that they believed in. I was looking around me, and we had some kids who were trying to lose weight to make the wrestling team, and others who were focused on the homecoming stuff. That was the time I thought beyond the walls of my high school and the culture that gets drilled into you."

At Harvard, Morello embraced his guitar playing as keenly, or more so, than his actual studies. Credited by some as being the founder of the first heavy metal interest group at an Ivy League university, he ramped up his practice regime until he was putting in a close-to-unhinged eight hours per day. Explaining that "None of the guitar players that were my heroes started [at 17 years old], I panicked. I was way behind." He added that "There were a few crossroads in my history as a guitar player. A key one was when a guitar-playing friend of mine back in Illinois communicated to me a simple sentence that would change my life as a musician. He said, 'You'll get better if you practise just an hour a day without exception'. I just took that to heart, and over time I was able to form chords and learn songs better. With that victory in hand, I said, 'What if I practised two hours a day?' And I found that development, the growth curve, seemed to be exponential. I was improving more than twice as much at two hours a day. So I said, 'Well, if that's the case, how about four hours?' Then, finally, eight hours a day."

He continued, "In my four years at Harvard, including summers, I probably missed two or three days of practice. Even then, when I missed a day, I suffered a tremendous amount of guilt. I'm telling you this not in any sort of joking way. It was a very unhealthy practice regime, as if I had some kind of disorder. People would say, 'Tom, you've got a fever of 102, you have an exam at eight in the morning, and it's three AM'. And I'd say, 'Yeah, that's cool, only two more hours'. It was unshakable. I wouldn't shave five minutes off of it. Not even 45 seconds. I'd watch the clock. It's part of my makeup. With me, once certain things are set, they're set in stone… I had this relationship with my guitar that made up for other human relationships."

Along the way, music was constantly a temptation, recalled Morello: "I had the opportunity to become a full-time musician the summer after my freshman year, when I auditioned for some bands at home in Chicago, and at the time to me they seemed like The Rolling Stones even though they were really just crummy cover bands. I was able to play in bars I was too young to drink in, and I could have chosen to stay there and keep playing, but I thought, 'I got into Harvard. I ought to finish what I started.'"

This infatuation with guitar practice extended as far as vacations with his mother. Carrying a Gibson Explorer – one of the quintessential heavy metal guitars – with him in a heavy flight case as he travelled from country to country, Morello never, ever stopped working on his technique. "I didn't even know what a gig bag was back then. So I'd lug this thing around Europe with my mom. It was like carrying a body around. But I'd practise, whether we were at a bus stop, or wherever; I'd log my time... I felt like one of those kids who said, 'This is what I'm going to do if it kills me'. There's that excellent montage [in the 1988 movie *The Decline Of Western Civilization, Part II: The Metal Years*] where the interviewer asks, 'What if you don't make it?' And the answer was, 'Well, that's not an option.' She says, 'What's your Plan B?' And the answer is, 'There is no Plan B'. I had no Plan B."

What's most interesting here is that Morello was not, by his own admission, a musician with much natural talent, despite his skills in other areas. He genuinely needed those gruelling practice sessions in order to evolve his playing. "I wasn't a poor actor, and I wasn't a poor writer, but I was a poor guitar player. I was awful. I was really awful," he sighed. "But that's the thing I just decided I really had to do. I had no natural ability. I mean none. I couldn't play many songs in high school. Just my own. There were guys who could play anything by anybody, but couldn't write to save their life. But in high school, it was a mark of shame if you couldn't cover the Doobie Brothers. You weren't getting chicks. Period. Okay?"

He added: "One thing that I learned later that I would have liked to have known earlier, was the fact that there are worlds of difference between practising – rehearsing in your garage or bedroom – and playing in front of people. There is no better way to become a better player than live... There are nerves and all sorts of technical variables involved that you don't have in rehearsal. And there's a certain vibe playing a song from beginning to end that you need to go for in front of the audience. My playing and confidence grew exponentially when I was in a bunch of crappy bands that actually played out regularly. I see it all the time, bedroom shredders get on the stage, and it's not happening. It's an important part of learning."

After graduating from Harvard in 1986 with his Bachelor of Arts degree, Morello moved from Illinois to Los Angeles, chasing the perennial small-town kid's dream of finding fame and fortune with a band. As is so often the case, the first few months of his time in LA were miserable: he couldn't find a job, being hugely overemployed, and rapidly burned through the $1,000 of savings he'd brought with him. He ended up doing a variety of low-income, zero-dignity jobs to pay the rent. At one point, he admitted much, much later, he even worked as a stripper.

"When I graduated from Harvard and moved to Hollywood, I was unemployable," he recalled. "I was literally starving, so I had to work menial labour and, at one point, I even worked as an exotic dancer. 'Brick House' by The Commodores was my jam! I did bachelorette parties and I'd go down to my boxer shorts. Would I go further? All I can say is thank God it was in the time before YouTube! You could make decent money doing that job – people do what they have to do."

More lucrative, if equally demeaning, employment came when Morello landed a job in the office of California senator Alan Cranston, a liberal Democrat who had become known in earlier years for his progressive stance on nuclear disarmament. At first Morello was a lowly member of Cranston's office, employed only to answer the phones; later he was promoted to the role of the senator's scheduling secretary. From 1987 to '88, Morello got to experience the political machine from the inside, a process which left him thoroughly disillusioned.

"I never had any real desire to work in politics," he said later, "but if there was any ember burning in me, it was extinguished working in that job because of two things: one of them was the fact that 80 percent of the time I spent with the Senator, he was on the phone asking rich people for money. It just made me understand that the whole business was dirty. He had to compromise his entire being every day. The other was the time a woman phoned up to the office and wanted to complain that there were Mexicans moving into her neighborhood. I said to her, 'Ma'am, you're a damn racist', and she was indignant. I thought I was representing our cause well, but I got yelled at for a week by everyone for saying that! I thought to myself that if I'm in a job where I can't call a damn racist a damn racist, then it's not for me."

Quitting his job with Cranston, Morello continued his search for a band, working his way through at least one embarrassing heavy metal outfit. Eventually he found a more like-minded group of souls in early 1988 in the form of Lock Up, a funk-punk-metal outfit fronted by singer Brian Grillo. Lock Up had been around for a while, having been founded by ex-Mau Maus guitarist Mike Livingston and drummer Michael Lee. The latter had been replaced for a while by a serious name to conjure with, DH Peligro of the Dead Kennedys, who was later a temporary member of the Red Hot Chili Peppers.

Grillo recalled those far-off days for this book, beginning: "I started the band in the mid-eighties, although I never said 'This is my band and we must do my stuff!' Tom had seen our band play at Al's Bar and some people told us that he was really good, but he was already in another band, some big heavy metal band that was playing the Sunset Strip. Apparently they would dress up like pirates, and he was way not into it at all. I was out in the Valley one night, and we were like, 'How are we going to get ahold of this guy?' Somehow we managed to get the phone number of that band's lead singer, and we got my friend's girlfriend Judy to call the guy and act like she was a big groupie for Tom. She called up and said 'I really, really like that guy, can I please have his number?' and the guy gave it to her, which is how we got hold of Tom. He came and auditioned and he was in the band from then on, basically."

Ironically, given his later acclaim as a guitar hero, Morello recalled that the opportunity to acquire some professional equipment on joining

Lock Up unnerved him: "When I was first signed to a major label with Lock Up, they insisted that we go out and get gear. But for me, it was horribly intimidating. 'I have to get gear? What kind of gear would I get? How would I plug it in?' Everyone else went hog wild, and I guiltily went to Guitar Center and picked out a piece of rack gear. I didn't understand the manual, and I seemed to ruin it just plugging it into the effects loop on my amplifier. It ruined the sound. Now it just gathers dust."

Grillo had some history, having worked some years before alongside sometime Killing Joke and Public Image Ltd drummer Martin Atkins in Atkins' Brian Brain band. His background was different to the heavy metal-worshipping Morello's to a significant degree, he explains. "Tom was introduced to a whole different world than the one he'd been in before. I was dragging us into leather bars to play shows!" he chuckles. "We were playing all the time: we'd play anywhere we could get a show, and we finally got signed to Geffen and they put out our record, which we called *Something Bitchin' This Way Comes*. Tom told me a few years ago that it was like going to college to learn everything not to do in the music industry..."

Life in Lock Up alternated between fun times in rehearsal and the deadly slog of the road, recalls Grillo. "We had our own rehearsal studio, which was more like a clubhouse. We would have parties and perform our new songs there, five times a week, making art and music. We had a game where one person would start playing a riff or lick and everyone else would jump in, and we'd do that until we got bored. Out of that, a lot of really good songs came to be. Nobody had any ego."

"Tom was living in West Hollywood at the time," he continues. "He was friends with Maynard James Keenan, who ended up being the singer in Tool, and he ended up going out with my cousin. They decided to put an inflatable swimming pool in their living room – I still have pictures of it. They had this big party with all these people over, and a few weeks later the pool got a leak in it and flooded the whole apartment."

These were good times, at least in part, recalled Morello. "In 1989, [Jane's Addiction singer] Perry Farrell asked us to impersonate Jane's Addiction [at a New Year's Eve show]. So the lights would go off and they'd say, 'And please welcome Jane's Addiction!' and it would be my band, you know, me with a Dave Navarro wig, the singer with little braids, and we'd play 'Pigs In Zen'. It was a joke on their audience, right? So, we stepped out on stage and it was dark enough so that the audience clearly thought that it was the band, and I have never felt anything like the rush and the electricity. It was really like grabbing a live wire standing on that stage, from the incredible intensity. We did our little joke. They came out and finished the set and I walked off the stage going, 'Man, that is unbelievable'. I had never experienced anything like that onstage in my life."

Recording the *Something Bitchin'...* album may have been fun for Morello, but for Grillo, it was a nightmare. "I hated that whole experience," he says. "The record label hooked us up with Matt Wallace, who had produced Faith No More, and he was really cool until we ended up recording the record out in Lucas Valley, north of San Francisco. We were holed up there for months and it was horrible. Computer recording was on its way in, and Matt had Tom punch in [ie record out of real time] pretty much every single lick that he played. The more he did, we didn't sound like the same band. It sucked. I ended up having a nervous breakdown: I was like, 'I wanna go home to Hollywood! I can't take any more!'"

Point your mouse towards YouTube, search for Lock Up and 'Nothing New' and you'll be in for something of a surprise. As Grillo says, Lock Up (not to be confused with the grindcore band of the same name which emerged a decade later) fell between two stools in musical terms: the dismal last gasp of the hair-metal scene and the new, alternative wave that dominated the early nineties. The cheesy day-glo spandex and flowing hairstyles of the former were there, but the lipstick and posing wasn't; the funk chops and the sub-Red Hot Chili Peppers sexual groove of the latter was present and correct, but the plaid shirts and downtuning were not.

Who knew what Lock Up were trying to achieve? Whatever it was, it was entertaining.

"Playing live was our main forte," says Grillo. "We did the record and toured and toured all over the United States and Canada. It was just the four of us in a van with a soundman. It was hard, because it was at the time when Guns N' Roses were big, but we were friends with bands like L7, who came and stayed with us when we were recording our album. There was a whole new scene starting in Seattle, while in LA it was still all about glam metal. We didn't really fit into either one, and Geffen didn't know what to do with us. We were a band with an Italian singer and a black guitarist: they were like, 'How do we market this freakshow?' Our live shows had amazing audiences, though, so we kept playing and playing, even though they weren't promoting us."

It wasn't just Geffen who were confounded by Lock Up's line-up. Certain audiences were taken aback too, especially in the Southern states, where the presence of an African-American in a rock band caused more than a few morons to react negatively. "When you have a black guitar player and a gay singer, touring the South for three months, you become political whether you want to or not," remembers Grillo. "I experienced a lot of stuff that wasn't as bad for me, because I'm white and I could pass, but I remember one night we were at a club in Florida and just worn out. I wanted to go home: I'd had it with being out every fucking night. Even on days off we were stuck in the middle of nowhere, and there was nowhere to go. We were in this club, exhausted, and Tom came up to me and asked me to get him a Coke. I said, 'Why can't you get your own Coke? The bartender's right there' and he said, 'They won't serve me'. I had my eyes opened. We toured the South for a long time, and I couldn't believe how little things had changed down there when it came to racism."

He concludes: "Finally Geffen ended up dropping us, a short time after the record came out, although we continued on anyway. We lost our drummer and got a new one, but it wasn't the same, because the four of us made Lock Up what it was. So I called Tom one day and I told him that I was out. He was going in a more metal direction at the time, and I really love his guitar playing now but at the time he was more into Steve Vai and Eddie Van Halen, when I was coming from a punk rock background. We just decided to go our separate ways because we were both growing out of it and wanted to do different stuff. We left on good terms and we still keep in touch today. A short time after that I formed a new band, Xtra Fancy, and he formed Rage Against The Machine."

So that was that for Lock Up. Their greatest success was probably the contribution of two songs – 'Punch Drunk' and 'Half Man Half Beast' – to the soundtrack of a 1991 comedy film called *Ski School*. Perhaps the musicians and the music scene itself were just too much in flux to make a real success of their band: Morello was still in the process of discovering his political side, after all, and deeper endeavours awaited him. Grillo remembers that "Tom's mom would always send him copies of *The Nation* magazine, and he was just starting to discover Public Enemy. There's one song that he wrote called 'Can't Stop The Bleeding'. He was a great lyricist as well as musician," and it's clear that whatever Lock Up represented, it was only a stopping-off point to another, more serious level of creativity.

It was time to get serious, and in 1990 Morello placed an advert in a local music paper. He wrote that he was looking for "a socialist frontman who likes Black Sabbath and Public Enemy". Now, who would respond to a weird ad like that?

BOMBTRACK 1

Wage Slavery: Is There An Alternative?

Before we look at this next, pivotal stage in Rage Against The Machine's career, let's examine the state of play when it comes to the average consumer of rock music in the Western world. These people, primarily but not exclusively conforming to the standard white, middle-class heavy metal demographic, would be responsible for Rage's swift ascent to the top of the music industry, and their concerns tallied more or less neatly with the things which Tom Morello and his band wrote about.

You, the reader, may be one of these people yourself. I know I certainly am. You probably do some kind of job from nine to five, or you've done so in the past or you'll be doing so in the future. The primary reason for working is to earn enough money to live. The secondary reason, for most people, is because their job is fun, but we all know that a lot of people don't remotely enjoy what they do for a living. They work and work and work until they become automatons, living for the weekend and some unattainable point years down the line when they won't have to work anymore. This is a miserable existence, highlighted by Rage Against The Machine in several songs, including 'Bullet In The Head' – in which the average wage slave is depicted as a walking zombie, shackled to a nine-to-five, controlled by advertising and devoid of independent thought.

Tom Morello expressed this dismal truth when he told one interviewer, "The problem is wage slavery. America touts itself as the land of the free, but the number one freedom that you and I have is the freedom to enter into a subservient role in the workplace. Once you exercise this freedom you've lost all control over what you do, what is produced, and how it is produced. And in the end, the product doesn't belong to you. The only way you can avoid bosses and jobs is if you don't care about making a living. Which leads to the second freedom: the freedom to starve."

Asked if his Harvard degree had helped him find security – not the first or last time that he was challenged to back up his statements with personal experience – Morello explained: "When I first moved to Los Angeles, I was wholly unemployable. I could not have been more overqualified. I just couldn't get a job. I was unwilling to enter into career paths where a Harvard degree typically leads you, where you have to devote your life to the corporation. I wanted to devote my life to music and needed a day gig, for which I was wholly unprepared. I did telemarketing, and mind-numbing temp work. For months, my job was alphabetising and filing. Basically, I was treated like a dog. Right now, the biggest employer in the United States is a temp agency, and I got to experience that first hand. Insecurity is such good business. When you have to call up every morning at seven to find out if you have a job or not, there's no way you're going to be organising a union or trying to get a higher wage. Those of us without computer skills were making four dollars an hour. That's wage slavery, and I was happy to escape."

A lengthy interview with the political thinker Noam Chomsky was conducted by Morello for the 1996 radio show quoted in this book's introduction, and it is one of the most crystallised examples anywhere of the left-wing logic espoused by Rage Against The Machine. As he did with his thoughts on the war crimes of the US presidency (more of which comes up later in this book), Chomsky discussed the lot of the average office worker – and its implications for those who exploit him/her – with great clarity.

Asked by Morello why people accept and submit to this exploitation, Chomsky replied: "That hasn't been easy. It's kind of interesting to read the working-class press in the mid-19th century, which was very substantial in size, I should say. It's like the scale of the commercial press in those days. And it was organised by ordinary people. I mean, artisans, what they called 'factory girls', young women off the farms who were working in the textile industry around where I lived and so on. There are definite themes that run through it, and one of them is strong opposition to wage slavery, which they didn't regard as any different from chattel slavery. In fact, after the Civil War, there were bitter complaints about the fact, look we fought down slavery and now we are being driven into another form of slavery."

He continued: "It was just taken for granted that, in their words, that 'those who work in the mills should own them'. If we have to labour at the command of others, we have lost our freedom – the freedoms we fought for in the American Revolution and that they thought that they were fighting for in the Civil War. We've lost them. In fact, they also bitterly opposed what they called 'the new spirit of the age' back in 1850, [in which] we 'gain wealth forgetting all but self'. Back then that was the new spirit of the age, which they considered an utterly degrading doctrine that no honourable person would accept... The idea that people should subordinate themselves to the command of others was regarded as highly offensive, and it has taken a long, long time to get that out of people's heads. Right into this century, it was quite broadly felt and articulated, for example by America's leading social philosopher, John Dewy, who comes right out of the mainstream, that unless the working people control their own institutions they are simply tools, they're not people. And I don't think that understanding is very far below the surface. It could come out very quickly."

Among his many points about the gap between rich and poor, its portrayal in the business media and other related issues, Chomsky painted a glum picture of the life of the modern worker-bee employee. "People are aware that they are working longer and with much less security and for lower wages and with rather dim prospects. That's an unmistakable feature of American life. No-one doubts it. The people's attitudes of what should be done are interesting. For example, *Business Week* just ran a poll which frightened them very much. They found that 95% of the population, which is just an incredible figure for a poll, you just don't get that on anything, 95% of the population thought that corporations had a responsibility to reduce profits because of the needs of their own workforce and their communities. It is interesting to compare that with a general understanding of working people in say, the textile industries in Massachusetts 150 years ago. They were not asking for the autocrats to be more benevolent the way people are asking now. They were saying that they just have no right to be there at all. Not 'please treat your subjects more kindly', but that 'you have no right to rule'. That's a big decline in sensibility, but it's still dramatic that almost the entire population condemns the practice of business enriching itself."

Cheerful stuff, eh? But firmly based in reality, unfortunately. Is there any way out of this depressing way of non-life? Certain thinkers believe so, and for the purposes of this book I interviewed an American writer, Pamela Satterwhite, who is convinced that none of us need to sell our souls to pay the bills. Advocating a new style of community, Ms. Satterwhite has written extensively on the subject of rewiring our approach to the daily grind, most notably in her 2009 book *Waking Up: Freeing Ourselves From Work*. For more information on her work, visit www.nas2endwork.org.

What led you to write *Waking Up*, Pamela?
I think I've been pondering 'work' my whole life, one way or another. And now that I'm a grandma of a two-year-old, and get to play with a lot of two year olds, I see that it's a question we all start out with, under 'class'. We start out honouring our body's truth: listening to what it tells us feels right, and what it tells us doesn't, but we get subjected

during the course of our lives to a lot of propaganda that convinces us to distrust that original 'truth', our original questions that arise from the conflict between what our bodies tell us, and what we're told we must do to be 'successful'. In my case I always loved words, but could find no way to honour that love, and live. It took an injury when I was working as an electrician to lead me back to writing, and to beginning to read more seriously about the issue of work.

What is your personal history when it comes to this subject?
I started out jumping through the traditional hoops – grades, higher education. After which, if you're a person of conscience, you're faced with the challenge of how to make a living without violating your principles. I think I've explored almost every available route to doing that, so I've done a lot of different jobs, most of which had nothing to do with my love of writing and words. When a job did involve those affinities – writing grants or whatever – they were serving someone else's agenda. And it's difficult to believe in one's gifts, until you wake up, when they aren't offered monetary compensation.

What is the nature of the system for which we work?
This is an interesting question, more complicated than it seems. Because the means it employs – acquisitiveness – is what we see, often the Left tends to reduce it to these observable practices, confusing means for ends. But I believe that what it is, is evident in its results: hierarchy, ranking, class, the privatisation of planetary resources, the systematic removal from the hands of we-the-people of the means to reproduce our lives independent of those in whose hands the wealth of the planet has been placed… ie we are made effective slaves, in the sense that we are not self-determinative. So I would say that it is a mechanism for appropriating planetary wealth and concentrating it in the hands of an infinitesimal few in order to maintain the dependence of virtually the entire population of the earth on that infinitesimal few.

But the question is made more complicated by our implication in it. Hierarchy by definition creates layers of reward ('salary' and 'recognition') and punishment ('low or no wages' and 'invisibility'), and all of us to some degree serve as representatives, or manifestations, of 'the system' as well. It was in fact the British philosopher Jeremy Bentham, writing around the turn of the nineteenth century, who explained how to accomplish this: how to implicate us in our own 'management' (enmeshment). Bentham provided the guidance to 'power' – not seen with the level of clarity and detail he offered since Plato – for how a tiny few can control the vast majority, by means of such 'layering' techniques and other mechanisms of social control – guidance that reflected and updated Plato. The system's fundamental goal and nature is not accumulation for accumulation's sake, but rather to establish rigid, fixed class divisions: its goal is fundamentally totalitarian. Wage work, therefore – by which I mean coerced work – is the crux of our diminishment as human beings in a class system, and as such, ending this practice of forcing us to market our gifts would usher in our freedom.

What is the currency of that system?
I believe that human beings are the key wealth that must be kept in private hands. It is only by commodifying the energy of human beings that the system – based on reproducing increasing disparities, creating 'winners' and 'losers' – can exist.

Surely everyone should expect to have to work?
Jeremy Bentham, the British philosopher, said in 1781 that 'labour is our inevitable lot' – but it is not. And the very absence of any discussion of the question – of whether it makes sense to commodify human energy – seems to me to speak to the existence of an organised elite determined to thwart our beginning to have these discussions, generally, across the globe.

Consider these excerpts from this poem, titled *Sweet Content*, by Thomas Dekker (1575–1641):

"Art thou poor, yet hast thou golden slumbers?
    O sweet content!
Art thou rich, yet is thy mind perplex'd?

> O punishment!
> Dost thou laugh to see how fools are vex'd
> To add to golden numbers golden numbers?
> > O sweet content! O sweet, O sweet content!
> Work apace, apace, apace, apace;
> Honest labour bears a lovely face...
>
> Swimst thou in wealth, yet sink'st in thine own tears?
> > O punishment!
> Then he that patiently want's burden bears,
> No burden bears, but is a king, a king!
> > O sweet content! O sweet, O sweet content!..."

Until I entered the trades I'm not sure I would have understood or appreciated what Thomas Dekker knew and appreciated. He knew that it is force, the pressure of necessity, that weighs our backs with worry... it is the whip of command over us that wears raw our nerves, and that, under the command of our own intelligence, our own powers of analysis – and sweetened with the honey of communion – work once again becomes but life.

So we can really live our lives free of work?
If we agree that ending coerced work would usher in freedom from necessity, or generalised human leisure, why do we not believe we can achieve it? Particularly as the arc of history does bend toward generalised human freedom – and it's bending fast right now because of the internet. These times present us with altogether new terms for our resistance: the capacity to unify globally, within a single generation, and our thoughts must catch up to these new terms.

Who are the shadowy paymasters who enslave us?
I used the term 'pitiful power-drunk few', and drew on the vampire image – people who feed on other people – to describe them in *Waking Up*, but it's not accurate to paint them as malevolent. I believe these 10,000 or so guys are not malevolent but rather loyal to their tribe,

although going by results alone, it's difficult to tell the difference. They certainly don't see themselves as malevolent. Jeremy Bentham believed he was 'the most benevolent man who ever lived...' despite devoting his life to trying to figure out how to make the majority better servants to their 'betters'. If anyone's a villain it might be Plato. And I give constant thanks to Karl Popper and his work *The Open Society And Its Enemies: The Spell Of Plato*, for helping me to understand power's motives. He wrote during the spread of fascism across Europe and was trying to call attention to the roots of totalitarian thinking in Plato.

But these people are not evil?
These would-be philosopher-statesmen are born into a carefully-sculpted reality, an experience that creates a belief in inherent, natural class divisions. From their perspective, and Plato's, the people are childlike, if not beasts, requiring patriarchal guidance. And, of course, it must be a very heady feeling to feel one is part of a governance structure for the world.

Isn't it a normal human trait to want to conquer and succeed, corporately as everywhere else?
A recent examination of archaeological evidence found that prior to 13,000 years ago, human remains bore no evidence of violence. The author argued that war was an invention, like art. In *Man Makes Himself*, V. Gordon Childe described the invention of slavery in the discovery that human beings could be domesticated like non-human animals. But these were self-reinforcing departures from an inherent tendency toward co-operation, sharing and mutual aid. Peter Kropotkin illustrates this in his book *Mutual Aid: A Factor in Evolution*, arguing that mutual aid is an evolutionary advantage across species.

Do you suggest a socialist model for your new society?
Jeremy Bentham warned those in power about the importance of 'controlling the lexicon', which means controlling the definitions, in other words controlling the very thoughts we can think. What I've learned, with the help of Karl Popper and others, is that a key tactic of power is to seize upon ideas that reflect our deep human longing for

solidarity, for sharing and cooperation, for good fellowship – and try to own them, turn them into concepts that do work for power itself. This is certainly true for the words 'socialism' and 'communism'. So I believe it's time to describe – using 'earth-terms' – the future we want, in very concrete terms that cannot be co-opted.

Define power in this context.
The image I use for power (meaning, this narrow elite of philosopher-king-hopefuls) is an invisible boulder sitting on top of all of us. Now, power must conceal itself to exist, Bentham schooled power well on this, so this heavy weight of power is never consciously seen or acknowledged. It's never discussed, so it's invisible to us. All that is discussed, and so all we see are these stunted versions of ourselves... bent, deformed and damaged. But once organised power is off our backs, we can begin to grow straight again.

Why has no large-scale socialist society lasted long?
I think because we have been misled, and encouraged to define the problem inaccurately, as not one fundamentally of class, management, rank and hierarchy, but rather of greed. This misdirection is of course intentional. Our future freedom can only be achieved by working together as a global humanity.

Surely our society is one of our own making, and exploitation in the workplace effectively our own fault?
We unwillingly reproduce the terms of our own enslavement, which is why thinking through how this happens, and developing an accurate analysis of how it is we find ourselves nose to the grindstone, in survival mode, unable to develop our earth-given gifts, is a necessary first step – because the terms need to be established before change can occur. So when Rage Against The Machine calls for a revolution, there needs to be discussion both of the basic premises of the system that exists, and simultaneously discussion of what the basic premises of that new world will be. The problem needs to be defined accurately in order for us to see the contours of its alternative.

People often feel crushed by their jobs because of the vertical boss-dominating-underling hierarchy of the corporations in which they work. But isn't that structure necessary?
Some people think that hierarchy is natural, and that corporations, or organisations in general, reflect this supposed key divide between those who need to be guided and those who gravitate to leadership and control. It's possible you could have said of me as a young woman that I tended to hang back and require guidance, but what a person is at any one time does not define them. Over the course of our lifetimes, all of us go back and forth between many roles. Studies on 'hierarchy' tend to be snapshots, reflect moments in time, abstracted out of the movement and flow and trajectories of our lives. The few cannot govern such that the interests of the many are honoured. The more who directly participate in decision-making, the more perspectives are represented, the better the decisions.

In *Waking Up*, you mentioned a general strike as an objective. On this scale, the general strike you're calling for is effectively a revolution.
As John Trudell said, we don't want revolution: we want evolution, because with revolution you just get back to where you started. I think of the progressive claiming and developing of our unique gifts as a spiral, sweeping ever out – embracing more and more – and up, as we develop them. I like the way Maxim Gorky put it:

"I know the time will come when people will wonder at their own beauty, when each will be like a star to all the others. The earth will be peopled with free men, great in their freedom. The hearts of all will be open, and every heart will be innocent of envy and malice. Then life will be transformed into the great service of Man, and Man will have become something fine and exalted, for all things are attainable to those who are free. Then people will live in truth and freedom for the sake of beauty, and the best people will be accounted those whose hearts are most capable of embracing the world and of loving it, those who are most free, for in them lies the greatest beauty. They will be great people, those of the new life!... And for the sake of that life I am ready to do anything at all. (Maxim Gorky, *Mother*, Chapter XXIV)

This future will be the opposite of what we have now, because now everything is based on our selling our gifts. The opposite of that is expressing our gifts rather than alienating them. As Emily Dickinson said, 'Reduce no human spirit to disgrace of price'. What we are born with is inherently co-operative, curious and joy-seeking. In the world that we create, power will be indistinguishable from beauty, and 'work' indistinguishable from 'life'.

Are corporations, and the relative freedom in which they operate when it comes to making money, the root of the problem?

How the problem is defined is critical. Alfred O. Hirschman in *The Passions And The Interests*, pointed out, quoting the French thinker de Tocqueville, that if you can get the many chasing money, it leaves the few who play the higher stakes of power freer to pursue their ambition. And that ambition is global supremacy. In this global game of power, we-the-people serve as fuel. Our lives – consigned as they've been to power's purposes, have historically (from the perspective of self-creation) – been nullified. But the internet has finally shifted the terms in our favour.

If we see the problem as being caused by corporations, then the solution put forward is to limit the corporations' ability to make profits, which will do nothing to return our earth-given gifts to our exclusive use. Corporations serve as privatising means for 'power': consolidating the resources of the planet in private hands. So we need to ask ourselves what would put those resources in our hands. And of course the most determinative resource for how the world is shaped is we-the-people.

Isn't the problem simply the fact that most of us can't visualise any other way of life than getting up every morning to go and work in return for a monthly salary?

Our original truth and our unique gifts are ever with us, awaiting the conditions that validate them. I think we-the-people long to use our gifts, long for good-fellowship, long for that world based on different operating premises, but we never hear this truth expressed anywhere. The media does not allow discussions about ending class, ending the wage work system, over the airwaves. But there's a very real hunger for a world beyond rank, division and coercion. When Occupy Oakland was just starting in 2011, they called for a general strike and within days, 20,000 people came. The initial excitement was profound, the sense that what was being challenged was the core of the system itself. But then, as happens until we frame a more conscious resistance, there was infiltration, there were acts of violence, and power had its necessary cover for dismantling the encampment.

Do people generally assume that they can't give up their boring job because they need the money?
Definitely. People have to survive. That doesn't mean that we can't think about the broader global frame for how we should live our lives, and how to shift that frame to allow self-creation, at the same time. I think it's a process of giving ourselves permission, of taking ourselves seriously, of honouring our gifts, and trusting the source of those gifts – essentially redirecting our allegiance to these sources, and away from power. When enough people begin discussing how a world based on generalised human freedom (leisure) could work, and want to see a demonstration of how this world could work, there will be one. There is no technological or material reason why we sell our human gifts to the system. We don't have a knowledge problem, we have a power problem.

So what concrete steps should people take?
We need to get discussions going of what the fundamental premises of this system are, and therefore what the opposite premises would be. These discussions would open up a spiritual and mental space for those who want to create a world based on those opposite operating premises.

When the Egyptian revolution happened in 2011, they identified three initial operating premises: no division, no violence, no leaders. Those are useful beginning premises, but I've argued that we should substitute 'coercion' for 'violence' in our thinking, and in our defining of the problem. Perhaps the basic operating premises of those of us who want to establish a very different world and a future that's free must be 'no division, no coercion, no leaders' – because our ultimate goal is for the species to grow. If that movement were defined as 'a mass movement to end wage work', it would be very difficult for agent provocateurs to undermine.

Why do we need so much discussion?
Plato said that the most dangerous thing of all is to let the people think. 'The pen is mightier than the sword' means that our thoughts are mightier than the sword. One authentic thought leads to the next and to the next, until power can't contain them anymore.

Where could people go to set up this new life?
Public land, if sufficient numbers called for it, could be designated communal, as perhaps part of a pilot project to test the viability of self-sufficient communities.

What would these communities look like?
Michael Reynolds, the architect and designer of a solar-powered house called the Earthship, offers us a model for a community that is self-sufficient, requires zero energy input, recycles its own waste and so on. I use the Earthship as a device to make the case that there are no technological or material reasons why we sell our human energy. I believe we need that psychic space that discussion opens up for those who wish to build a self-sufficient community to do so. It's our future – working together freely, co-operatively, not under conditions of coercion.

So who will do the dirty work if this utopian ideal comes to pass?
Dirty work won't exist, because work can't be dirty when you're working with your natural gifts. That poem by Thomas Dekker –

'Work apace, apace, apace, apace; Honest labour bears a lovely face...'
– captures the truth of our bodies well. It was fun working on a crew as an electrician. I still miss it. It feels good to work with our hands, just as it does with our brains. We deserve it all.

Major change is at hand, then?
I believe so. It feels like an endgame, with the necessary convergence of both environmental and economic crises, and with the internet providing the means for our thought, our powers of analysis, to be shared and grow at a rate which it couldn't before. Power counts on being able to suppress alternative ways of thinking before they can build, which now can't happen. Immanuel Wallerstein has written that the US is a wounded tiger and not a paper one. Well, I believe that this power system, this system of class, is also a wounded tiger, which means that it's extremely dangerous because it's struggling for its very survival.

What's the bigger picture here?
As Wallerstein also said, the problem isn't capitalism or corporations. He said, 'Capitalism is doomed. It's no longer possible to have serious accumulation of capital because the costs are too high in terms of purchasing power. Capitalism as a system depends on lots of people working to create surplus value that ends up in the hands of the few, which results in polarisation. The issue is... what will replace Capitalism.' Our thoughts give us permission to go through that door to a very different future.

CHAPTER 2

1991–1992

Lock Up and Inside Out, although neither were destined to be the world's most successful rock or punk bands, did function as successful stepping-stones towards Rage Against The Machine. Both bands had toured, giving the members valuable experience in how to occupy a tourbus for weeks on end without murdering each other, as well as giving the musicians the opportunity to hone their performance and songwriting skills.

That said, in 1990 and early 1991, Tom Morello was approaching 26 years old, several years past the sell-by date of any musician looking to begin a career. It would be overdramatising the situation to state that his advert seeking a frontman to form a band was his last gasp, the final straw, his last bite at the cherry – but who knows how long he could have gone on trying to make it in a band had Zack de la Rocha and his high-school buddy Tim Commerford not answered the call.

It was Jon Knox, a drummer for Lock Up in the last stages of the band's existence, who suggested that de la Rocha and Commerford should jam with Morello to see if there was any spark between them. Brad Wilk had already been recruited to Morello's new project after connecting briefly with Lock Up: he had auditioned unsuccessfully for the band after placing an ad in *Music Connection* magazine after their drummer was fired. His own group, Greta, had formed in 1990, and went on to release a couple of moderately interesting albums for Mercury Records before calling it a day in 1995.

Wilk's back story is the classic drummer tale. As he recalled, he was introduced to the drums around 1981: "When I was about 13 years old, in Chicago, a friend of mine who lived a couple of doors down had a Ludwig Silver Sparkle drum kit with a big Kiss logo on the front head. I was totally infatuated with the drum set – period. So any time I could, I was on his kit, not knowing what the hell I was doing but banging away nonetheless." Already a fan of The Who, Wilk appreciated the skills of drummer Keith Moon in particular. "I was just fascinated by the energy and with The Who in general," he continued. "The excitement that they were portraying as a band had a huge effect on me, definitely... I love the fact that Keith Moon played with this unbelievable confidence, but he was on the edge of insanity. He was a driving force, but he was always just on the brink of completely losing his mind."

Also a fan of John Bonham and Elvin Jones as well as flamboyant rockers Van Halen, Wilk brought precision, power and economy to the drums: like Commerford and Morello, he is an adherent of the Miles Davis school of less-is-more, leaving spaces where other, less subtle musicians would play notes.

Together Morello and Wilk went to see de la Rocha rapping at a gig, and with him came Commerford. "I was totally blown away," recalled Morello, who recruited de la Rocha immediately. "It was the passion of his performance at rehearsal. We were playing in some guy's sweaty side room of his mom's house, and Zack was as intense as he is onstage. But the real clincher was when I looked through his book of poems and lyrics. It was like I'd found an ideological brother. And it wasn't just paragraphs about Mao and Paraguay. It was great poetry."

The bond between the musicians was immediate. "From the first time that the four of us got together in the room, something clicked," said Wilk. "I don't take chemistry for granted: it all has to do with the chemistry, and whatever happens was there from day one, and we knew it. We knew that we were onto something that was special to us and that we thought was unique."

"Zack was like a lightning bolt," added the drummer. "That's all I remember, just [the band] really feeding off each other. It was this kind of intense electricity that I hadn't really felt before. We started playing all this pretty insane punk rock and hip-hop fused with hard rock. It wasn't just me – everyone in the band was fully on that trip, whether it was Zack rhyming through a verse or just going off an intense punk rock session."

That said, after the fizzling-out of Lock Up and the descent into ideological dissent of Inside Out, none of the new musicians expected much to come of the new band, which was formed in August 1991. In fact, Morello in particular had underachievement firmly in mind. "We had no expectation of even being able to play a show," he recalled. "We were perfectly content to make a cassette and sell it for $5 to anyone who would buy it." He knew that the group, based on the connection between him and de la Rocha of radical politics, would also be more than a little off-putting to the heavy music scene of the day. "I thought the politics of the band would be alienating. I thought the music of the band would be alienating. I thought the racial makeup of the band would be alienating," he emphasised.

"We had no real hope of ever really having an audience when we first started," mused the guitarist some time later. "At the time, not only was the band ethnically alienating to club bookers, record companies or radio, but there was no precedent for a multi-ethnic rock band. Add to that a rock band with revolutionary politics playing the most hardcore elements of fringe musics – hip-hop, hardcore punk and hard rock. We didn't dare to dream we could have the opportunity to mould the disparate audiences. The music really came from our hearts. We were determined to be 100% pure and uncut, uncompromising politically and musically. With that we didn't even care if we were able to get shows, and it was through having that sense of conviction that I think we got an audience."

Whatever the members might or might not have been expecting in commercial terms, there was no doubting the creativity that existed between them right from the start. As Morello recalled, "One thing that I have always completely disagreed with is when someone says, 'It's the band's internal tension that makes the music great.' Bullshit. We wrote 12 to 15 songs in the first month that we knew each other and were getting along like peas in a pod... The better the band is getting along, the better the music is."

Those early rehearsals were explosive, he recalled. "From the very first rehearsals in 1991, when we were playing this first couple of songs we wrote – 'Bombtrack', 'Take The Power Back' and maybe 'Know Your Enemy'... different combinations of us had jammed those riffs with other musicians, but when the four of us played it, and Timmy kicked in the distorted bass, Zack was losing his mind, and Brad pummelled his stripped-down drum kit, the sound just blasted off. You just had to go 'Shit!' Even then, we still didn't know whether it was going to connect or whether it was going to be our own little private pleasure, until we played live. When we did, the magic was immediate."

The new band named themselves Rage Against The Machine for obvious reasons – the existence of the title of a song written by de la Rocha, and the group's shared beliefs, primary among them. While the four musicians weren't unified in their political thoughts, they all held certain causes close to their hearts – and it was obvious that socialist protest would be at the core of Rage's songs.

"We're all definitely into different things," said Wilk, "but the philosophies are in line. I'm more into doing things on a local level as opposed to a global level. I think they're both really important, but there are a lot of people who are concerned with global issues that walk out the front door with blinders on, and it's important for people to realise what's going on in their own neighbourhood. I work with the Los Angeles Free Clinic, which is right down the street from my house. There's a lot of homeless people around where I live, and this place gets them the medical attention and health attention that they otherwise would not have."

Of course, people chuckled at Rage's right-on political stance, or worse; the mockery has been incessant from day one – but times were changing back then, and opportunities to be taken seriously in rock were about to present themselves. A major change was coming in the whole of popular music, in retrospect, which the band sensed and exploited, and which audiences for rock music had long anticipated.

Look at the evidence. The biggest touring rock bands in the world in the previous year – 1990 – were Bon Jovi and Aerosmith, both of which had evolved by this stage into anodyne acts producing albums of boring music. However, the following year both were toppled by much heavier acts from the previously more niche realm of heavy metal: Metallica and Guns N' Roses. In August 1991 Metallica released their fifth, self-titled studio album, a ponderous but radio-friendly behemoth that introduced a whole generation of previously metal-illiterate music fans to the joys of the moshpit, thanks to its hummable, air-guitarable riffs and song structures. Metallica themselves had undergone something of a style change during the recording of the album, moving from fast, progressive thrash metal to a simpler, more digestible style that propelled *Metallica* (the 'Black Album') to eventual sales of 20 million and beyond. Established fans stood and stared as 'their' metal band hit the charts – but with the benefit of hindsight, we can see that the fertile mood of change that enveloped the music scene at the time made such a development not only possible, but probable.

As for Guns N' Roses, a highly unstable five-piece supported, it seemed, only by booze and narcotics, GNR had recorded their much-loved debut album, *Appetite For Destruction*, in 1988 and toured incessantly, scoring radio airplay along the way with a series of cheesy, if hummable, singles including 'Paradise City' and 'Sweet Child O' Mine'. The band's hubris reached its logical limit in 1991 when they released two double albums on the same day, entitled *Use Your Illusion I* and *II*. This over-the-top move had attracted an enormous fanbase – and Metallica and GNR realised that a double-headline tour with both bands would be mutually beneficial. Taking the funk-rock act Faith No More along as support, the bands toured the planet, making 1991 (and 1992) their own.

Let's not forget grunge, though, the abysmally-titled wave of emotional heavy metal whose biggest (but not first) group was Nirvana. Of that band, much has been said, with the grunge wave they rode a brief but bright flash of activity. A whole raft of grunge, grunge-influenced and post-grunge bands followed in Nirvana's wake, including major acts in their own right such as Pearl Jam, Soundgarden, the Screaming Trees, the Smashing Pumpkins and Hole. However, the initial impetus of the movement had already stalled by the time Nirvana singer Kurt Cobain killed himself in April 1994, with the generic 'alternative rock' tag a more enduring label – later applied to any guitar-heavy act with a raw or confessional edge.

And then there was the small matter of the Red Hot Chili Peppers. Funky to the point of ridicule, this LA quartet were responsible for the rise of a whole host of bands, especially after their 1992 album *Blood Sugar Sex Magik*. Genuinely or otherwise funk-influenced, but almost all categorised by a bass player who slapped and popped on his instrument, the Chilis' contemporaries included 24–7 Spyz, Catfish, Fishbone, Guano Apes, Infectious Grooves, Primus, Living Colour, Madball, Mr. Bungle and finally Rage Against The Machine.

The point of all this namechecking is to remind ourselves how much rock music was changing back in 1991 and '92. However, we also need to take into account the social turmoil in which Rage Against The Machine first formed. Remember the LA riots? They made an appropriate backdrop for the subjects which the group were about to address on their first album: in fact – as the famous song goes – while the album was being recorded, a riot was literally going on.

The reasons for the riots were essentially the same issues that Rage protest against in their songs. Take the US government, for example: like all governments, its representatives in the public eye often say the wrong thing. "I want to be Robin to Bush's Batman," said US Vice-President Dan Quayle in the early nineties.

An appropriately useless sentiment in this context, given the feeble nature of his government's response to the riots of April 1992.

On April 29, 1992, the announcement came that a jury in Simi Valley in California's Ventura County had come to a verdict after almost 14 months of trial and deliberation. The case at hand centred on the alleged brutality of four police officers towards a motorist in northern LA, and the verdict that the jury returned was that all four cops were not guilty. The motorist's name was Rodney King. The four policemen were Sergeant Stacey Koon and Officers Larry Powell, Theodore Briseno and Timothy Wind.

The Mayor of Los Angeles, Tom Bradley, said: "We must express our profound anger and outrage [at the acquittal], but we also must not endanger the reforms that we have made by striking out blindly." He continued, "We must demand that the LAPD fire the officers who beat Rodney King and take them off the streets once and for all." California State Senator Ed Smith said that he was shocked by the verdict, and was quoted by the United Press as saying, "It's hard to believe that there was no sustaining of the charges at all... the world saw the videotape, and if that conduct is sanctioned by law in California, then we have to rewrite the law." Executive Director Ramona Ripston of the American Civil Liberties Union labelled the verdicts "a travesty of justice".

It seemed that many of the residents of Los Angeles agreed. As the nation watched, transfixed, reports of the biggest civil disturbance in US history began flooding in. Rodney King's beating was merely the last in a long line of incidents, each of which raised the temperature of inner-city LA (and most prominently, in poorer areas such as South Central) until the anger felt by many of the city's oppressed residents reached breaking point.

The *Washington Times* journalist Lou Cannon wrote a book entitled *Official Negligence: How Rodney King And The Riots Changed Los Angeles And The LAPD*, in which he analysed the roots of the conflict between LA's police and citizens and the riots to which it led. In it he revealed that the LAPD was riddled with institutional dysfunction, embracing racism wholeheartedly and applying those principles to the execution of their work. Cannon's findings were largely endorsed by the independent Christopher Commission, which undertook an extensive survey of the LAPD after the riots had died down.

The Commission's report stated that "...there is a significant number of officers in the LAPD who repetitively use excessive force against the public and persistently ignore the written guidelines of the Department regarding force... complaints filed in recent years show a strong concentration of allegations against a problem group of officers... Graphic confirmation of improper attitudes and practices is provided by the brazen and extensive references to beatings and other excessive uses of force in [police communications]." The report went on to conclude that the failure to control these officers indicated "a significant breakdown in the management and leadership of the Department" and that "the Police Commission, lacking investigators or other resources, failed in its duty to monitor the Department in this sensitive use-of-force area".

A little-known fact about the events of April '92 is that of the many people detained by the police, 51% of the people arrested were Latinos, 'only' 38% were African-Americans, 9% were white and 2% were Asians or of other ethnic background. Although the riots are widely regarded as a black uprising, much of the violence that occurred took place between the Latin American population and the police. The Latinos themselves claimed that that the Chicano population of the city, rather than the African-Americans, were more likely to suffer police malpractice in the form of aggression, harassment and racially-biased policing – and factual evidence bears them out. In the autumn of 1991, a Latino gang-member was shot and killed by LA County Sheriff's Deputies at the Ramona Gardens housing project – just another reason for public dissatisfaction with the police force.

Despite this fact (that the LA cops and the Chicanos are most likely to clash at any given time), a report prepared by the District Attorney in 1992 stated that after studying the LAPD's gang database, it had discovered that "the police have identified almost half of all black men in Los Angeles County between the ages of 21 and 24 as gang members. That number is so far out of line with other ethnic groups that a careful, professional examination is needed to determine whether police procedures may be systematically over-identifying black youths as gang members".

Rage Against The Machine wouldn't have been impressed by the first response of the LAPD to the riots. LAPD chief Daryl Gates had chosen to attend a political fund-raising party in the wealthy beach community of Pacific Palisades, 20 miles from the centre of the riots. The police department was understaffed and unprepared for an insurrection of this scale, and pulled out of one of the hot spots (the Florence and Normandie intersection in LA) on the first day. This didn't help matters – the area quickly became a war zone. Fidel Lopez, a Guatemalan immigrant, was beaten to within an inch of his life, the attack being captured on video. His assailants smashed a stereo speaker into his forehead, his genitals were spray-painted black and his body was doused with gasoline, presumably in order to set him on fire. However, his life was saved by a black clergyman who threw his body on Mr. Lopez's, persuaded the attackers to leave and then drove him to a hospital, when it had become clear that no ambulance crew would enter the area. Earlier that day, Choi Sai Choi, a Chinese book-keeper, had been dragged from his car, beaten and robbed at the same intersection. After some hours of destruction without a police presence, the National Guard was called in.

Within hours of the first reports of violence and theft, the Bloods and the Crips entered the fray, bringing a degree of motivation, organisation and firepower that was far beyond the scope of the average street thug. At one stage no fewer than 22 members of a Crips set were arrested after they had systematically removed over $80,000 worth of products from electronic goods stores. Reports of arson came flooding in as building after building was set on fire, and an unceasing flow of panicked phone calls from citizens reporting assaults, murders and looting continued through the night. Even the National Guard began to feel outgunned as weapons stores reported the theft of over 4,000 guns over the six days. Worse, the gang-members had started to paint anti-police graffiti on walls, including 'Open Season on LAPD' and '187 LAPD' (187 being the California Penal Code section for homicide).

Things would get worse before they got better. The Los Angeles Fire Department reported that nine large stores were ablaze and that numerous cars had been deliberately torched in order to block the roads. An LAPD sergeant told reporters that the police department had called for a tactical recall, cancelling leave for all officers. Many cops were patrolling the streets in full riot gear by this stage. Shockingly, many firefighters had reported sniper fire as they tried to extinguish the flames of burning buildings. Mayor Bradley was calling for calm among the city's black community every few hours, but his office was confounded by reports that many of the looters were Latinos and whites – many of the latter decidedly middle-class. Commentators revealed with genuine shock that some of the looting was being carried out by entire families, who were entering shops and exiting with armfuls of merchandise. Far from being a riot of black people against their white oppressors, this appeared to be a free-for-all in which people of all ethnic origins simply took what they wanted when the cops' attention was diverted elsewhere.

Bradley declared a local state of emergency, with a night-time curfew in effect that would make a lockdown from dusk till dawn mandatory. He also prohibited firearms sales, banned petrol sales (unless gasoline was loaded directly into vehicle fuel tanks), closed down all schools in southern LA, called in 2,000 extra National Guardsmen and arranged with President Bush for federal assistance to be invoked if required. At the end of the second day, an unidentified police officer commented to the news crews: "Things are totally out of control here... and we expect it to get worse when it gets dark. I hope we all live to see tomorrow."

By the time the riots in LA died down on May 4, the violence had spread to other cities, notably in San Francisco, where 1,400 people were arrested, with a state of emergency and curfew also in effect. In Las Vegas 200 rioters embarked on an arson and drive-by rampage.

Downtown Seattle was struck by mobs of up to 100 people, looting cars and attacking property. In New York, groups of up to 400 people stormed shopping malls. In Atlanta, police clashed with hundreds of black rioters. And in Tampa, Pittsburgh, Birmingham (Minnesota), Omaha and several other cities, black and Latino protesters demonstrated their sympathy with the LA rioters — either that, or a quick eye for an opportunity.

By the time the smoke had cleared, damage assessors were announcing that around a billion dollars of damage had been done to Los Angeles. Many thousands of arrests had been made, over 500 structures had been destroyed by fire, about 2,500 people had been injured and between 40 and 60 citizens had died (even 22 years later the official body count varies, according to the source).

Clearly there were investigations to be made — and while the Christopher Commission was uncovering the LAPD's institutionalised racism, another investigation was held into the Department's management practices. The latter was headed up by ex-FBI chief and sometime CIA director William Webster, who advised that community policing should be set in motion and that police officers should "treat all individuals with equal dignity and respect". Webster's team also found that the lack of leadership both in the police department and in city government had led to the lack of riot strategy, leaving no coherent decision-making structure in place and allowing the rioters to spread with little restraint. Following the report, LAPD head Daryl Gates resigned his post and was replaced by Philadelphia PD chief Willie Williams.

As for Rodney King, his trial dragged on as far as the Supreme Court, which found some parts of earlier sentences acceptable and other aspects unacceptable. The officers who had attacked him each received varying penal sentences and he himself was awarded $3.8 million in compensation for loss of work, medical costs, and pain and suffering.

Got all that? This was the background for the arrival of Rage Against The Machine. In 1991 and 1992, chaos reigned on musical and social levels, at least in Rage's home state of California. Eighties music began to seem a mite old-fashioned, especially given the new and abrasive edges of bands such as Nirvana, the occult fixations of Tool and – soon – the real-world concerns and confrontational lyrics of Rage Against The Machine. This was the environment in which Rage flourished, and no-one needed to tell them twice: they saw their chance and took it with a vengeance. Working up songs and refining the stripped-down one-microphone, one-guitar line-up (Morello joked that "at one of the very first RATM rehearsals in 1991, Timmy and Zack removed the microphone from in front of me, thus denying the world of the opportunity to hear my rich baritone"), the band soon came up with a sequence of songs.

"It was shocking! It was really, totally shocking," said Morello, asked how Rage Against The Machine's first few shows were received. The band's first public performance occurred at a private house party in Orange County, although their first formal gig took place on October 23 at California State University. "During our first couple of club shows," he added, "we amassed a rabid following. It was amazing how quickly people learned the words to the songs. One guy from each show was obviously telling 20 more guys about us, based on how the shows grew from the start. There was a kind of feral intensity at those shows due to the political content. It was like a scorched-earth policy at the little club, as if to say, 'You don't have a clue what you're in for right now!'"

Within weeks of their formation, the group members had decided to record a demo tape, copies of which were initially sold at a Los Angeles club called Jabberjaw. "We rehearsed for two or three months and decided to fuck the record companies and just sell the tape ourselves at the show," said Brad Wilk. "The crowd reaction was so intense that it was a big celebration of frustration and anger. It was a remarkable feeling. I realised that we had something special and that maybe we could take this thing further. There's nothing like it. I love it."

Commerford later stated that it was Morello's initiative to record the demo cassette. "Businessman Tom Morello, cracking the whip," he smiled. "I remember going, 'Man, we can stop at eight songs.

Eight will be fine'. He's like, 'No, we need more. We need 12'. And that's what we did."

Morello shared the rush of adrenaline which live performances as a member of Rage gave him, saying: "The relationship that I have with the RATM audience is the most satisfying relationship I've ever had in my life. It's really incredible... that thing with the audience has always been intact and precious. We can walk out onstage, and, before even playing a note, the connection is unbelievable."

"For the longest time until I was in RATM, I was unable to, for the most part, write music that I loved," he continued. "I was in a hundred bands, writing a thousand songs, but it wasn't until this band and the interplay with these musicians that I could write the music I loved. For all the countless hours that I have practised playing guitar in my life, Rage is just something that came together without any particular rhyme or reason. Now I can regularly toss out stuff I love... I have somehow been able, with the combination of Tim and Brad, to write music that greatly pleases me."

The first Rage Against The Machine demo cassette, which began circulation in December 1991, was either self-titled or called *American Composite*, depending on which source you consult. Recorded at Sunbirth Studio in LA, the demo was sold for five dollars at shows in spring 1992 and sold an unexpected 5,000 copies, primarily to gig-goers, although it would also have been copied endlessly for others. Rage sent the demo to various record companies, with a surprise visitor in 1992 none other than Madonna, who was considering signing Rage to her Maverick record label. Asked by the *NME*, "When Madonna kept on making appointments to come and see the band in rehearsal, did – and I want an honest answer here – the thought that you might just possibly cop off with her ever cross your mind?" Morello laughed and retorted, "Oh hell! I thought of little else all week! I mean, come on!"

The tracklisting of the demo will be familiar to anyone who enjoyed Rage's subsequent debut album, running 'Bombtrack', 'Take The Power Back', 'Bullet In The Head', 'Darkness Of Greed', 'Clear The Lane', 'Township Rebellion', 'Know Your Enemy', 'Mindset's

A Threat', 'Killing In The Name', 'The Narrows', 'Autologic' and 'Freedom'. Although most of the songs were different to the later versions in some way or other – slower, or arranged differently, or featuring alternate solos – the majority packed a mighty punch thanks to the rock-solid precision of the performances and the incendiary lyrics written by de la Rocha. The songs omitted from the debut album – 'Darkness Of Greed', 'Clear The Lane', 'Mindset's A Threat', 'Autologic' and 'The Narrows' – were eventually used as single B-sides (remember them?) or remained largely unheard, until the rise of YouTube a decade later and ultimately a box set in 2012.

The slightly curious statement "No samples, keyboards or synthesizers used in the making of this record" appeared on the cover of the Rage demo – at least curious until you heard its contents. In a step away from the frat-boy riffs and solos of his Lock Up days, Morello had focused his attentions when playing guitar on a new approach. Now, far be it from this book to enter the tedious (to most) world of amp settings and effects pedal controls, but in the case of Tom Morello, it's important to understand his approach to the guitar in order to understand a large part of Rage Against The Machine's musical impact.

Together with the funk and hip-hop influences brought to the band by Commerford and Wilk, Morello was able to bring an entirely new sound to metal. Although his command of traditional heavy rock soloing and riffing is miraculous, he often prefers to create machine-like or industrial noises using a variety of unorthodox techniques – removing the cable jack from his guitar and letting the resulting chainsaw buzz ring out among them. Plucking the strings with objects other than a pick, such as an allen key, and even scraping his guitar's cable over the pickups for a rubbing, scratching sound, he makes extraterrestrial noises which don't usually enter the guitar's vocabulary.

"Those odd noises really feel very comfortable," he told Bob Gulla of *Guitar One* magazine. "It's what naturally spills out. I was looking at a noise chart that I had in the studio... it helped me remember solos and noises. Back then, it was almost a bible to refer to, but now it looked very outdated. 'Oh, how remedial that one was.' Now, it's just a case of strapping on the guitar and letting the stuff sort of leak out... [I'm] feeling comfortable with this style of playing, growing and getting in touch with the subtleties of it, as opposed to going, 'Okay, here is a noise that sounds reminiscent of something off of [Dr Dre's 1992 hip-hop album] *The Chronic*.' It's now a matter of which shades of the lawnmower sound I want to inflict on the listener!"

But the guitar noises were only a small part of the picture: one that took up more than its fair share of attention, in retrospect. The most attention-grabbing element of the first 12 Rage Against The Machine songs was their lyrical content, devised by de la Rocha and a pulverising denunciation of almost everything which Western society was based on in 1991. Poverty versus wealth, exploitation of the masses by vested interests, the war crimes of the elite, the failure of education, the mental and physical enslavement of you and me... all of these things were spat out and stamped upon by this passionate kid with the dreadlocks.

Morello backed his singer's violent, apocalyptic poetry all the way, explaining: "Everybody has complete confidence in him to come up with the lyrics and the poetry that ideologically defines what the songs are about. I think there's a great deal of sensitivity in our songs. We sing about things like solidarity, resistance, and struggle. Those things are every bit as much a part of the human experience as love and break-ups and cars and nookie, but it is a corner of human experience that is often neglected in the realm of pop music. There are plenty of bands that cover the other end of it."

He added, "You don't treat extreme illnesses with mild medicine. We are completely unapologetic about that... We've tapped into a vein of indignation the same way The Clash and Public Enemy had a resonance you were not getting on the news." De la Rocha refined this statement, saying, "Anger has always been at the centre of music, [but] ultimately, every revolutionary act is an act of love. It's about love for people. And so I think every song I've ever written has been a love song." A mixed message, perhaps, but hold on: the band were just getting started, and we'll take them to task for some of their more extreme rhetoric in due course.

Record labels had continued to express interest in signing the group, and it was Epic, a subsidiary of Sony, whose A&R executive Michael Goldstone eventually secured the Rage deal in early 1992. "Once we sat down with the company at those early meetings, there was only one question that we absolutely demanded even though were literally starving at that time," said Morello. "And that was absolute creative control over every aspect of our careers in perpetuity. We told them you're just gonna get RATM without compromise, and we're gonna push the boundaries of what it is to be a rebel rock band. It was during that period between Jane's Addiction and Nirvana, where labels had the attitude that they should give these crazy kids what they want because it seems to be selling. So we were shocked to get a green light at meeting after meeting for the right to be unmolested for the rest of our career."

Morello's previous experience with Geffen, when he was a member of Lock Up, was invaluable when it came to dealing with the suits at Epic. Quizzed about his thoughts on the record business in later years by the venerable *Los Angeles Times* critic Robert Hilburn, he explained: "I've come to think of the music business as this layer of people – the managers, the attorneys, the record company executives – who are like the landlords of this building that is the music industry. Whether we are talking about the eighties or the nineties, the bands just rent a room for a short time. These landlords all know one another and have business dealings with each other, long before you put your band together and long after your band is dropped from the label. Their interest is more in keeping the building in good shape than in the interest of the people who check in and out. When you are fortunate enough to be in a band as successful as Rage Against The Machine, you get to rent the penthouse suite – but only for as long as you are able to sell records... The important thing is to know what you are up against. Unfortunately, I think that artists suffer from a lot of naiveté. I know I did when I came out here from Illinois."

Looking back on his Lock Up days, he explained: "We had a two-album guaranteed deal. But when our first album flopped, the label dropped the band. We asked about the second record and they said, in effect, 'Do you have the money to sue us?' And, of course, we didn't. So with Rage Against The Machine, we made sure we wouldn't be powerless again. We said the company had to not only guarantee that we would be able to make three albums, but if they reneged on the deal, there were specific amounts of money they would have to pay the band if they didn't make album two or album three. And it was substantial amounts... enough to make us feel their commitment was genuine. Plus, Michael Goldstone, who signed the band, also had Pearl Jam, which was the biggest band in the world, and Michael was saying we were an important band, too. That helped our standing... We stipulated that we would have 100% control over every aspect of our careers, from album covers to videos to T-shirt design. That's something bands should remember. If a lot of labels are competing for you, take advantage of it. Set your own ground rules."

Creative freedom or not, the Epic deal marked a long, in fact never ending, confrontation between Rage Against The Machine and their critics about the legitimacy of signing up with a major corporation when the message of the band was wholly anticorporate to the point of being both anarchist and revolutionary, as we'll see.

"We never saw a conflict as long as we maintained creative control," was Morello's summary of the partnership, a statement which sums up Rage's position succinctly. However, it was difficult to understand – and remains so to this day – how group and label, the one concerned with freedom and the other with profits, could reconcile. Presumably Sony couldn't give a damn about Rage's politics as long as CD sales were healthy: that part is easy to grasp. What was less apparent was how Rage viewed their paymasters, or at least it was until Morello and his band had explained the issue a few times – or hundreds of times, as it turned out.

"That sort of criticism never comes from political activists," explained the guitarist in an online chat with fans hosted by MTV, a few years down the line when such interactions became the norm. "More often it comes from well-heeled suburbanites typing on the computer Mommy and Daddy bought them. [Imprisoned activist] Leonard Peltier, for example, couldn't care less what label we are on. We're interested in freeing him from prison, in getting a new trial for Mumia Abu-Jamal, in combating sweatshops, in stopping the rise of neo-Nazism in Europe... We're interested in donating as much food as possible to our nation's food banks and providing as much assistance as possible to our nation's homeless. These are all endeavours which we are able to undertake in part because of our affiliation with Epic Records. Grass-roots activist organisations, people who really work for social justice and don't just sit smugly with self-righteous indignation, have been supportive of our efforts. I believe that we can do much more in this area than we've already done. I believe it is our responsibility to continue to amplify the band's message by any means necessary."

Elsewhere, he said: "You have two choices. I admire bands like Fugazi that take the other route. They are completely self-contained and independent. But if you do that, then you have to be a businessman. Then I have to sit there and worry about the orders to Belgium and make sure they get there. That is not what I'm going to do. We've had, in Rage Against the Machine... complete artistic control, 100 percent over everything. Every second of every video, every second of every album, every bit of advertisement comes directly from us. I don't even look at it as a trade-off. You live in a friggin' capitalist world. If you want to sell 45s out of the back of your microbus, God bless you. And maybe that works better, I don't know. I'll see you at the finish line."

Most of the songs from Rage's demo from the previous year were re-recorded for the group's debut album for Epic, the long-since-declared classic *Rage Against The Machine*. Produced by Garth Richardson (affectionately nicknamed and credited 'GGGarth' because of his vocal stutter) at three Californian studios including the fabled Sound City in Van Nuys, the album was laid down in a few short weeks. As Richardson recalled, "We did that record minus the mix in 30 days. It was a really quick recording, but a lot of work. I think with that record, we made a record that in 10 or 20 years' time will still be one of those records that like a Zeppelin record, or a Mötley Crüe record, or a U2 record, continues to stand the test of time." He was right, it turned out: but who else would have predicted it, given its lyrical concerns?

Richardson bonded with the band from the very beginning, reported Morello, despite the occasional divergence in recording approaches. "I'll tell you a story of how to ruin a perfectly good groove," chuckled Morello, years later. "Our first record was produced by GGGarth, who is a great guy. He decided that I play behind the beat, and that was unacceptable. So without telling me, he did some sort of calculation – 'Tom plays this many milliseconds behind the beat' – and edited my tracks in Pro Tools until they were dead on. I came in, took one listen, and said, 'What happened? The tracks don't sound like me or the band any more. Change them back!' He did."

While they waited for the album to appear towards the end of the year, Rage Against The Machine took their songs to the people. Two shows in March in San Luis Obispo and Long Beach readied the quartet for crucial support dates with Pearl Jam at the Hollywood Palladium in May, and a string of career-making appearances on that year's Lollapalooza festival, the perfect vehicle for them. If ever proof were needed of the chaotic state in which popular (but not pop) music found itself in 1992, the line-up reveals all you need to know. The Red Hot Chili Peppers, fresh from a musical about-turn with *Blood Sugar Sex Magik* that reinvented them utterly, headlined over the then-massive Pearl Jam. Soundgarden rubbed shoulders with Stone Temple Pilots, delivering their brand of not-quite-grunge to a receptive audience, while the rapper Ice Cube, who was undergoing a sort of conversion to prophet status after his startlingly violent late-eighties work, took the stand alongside hip-hop artists House Of Pain and Cypress Hill.

Running until September, Lollapalooza attracted the perfect crowd for Rage's message: young, energetic and looking for music with conviction. As the year passed, festival dates with Porno For Pyros, Tool, Smashing Pumpkins and the Beastie Boys continued Rage's arrival in the consciousness of the rock fans of the day, leading up to the band's first full American tour in the autumn. Received wisdom has it that the teenagers and twenty-something rock fans of the time were slackers, members of 'Generation X', ignoring the fact that many of these kids were the product of the Reagan era and as concerned with their own financial futures as they were with wallowing in misery. Don't believe what the magazines tell you...

CHAPTER 3

1992–1993

On November 2, 1992, the first single from *Rage Against The Machine* was released. It was titled 'Killing In The Name'.

How to explain the nature and impact of this song without indulging in simple-minded hyperbole? Perhaps by stating that it is one of the most exhilarating songs ever released, not merely from the then-nascent rap-metal movement, a largely tedious genre at best, but also the best politically-focused heavy metal song ever written. If you have a better suggestion, I'd love to hear it.

Catchy as hell because of its central riff, a funky little number in drop-D tuning (an unusual tuning that became ubiquitous soon after, at least in modern metal), and focused on a minimum of striking lyrics, 'Killing In The Name' immediately became Rage's signature song, which it remains 22 years later as I write this. The song's main riff was an old one, Morello remembered. "I came up with that riff [when] I was teaching guitar lessons and I was showing someone how to do drop D tuning. That riff just happened to spill out of my fingers. I had to stop the lesson and go and record it. I feel very lucky that I did."

Less is more is the principle behind 'Killing In The Name', which repeats two lines throughout each verse, two more lines through its choruses and builds to a climax with a devastating reiteration of "Fuck you, I won't do what you tell me!" throughout its final breakdown to the end, which ends with an extended shriek of "Motherfucker!" Then as now, you couldn't play this stuff on mainstream radio, although by chance, the song's profile in the UK received a mighty boost when it appeared on the most mainstream channel of them all.

"Just recorded an interview for the BBC documentary *60 Years Of The #Top40*," tweeted sometime BBC Radio One DJ Bruno Brookes, adding "Rage Against The Machine came up a lot..." His tweet came on August 15, 2013, not long before this book was completed, indicating the unbreakable link between 'Killing In The Name' and the erstwhile DJ's radio career. On February 21, 1993, Brookes – one of the 'Smashy & Nicey' generation of grinning, sweater-wearing radio presenters of the day – was playing 'Killing In The Name' as part of the chart rundown that week. Headphones off while it played, he was engrossed in other tasks and unaware of the screaming, expletive-laden lines which were blasting out of his listeners' radios. A producer hurriedly informed him what was going on and he reacted by fading the song out, following up with an apology.

Nowadays few people would give a damn if something like this occurred anywhere other than a children's TV show: in our jaded era, adult language is fair game. Back then, before we all grew up, it was a different story, and the fact that a leading Radio 1 DJ had broadcast the dreaded F-word not once but multiple times, from the heart of the nanny state, was a genuine PR catastrophe. Complaints flooded in and Brookes never heard the end of it, although all these years later he is the CEO of a private media company and doing just fine, it appears.

This was the best possible launch for 'Killing In The Name', in retrospect. The metal kids of the day regarded it as a triumph. Kids who didn't give a toss about music liked it because it represented a kick in the teeth for authority. Everyone else was at least informed that a four-word band and its four-word debut single existed, a marketing coup if ever there was one. This is the song which introduced Rage Against The Machine's self-titled debut album, released on November 3, and it's among the most memorable that the group ever wrote, whether you happen to like it or not.

Of course, more than a few interviewers asked if Rage thought their audience simply liked the swearing and riffage, rather than the message. "There's always those kids who are into it for the aggressive style of music," shrugged Commerford, "and I respect that: I have a certain amount of that in me. Then there's always going to be those kids who know more about the political topic of a song than we do. I feel like music transcends words, it's the universal language. And we go up there, and whether we're in Japan or America it doesn't matter. There's kids that understand what's being said and there's kids that don't understand, but they feel it. They know that we're giving every ounce we have, and that's the coolest thing. We've achieved our mission."

Years after its release, the song continued to irritate and intimidate its naysayers. For example, in 2008, in a Preston, Lancashire branch of Asda, the Walmart-owned British supermarket which sells products in huge quantities at low price points, 'Killing In The Name' was played in error over the public address system. Customers complained. Metal fans chuckled. Four years later it came to Morello's attention that the song was being played at rallies of the UK Independence Party (UKIP), accompanying the entrance of party leader Nigel Farage onto the platform. It was a bewildering choice of song anyway, given UKIP's right-wing stance when it comes to immigration and other issues, and Morello tweeted: "Hey UKIP & Nigel Farage: Stop using 'KILLING IN THE NAME' for your racist/rightwing rallies. We are against everything you stand for. STOP. IT."

On the actual album, 'Killing In The Name' comes after 'Bombtrack', an opening salvo of immense and immediate impact which introduces the band's deft grasp of a stripped-down, funky lick and Zack de la Rocha's slick rhyme flow. "Landlords and power whores", barked de la Rocha, deserved to "burn" in punishment for exploiting others. An accompanying video depicted the Peruvian Shining Path movement and its leaders Abimael Guzman, a group which Rage partly supported, although they later amended their views on the subject, as we'll see.

'Take The Power Back' follows 'Killing In The Name' and after the screamed invective at the end of that song, it has some catching up to do. A more lightweight track introduced by Commerford's slapped bass-line, it's one of the more commercial songs from the album, in terms of a memorable dynamic that people could hum along with. The next song, 'Settle For Nothing' is much tougher, a doomy, threatening wall of riffs alternating with near-silent, whispered passages that is unexpectedly leavened towards its midsection by Morello's sweet, jazzy guitar solo.

Next up is the unforgettable 'Bullet In The Head', which begins with a chorded bass riff and slips quickly into some of de la Rocha's most venomous lyrics. Addressing themes such as the manipulation of our minds by advertising, the song paints a picture of a zombified population ("believing all the lies that they're telling ya / buying all the products that they're selling ya"), sleepwalking through life as if brain-dead. The singer refers to TV as an "in-house drive-by", and audiences as the victims who are dispatched for corporations' convenience. Grim stuff, but delivered in a funky-as-hell manner, with Commerford's relentless bass groove devolving at the song's end into Rage's most famous riff, a spidery, descending figure that is still heard all these years later in guitar stores worldwide.

By 1992 Morello's old schoolfriend Adam Jones had found fame with his band Tool, whose singer Maynard James Keenan observed life via his sardonic, opaque lyrics. When Rage invited Keenan to guest on the song 'Know Your Enemy', it seemed like an obvious step. The song featured a softly-played midsection between the heavy riffage of its beginning and end, in which Keenan sang the lines "I've got no patience now / So sick of complacence now" twice before yelling "Sick of sick of sick of sick of you / Time has come to – pay!", with the last word an extended roar.

De la Rocha makes the target of his wrath explicit when he shouts "Yes, I know my enemies / They're the teachers who taught me to fight me". However, Keenan's short stanza is more subtle, naming no-one in particular and merely venting his general dissatisfaction. Rage and Tool diverged in style soon after this, a fact which Jones made clear when he said: "We're not a band like Rage, who I respect a lot, but they're very political… they're trying to change people's thinking and all that kinda stuff, and all we're doing is going 'Hey, this is what we're about'… I can't do anything. All I can do is just try to open my own mind. And that's what we're expressing through our songs." (For more on the frankly mindblowing Tool, see *Unleashed: The Story Of Tool*, by the same author, also on Omnibus Press.)

After 'Know Your Enemy', which concludes with de la Rocha's unaccompanied yell of "Compromise, conformity, assimilation, submission, ignorance, hypocrisy, brutality, the elite… All of which are American dreams", the last six words repeated four times, the next song fades in with focused drama. A single-note drone not unlike the main riff of Led Zeppelin's 'Kashmir', the intro gives way to a groove that is indebted to funk as much as 'Take The Power Back'. Like that song, 'Wake Up' is a call to action, in this case against governmental racism, citing as inspiration a famous speech by the late Martin Luther King nicknamed 'How Long, Not Long'. In this speech King referenced a Biblical verse in which the lines "Whatever a man sows, this he will also reap" appear: he adapted these words to "How long, not long, because what you reap is what you sow" – a line which de la Rocha shouts as the song crashes to a halt.

'Fistful Of Steel' and 'Township Rebellion' form a collective one-two punch in which de la Rocha flaunts his rapping skills and likens the mike in his hand to a gun, and then delivers a message about the meaning of freedom. Of the two, the latter is more powerful, largely down to the intense chorus of 'Why stand on a silent platform? Fight the war, fuck the norm!', a line designed for festival crowds if ever there was one. Both songs rise and fall in the huge sweeps required to energise large venues: it's almost as if Morello's experience with mid-sized crowds, de la Rocha's impassioned sentiments and the supremely groovy rhythm section of Wilk and Commerford united in perfect synch at these moments.

Finally, *Rage Against The Machine* ends with 'Freedom', a more considered composition that segues from riff to riff while de la Rocha intones his wisdom. The video clip for 'Freedom' focuses on the case of Leonard Peltier, the imprisoned Native American activist whose cause Rage had discussed and who is discussed in greater detail below. Ending with a chaotic finish, the song drags the album to a halt, leaving the listener breathless and with much food for thought.

And this was before we even got to the album cover. A simple black and white photo, the sleeve of *Rage Against The Machine* could not have been more appropriate given the contents. It depicts the Vietnamese monk Thich Quang Duc, engulfed in the flames of his self-immolation on a public street in Saigon in June 1963. Protesting the persecution of Buddhists in his country by its government and president Ngô Đình Diệm, Quang Duc took his own life in the most dramatic manner possible, with the photo – taken by American photographer Malcolm Browne, who won a Pulitzer Prize for it – bringing international attention to the policies of Diệm, who was assassinated in a coup d'état the same year.

What all this had to do with heavy metal fans in 1992 might have been opaque at the time, but those who took the time to investigate de la Rocha's lyrics in depth would have found plenty of resonating themes. In their first salvo, Rage Against The Machine targeted some pretty ambitious targets: the policies of various governments, including their own; the institutionalised racism of America and its representatives; the media; the enslavement of the masses; and in effect, the entire financial and administrative systems of the Western world. There's significance there for all for us.

Morello brought the relevance of these things home for Rage's fans when he explained: "It's very fashionable now among intellectuals and politicians to claim that history is over, that the world is no longer amenable to radical change. We know better. We prove otherwise at every show. But in order to disentangle yourself from that way of thinking, you have to perceive how people become their commodities. They find their soul in their automobile, or their stereo, or their guitar. People tend to think that if the worker and boss enjoy the same TV shows, or own some of the same commodities, then that represents the disappearance of class antagonism. But the splendour of Beverly Hills could not exist without the sweatshops of Indonesia, and without the layoffs in Flint, Michigan. Or, for that matter, without centuries of black slavery, the genocide of Native Americans, numerous imperialist wars, foreign death squads, fascist dictators supported with our tax money. That's what props up the consumer paradise of Melrose Avenue. Americans are fans of democracy, right? In the sphere of life that has the most to do with who you are, and what you do on a daily basis, there's no democracy whatsoever. There is no more hierarchical pyramid of control than the multinational corporation."

He added: "Whether it's an article or a song, the bottom line is: are you telling the truth? Does it come from the heart and connect with the people who are listening to it? Everything else is irrelevant." True from his point of view, and that of his supporters, but others could still not accept the brashness of a band who would align themselves with a major record label and then embark on a destructive critique of the very system which supported and enriched them. Addressing this point one more time, Morello argued: "Regarding the music business, it's almost laughable that interviewers are still asking how we reconcile our beliefs with being on a major label. We would happily sign to the socialist record label that would distribute our propaganda to the four corners of the globe, but those are not the historical circumstances in which we were born."

Morello has never convinced all his doubters that this argument was valid, and indeed support was not universal across the board even in the ranks of alternative rock. The hardcore band Suicidal Tendencies' spinoff band Infectious Grooves released a mocking parody of 'Killing In The Name' called 'Do What I Tell Ya!', for example. To his credit, Morello continued to place his view in a clear and calm manner, saying: "When you live in a capitalistic society, the currency of the dissemination of information goes through capitalistic channels. Would Noam Chomsky object to his works being sold at [major bookseller chain] Barnes & Noble? No, because that's where people buy their books. We're not interested in preaching to just the converted. It's great to play abandoned squats run by anarchists, but it's also great to be able to reach people with a revolutionary message, people from Granada Hills to Stuttgart."

As for the subject matter of Rage's songs, some cynics wondered if modern young people were up to the intellectual challenge of appreciating its depth. Of course they were, Morello told the *NME*: "All American kids grow up thinking that history is the most boring, stuffy topic. People are taught to see themselves as completely removed from any process of historical change and, if you think that, then it doesn't matter what you do as long as you make it to the next six-pack, the next pair of stone-washed jeans so you can meet the perfect girlfriend, just plugging into that consumer culture. What we're saying is that what you do does matter."

As 1992 passed and more singles emerged – 'Bombtrack' came out in June on the heels of 'Bullet In The Head' some months earlier – word spread about this unusual, definitely unprecedented rap-rock band. In an era when one-word band names were all the rage, the lengthy group title seemed portentous, or pretentious, to many. What was this machine against which the four musicians raged, people wanted to know?

"The machine," said Morello, "is police who pull motorists from their cars and beat them nearly to death on the city streets. A month after the Rodney King verdict, a black Detroit motorist was dragged from his car and beaten to death by police, [but] it wasn't such a big media event because they didn't have it on video. The overall capitalist corporate bureaucracy which we are trained from birth to obey through propaganda in the school, teaching us how to be just another cog in the machine. It's the learned sexism and hatred of women through the media – it's all the machine which we are raging against."

The album, one of 1992's most ferocious, drew a line in the sand. Rage Against The Machine became well-known at incredible speed, with an ascent to the musical stratosphere unprecedented for a band with such uncompromising – and for many, uninteresting – views. Let's face it, most of us don't spend many of our waking hours pondering our corporate paymasters, or wondering how extensively we are controlled by the media: we're too busy trying to pay the bills. Multiply that indifference by 10, in the case of the under-twenties in Rage's fanbase, and it's all the more miraculous that the band and their album reached such a high point in so short a time.

"A tremendous number of people have picked up on the politics of [our music]," observed Morello. "We hear from them every day. The glut of mail and email we receive is astounding. But I think our audience in general is a very intelligent one. There are always going to be people who are just coming for the aggression in the music, and that's perfectly fine – we don't play this elitist music that's for New England coffeehouses. It's not this kind of political folk music for the converted. But some of the people who come for the rock will leave with something very different than what they came with. When you sell nine million records, you can't expect there to be nine million ideological adherents. And that's okay – if you get 10 percent of them, that's still 900,000."

"It's happened fast as a head rush," wrote the critic RJ Smith in *Spin*. "In 1991, they played their first public show. A year later they had signed with Epic. They released *Rage Against The Machine* that year, and industry approval was instant. *Billboard* editor-in-chief Timothy White and *Los Angeles Times* pop-music critic Robert Hilburn, critical biz barometers, wrote paeans. They landed a Lollapalooza slot. If the Black Panthers, to cite one of their heroes, had packed this much industry heat, today we'd all be eating free lunches."

Why were Rage so eagerly received by the people? That's the millon-dollar question, which I've attempted to answer in part by looking at the fragmented music scene and the sociopolitical upheavals in America of 1992. But there's so much more to it than that. Rage Against The Machine's music was real, angry and vitriolic – so much so that cynics and sceptics who sneered at their propaganda were overwhelmed by the sense of genuine outrage that lay behind it. Sure, Morello and his colleagues came out with some over-earnest rhetoric at times, such as the instructions for making a Molotov cocktail which they explained to the *NME*. "You get your wine bottle, get a little gasoline, a little kerosene maybe, a little bit of oil, some soap shavings and a rag," Morello said. "Make sure the rag is touching the oil, hold it away from your body when you're lighting the rag and throw it at the target. It's an effective and cheap weapon of the people. You can certainly disable police cars – in Czechoslovakia they disabled tanks. People have a right to this information."

Stuff like this was open to ridicule, of course, as is all political agitation. But Rage rose above their detractors, stuck to the message and watched as album and ticket sales flowed in. Family members weighed in with their support, in particular Mary Morello, Tom's mother, who had spent the previous five years operating Parents For Rock And Rap, an anticensorship counterweight to Tipper Gore's nauseating Parents Music Resource Center. It's worth taking a look at the PMRC, one of the more irritating inventions of modern America, to illustrate what Mary, her son and his band were up against, as it clarifies exactly who Rage's enemies were – and why the band's songs raged so energetically against them...

Censorship of music that is regarded as threatening or unsafe has been going on for decades, of course, and not just in the USA. As far back as 1951, Dean Martin's harmless but slightly smutty 'Wham Bam, Thank You Ma'am' had been refused radio airplay; four years later Elvis Presley was warned by the cops not to swivel his hips on stage; and songs such as 'The Twist' were banned in Catholic schools for years, thanks to their supposedly maddening qualities.

But the culture of intolerance and suppression only gained a serious political context in 1984, when the Prince album *Purple Rain* caused a bit of a stir in PTA meetings across the USA thanks to its song 'Darling Nikki', in which the eponymous female is said to be "masturbating with a magazine". Not particularly relevant to heavy metal, you might think – but the reaction to the album, which went all the way up to Ronald Reagan's office and back, was unprecedented. The issue was picked up by Tipper Gore, wife of Bill Clinton's future Vice-President Al Gore, who recruited 20 wives of Washington politicians and businessmen to form the PMRC. The aim of this pressure group was to persuade the US recording industry to censor itself in order to protect minors from the more extreme music of the day.

As it happens, the idea of the public policing its own activities is neither new nor controversial: any society needs to regulate itself. But what was slightly sinister about the PMRC was that it presented an agenda which crushed anything and everything that was slightly off its safe, middle-of-the-road, bland, approved list. This included most heavy metal, of course, but it also meant that the freedom of speech of many mainstream pop and rock artists was compromised too.

"Never mind the PMRC," said the nation's headbangers to themselves: "They'll never stop artistic expression." But they were in for a shock. Rather than telling Tipper and her twin-set-and-pearls cronies to fuck off back to the Washington golf clubs where they belonged, the Recording Industry Association of America (RIAA) bowed to the PMRC's demands and introduced the infamous 'Parental Advisory' stickers that adorn CDs, DVDs and books to this day.

The censorship virus spread rapidly. As public and performers watched aghast, the PMRC muscled its way into all sectors of the entertainment industry, beginning with TV and radio – the most potent disseminators of 'undesirable' music to the masses. After being told of the PMRC's concerns over rock lyrics, Eddie Fritts – the head honcho of the National Association of Broadcasters – contacted the bosses of 45 record labels asking that lyric sheets accompany all songs scheduled for radio airplay (back then, of course, there were more than four record companies).

The PMRC's next move was to draw up a list of 15 artists whose work they found offensive and circulate it to anyone who would listen – unfortunately, quite a lot of powerful people. Instantly labelled 'The Filthy Fifteen' by sarcastic journalists, the artists were AC/DC, Black Sabbath, Cyndi Lauper, Def Leppard, Judas Priest, Madonna, the Mary Jane Girls, Mercyful Fate, Mötley Crüe, Prince, Sheena Easton, Twisted Sister, Vanity, Venom and WASP.

Notice how much metal there is on there? The genre's much-loved lyrical themes – sex, drugs, the occult and all-round debauchery – had caused Tipper and her buddies to get into a righteous froth. As for the pop acts Mary Jane Girls, Vanity, Sheena Easton and the rest of them, most were both harmless and obscure. It really was laughable.

A line had been crossed, though. The eighties was, from that point on, the decade of censorship for rock and metal, especially if it contained even the slightest reference to Satan or Satanism. The most famous recipient of a PMRC-inspired ban was probably the perennial court jester Ozzy Osbourne, whose early solo albums *Bark At The Moon* and *Speak Of The Devil* were the stuff of nightmares for the PMRC. It's no coincidence that Morello's idol Randy Rhoads played at his finest on many of Ozzy's best albums.

Post-Ozzy, most heavy metal censorship focused for the next few years on lyrics and images that were sexually graphic or violent in nature, rather than Satanic. For example, the big chain Wal-Mart, deeply shocked by the cover of the Scorpions' *Love At First Sting* album (which features a half-naked couple embracing while the man gives the woman a tattoo) complained to the Polygram record company, who changed the artwork accordingly. Remember this next time you go to Asda and there's a cheery sign saying 'Part of the Wal-Mart family'.

The madness continued, with Wal-Mart discontinuing sales of rock magazines such as *Rolling Stone* and *Spin*, and MTV being banned on a local, institutional and national scale by various Christian groups and protesters gathering with placards at more or less every large-scale rock show. But it wasn't just the big bands:

even minor acts like Degarmo & Key, a Christian rock band, had material banned; in their case a video for their single 'Six, Six, Six'.

In 1985, just as another court case involving Ozzy kicked off – this time alleging that his song 'Suicide Solution' had "aided, or advised, or encouraged" a teenager to commit suicide – the US Senate got involved in the censorship debate at the request of the PMRC. The big cheeses in Washington wanted to know exactly how dangerous rock music was to the youth of America, and brought in three musicians – jazz-rock legend Frank Zappa, Dee Snider of Twisted Sister and country star John Denver – to speak in defence of popular music at a series of hearings. Zappa was most incisive in his comments: he echoed most sane people's opinions when he said, "The PMRC proposal is an ill-conceived piece of nonsense which fails to deliver any real benefits to children, infringes the civil liberties of people who are not children and promises to keep the courts busy for years... the PMRC's demands are the equivalent of treating dandruff by decapitation."

However, an interesting social trend began to emerge towards the end of the eighties. The authorities had forgotten one simple fact, which was that the young consumers of so-called 'deviant' music were not stupid, and the majority understood that this extreme art was just that: art. As ban followed ban and concerned parents filled the airwaves with their bleating, overkill inevitably followed and the kids became impatient with being constantly forbidden to listen to what was, for them, just another album. Asking themselves and each other what was wrong with listening to lyrics that dealt with sex and death – perfectly valid themes for discussion, then as now – the teenagers began to mock, and then to actively defy, the censorship which they perceived as petty and insulting.

The strength of this defiance was shown in the immense commercial boost which the banned artists received – both in marketing terms (a banned act was easy to promote as shocking, scary, evil and so on) and in hard cash: fans flocked to the shows and queued up to buy the albums, 'Parental Advisory' stickers or not. Three huge-selling albums were all banned in 1987 and '88 – Jane's

Addiction's *Nothing's Shocking* (banned from some stores thanks to its sleeve art), Prince's *Lovesexy* (which faced distribution problems because of its cover image – a naked Prince, albeit with genitalia well hidden) and Guns N' Roses' debut album, *Appetite For Destruction*. The latter faced accusations of tastelessness on several counts – the drug references ('Mr Brownstone'), the shots of the band members cradling massive containers of booze, and its controversial first sleeve, a cartoon of a scene in which a woman appears to have been raped. The latter was quickly replaced with an inoffensive logo.

The end of the eighties marked a hiatus in the endless war between metal bands and the industry, thanks in part to the rise of gangsta rap. Although the PMRC and the showbiz organisations in its pockets still fought hard to restrain albums by the few metal bands that had survived the grunge wave, their new targets were Ice-T, 2 Live Crew and NWA, whose lyrics were far more aggressive and reality-based than anything the metallers had come up with. When 2 Live Crew rhymed "With my dick in my hands as you fall to your knees / You know what to do, 'cause I won't say please", they made Mötley Crüe's 'Girls, Girls, Girls' sound like a feminist anthem. And when rapper Ice Cube yelled "Fuck the police, coming straight from the underground", he made Black Sabbath's pastoral croon of "Satan laughing spreads his wings" seem juvenile, inoffensive and – worst of all – irrelevant.

Of course, the ceasefire was temporary, and once gangsta rap had matured into the more politically astute G-Funk, the PMRC's sights were firmly targeted on metal and the new wave of alternative rock once more. Ice-T, who had bridged both worlds with his unremarkable metal band Body Count, was at the centre of a huge furore with 'Cop Killer' in 1992, and Oderus Urungus of GWAR was arrested in North Carolina, on charges of 'disseminating obscenity' at a gig. Meanwhile, Nirvana were in trouble over the song 'Rape Me' on *In Utero* – Wal-Mart and K-Mart refused to stock it, only relenting when the album topped the charts and a renamed version was manufactured: a perfect example of a) consumer buying-power being entirely indifferent to censorship and b) the hypocrisy of the industry.

Little wonder Mary Morello, a perennial activist all her life, chose to found her opposing group to the PMRC in 1987, at the height of the moral panic: there was plenty of work to do if sanity was to be restored. When Rage Against The Machine found its platform, she supported her son to the hilt, even appearing on stage to announce them.

"My mom has been tremendously political her whole life," recalled Morello some years later, after the PMRC and his mother's group had dissolved. "She was involved in the Urban League and other civil rights organising in the Chicago area. For 12 years, she ran an organisation called Parents For Rock And Rap, which is kind of the anti-PMRC, for those readers who remember the Parents Music Resource Center fronted by Tipper Gore. My mom combated pro-censorship forces on Oprah, CNN, and radio talk shows. She befriended Ice-T and 2 Live Crew and people like that. For another 10 years, she taught adult literacy at the Salvation Army, and now she volunteers her time in underprivileged schools. She's a great lady, and she gives spirited introductions to Rage Against The Machine. My mother, who looks very much the part of the retired suburban high school teacher, will get on the stage with a militant fist raised high and say, 'Please welcome the best fucking band in the universe'."

While the political speechmaking batted back and forth, Rage Against The Machine had an album to promote and went on tour throughout 1993, initially playing on that year's Lollapalooza and then heading to Europe to support spinoff band Suicidal Tendencies (whose piss-taking 'Do What I Tell Ya!' was presumably dismissed as a bit of good-natured banter). American dates with House Of Pain also took place, but the year's most memorable concert by some distance came at a Lollapalooza show in Philadelphia on July 18.

When show time came, the members of the band realised that they had a problem: de la Rocha had damaged his voice through too much live performance and would be unable to sing with his normal commitment that day. A hasty pre-stage time conference led to an unconventional solution. Stripping naked, painting the letters P, M, R and C on their chests and sticking duct tape over their mouths to represent censorship, the foursome generated a wall of guitar feedback and strode on stage to face the crowd. For 25 minutes, they stood side by side, staring down the crowd, while the electronic storm raged around them.

"The brilliant reason for that," Wilk explained later, "was that Zack blew his voice out that day. Couldn't sing. It was either cancel or do a half-ass show. We were in Philadelphia [the birthplace of American independence] and thought, 'We need to take advantage of this', 'Is everybody cool with being naked?' 'Yeah, yeah, yeah.'"

"After about 10 minutes," Wilk added, "people realised all they were going to hear was feedback. I got hit with a lighter, some other shit people were throwing. I remember my hand sliding from my waist down to my private parts, going, 'Please don't hit there...'"

More – and more conventional – gigs followed, including a sold-out Anti-Nazi League benefit show at London's Brixton Academy. The UK had taken to Rage with ardour, despite the many America-specific causes which the group espoused, as was seen most keenly in 2009 (we'll come to it). In October Rage began their American tour with a 'Rock For Choice' benefit in Hollywood, supporting the pro-choice side in the battle over women's abortion rights, a political hot potato in many countries but especially so in America.

As the tour income continued to roll in, Rage established a policy of donating a portion of it to various charities in the cities in which they played – homeless shelters and food banks among them. "It's not just about being active," said Morello. "It's about serving the communities that you play in and not just going in like a robber baron and walking off with a big cheque from each city." These sums began to pile up: according to Morello a few years later, the band had given hundreds of thousands of dollars to various causes, while de la Rocha estimated that he gives away 10 to 15 percent of his income.

The members themselves eventually accrued healthy bank balances, of course, and this inevitably became something of a common theme in interviews. Asked if they felt guilty about their personal wealth, the Rage musicians offered differing responses: Morello not remotely so, de la Rocha to an extent. "There have been times when I've felt removed from the community I'm struggling for," he once pondered.

Dates with hip-hop crew Cypress Hill followed, before the release of the video for 'Freedom', premiered on MTV's *120 Minutes* on December 19, although the single itself was not released until the following August. By now, Rage were expected to deliver incendiary messages in their songs, and 'Freedom' proved to be no exception. Taking up the cause of the imprisoned Leonard Peltier, the video recreated the events leading up to his arrest and provided text on screen to inform viewers about Peltier's case.

In brief, Rage's stance is that Peltier, imprisoned in 1977 with two life sentences after being found guilty of the 1975 murders of two FBI officers at the Pine Ridge Indian Reservation in South Dakota, did not receive a fair trial and should be released. Various organisations and governments agree with this view, including Nelson Mandela, Amnesty International, the United Nations High Commissioner for Human Rights, the Zapatista Army of National Liberation, the Dalai Lama, the European Parliament, the Kennedy Memorial Center for Human Rights, Archbishop Desmond Tutu and Reverend Jesse Jackson. Supporting factors for Peltier's release include the hiding of key forensic evidence during the original trial and unreliable testimony by certain witnesses. Although pleas for clemency have not been granted, the most recent plea rejected by George W. Bush in 2009, Peltier remains in prison, where his term comes to an end in 2040, when he will be 96.

It is fair to suppose that most young heavy metal fans had not heard of Leonard Peltier's predicament prior to the release of 'Freedom' – but once the video had become a chart-topping phenomenon in February 1994, it is equally fair to assume that his case had received its greatest publicity in years.

Evidence, if any were required, of the usefulness to Rage Against The Machine of collaborating with their enemy – that is to say, allying themselves to a major record label. "You labour and you slave away to try to get one column inch on page 36 of *The Daily News*," explained Morello, "when Rage can bring the case of Leonard Peltier into 60 million homes on MTV because we're on a major label – make no mistake about it. As far as tactics, it's just much more viable. We're not one of those bands that are pious rebels and into self-righteousness. Peltier does not care what label we're on, he needs to get out of jail. That takes more people, not less people."

CHAPTER 4
1994–1996

Proof that activism in music can yield financial benefit came when Rage Against The Machine presented a cheque for $75,235.91 to the Leonard Peltier Defense Fund in April 1994. That's serious progress for a band only two and a half years into their career, especially one that supposedly plays niche, 'difficult' music and whose followers (say their detractors) are nothing more than a bunch of disaffected stoner youths who don't appreciate the luxury of their lifestyles. The 75 grand was raised at a single show on 28 April, played at California State University alongside Cypress Hill, Quicksand, Mother Tongue, X and Stanford Prison Experiment, with a guest appearance by the Beastie Boys. That's activism at work for you.

None of this was easy to achieve, despite the rewards. The constant pressure to express their indignation about so many issues was tough for the members of Rage, not least because they had set the bar so high with their first album, and also because the highway of protest music was littered with bigger, more popular bands than them. "When you choose the path of being a political rock band, the road's a lot steeper for you," explained Morello, as always the band's spokesman on matters political. "If you're going to sing about Leonard Peltier, you've got to be pretty great in order to get over. At any given time there are bands who are overtly political, but they may not be artistically viable. We're fortunate to have nosebleed seats in the arena built by the MC5, Bob Marley, and Public Enemy. It's not like I'm wringing my hands that there's not a lot of political bands, [though]. I have two interests: one is doing my best with Rage's music and politics; the other is doing my best for the world of activism. I also think it would be horrific if bands that had no political convictions all of a sudden started making political pronouncements."

Asked if Rage's perennial lyrical angst might be replaced by love songs one day, Morello showed class by not rising to the bait. He replied, "Emotional conversations in rainy phone booths are all very much a part of the human experience, and deserve to be commented on. So too, are resistance and struggle and solidarity. They are important parts of the human experience which are normally ignored across the pop continuum. The better question would be to ask the more escapist artist, 'Why do you ignore these essential parts of life?' rather than ask us why we don't write love songs, since there are plenty of bands already covering that territory... As the band grows in popularity, so too do we, it seems, become more of a threat, and we've never had more resistance, whether it's from corporations... or police organisations who have tried to shut down our shows on certain occasions. So that only means that we're doing the right thing. When they start pushing back like that you know you're on the right track."

Although more live dates occupied the band throughout 1994, specifically a benefit for the Leonard Peltier Defense Fund, United Farm Workers, and Para Los Niños in LA called Latinpalooza, new music was expected from Rage in the wake of the hugely successful debut album two years previously. *Rage Against The Machine* had sold over a million copies by August, nabbing a platinum award by doing so: little wonder the board at Epic were thirsty for a follow-up.

While no new album was forthcoming, Rage did record a new song, 'Year Of The Boomerang' (with the definite article changed to 'Tha', hip-hop style, for a later release). This appeared on the soundtrack to the John Singleton-directed film *Higher Learning*, starring rapper Ice Cube. It's another slab of abrasive funk, with de la Rocha creating what must be the only heavy metal song to reference the French philosopher Jean-Paul Sartre: his repeated reference to the title comes from Sartre's quotation "It is the moment of the boomerang", itself referring to aggression from oppressed peoples. While other references to the Nazi concentration camp Dachau and Haiti aren't clarified, de la Rocha is plainly speaking out against a whole range of social ills, sexism, racism and the exploitation of the poor among them. His words "All power to the people" are the motto of the Black Panther Party, one of the more obvious inspirations for 'Year Of The Boomerang'.

At the opposite end of the spectrum in most conceivable ways came a cover of 'Calling Dr. Love', a Kiss song recorded for a tribute album called *Kiss My Ass: Classic Kiss Regrooved*. Morello and Wilk played guitar and drums while Maynard James Keenan of Tool sang and Billy Gould of Faith No More supplied bass in a line-up that was something of an alternative rock supergroup: its name was Shandi's Addiction. Their version of Gene Simmons' 1977 classic was a fun-free, stripped-down take on the lascivious original, ripping out most of the melodic content and replacing it with semi-industrial noises and Keenan's indistinct vocal.

As a depiction of where rock music was in 1994 as opposed to dinosaur bands like Kiss, the Shandi's Addiction song was revealing. Back then, the classic rock boom had yet to kick in, and glam-rock groups of the eighties and seventies were possibly at their most unfashionable. The climate of musical uncertainty which had allowed Rage and Tool to flourish was at its hottest: if anyone enjoyed this fragmented Kiss song, they probably felt guilty about it. All these years later, things have changed for the better – as the members of Rage would no doubt be the first to admit.

In fact, as 1994 ended, fun was in short supply within Rage Against The Machine. The sudden acceleration of the band's career over the previous 24 months or so had left the members in conflict, not constantly but enough to prevent any serious work being done on the next album. Epic wanted songs: the band were unable to provide any. To usher things along, the record label confined the four musicians for four weeks to a house in Atlanta, Georgia of all places, presumably hoping that Rage would emerge after that period of time clutching a demo.

It was not to be, of course. As Morello recalled, "There was no musical or personal communication going on. We were unable to agree on anything – to write music or choose a T-shirt design. Our A&R guy, Michael Goldstone, said, 'Let's get rid of every distraction. You guys live in a house down there. Either write a record or don't be a band any more. It was like MTV's *Real World* times ten."

"My frustration," said Goldstone later, "was, 'How can I be involved with a band this great and not figure out a way to get them to make records?' The differences made it difficult to move the process along, but it was the conflict that made the band so great."

Shelving the songwriting sessions and moving on to tour dates in 1995, Rage organised another benefit show, this time for an organisation called the International Concerned Friends And Family Of Mumia Abu-Jamal. Like Leonard Peltier, Abu-Jamal is thought to be wrongfully imprisoned for murder, and like Peltier the case for his release hinges on uncertainty of evidence and witness reports from his original trial. However, unlike Peltier, Abu-Jamal was on death row, with his execution scheduled for the winter of 1995 unless a pardon was granted.

Rage's involvement in the Abu-Jamal case took a more serious turn in 2000, as we'll explore, but back in '95 their views towards his imprisonment were already solid. Looking back, Morello explained: "When we heard the news item about Mumia we began doing some research into it. When one even probes the surface of the case and what went on at the original trial, it's so shocking. What initially caught my eye was that Amnesty International was calling for a new trial for this guy. I started looking at the case. It's really unbelievable. The core of this case, I believe is simple, straightforward and unambiguous, and that is Mumia Abu-Jamal did not receive a fair trial – period. In the United States of America, you can't execute political dissidents who haven't been tried fairly."

He continued: "We became actively involved in the case in 1995 – the last time they tried to kill Mumia, the last time a death warrant was signed. At that time Mumia was 10 days away from execution when he received a stay, in large part because of the huge international protest about his impending execution – hundreds of thousands marched both at home and abroad to try to stop that travesty of justice from happening. That's what we're shooting for this time as well – just to raise awareness to the kind of level where people aren't willing to stand to see a political dissident be executed, when he did not receive a fair trial and there's a great likelihood that he's innocent."

The Abu-Jamal case, which had been a cause for international concern since his death sentence in 1982, was just one of the causes occupying Rage's collective attention throughout 1995. The abortive attempts at a new album the previous winter had not been resolved, with the members at odds with each other on multiple levels – the direction of the new music, how the songs should be credited, and whether songwriting should take precedence over the various issues were all occupying their time. The excitement had temporarily gone out of being in Rage Against The Machine, it seemed, at least when you examine the statements made by the musicians at the time and after the fact.

"We were having problems writing songs and agreeing on what we thought was good. That was hard," recalled Commerford. "There were drastic differences in musical tastes in the band at that time. It used to be kind of a war between hip-hop and metal. And then I have to bring up the punk side of it too. The punk was the one we all agreed on. We wanted to be a punk band, but we wanted to play some heavy music and we wanted to play hip-hop [too]. It was kind of unsaid, but I felt the battle."

"The tension for me really revolved around the idea that as a songwriter and as a poet I wasn't being recognised," said de la

Rocha. "I had written over half of Rage's music as well as the lyrics, and I was having a hard time hearing that the effort on my behalf was being reciprocated and recognised by my bandmembers. And also we approach music so passionately and we took so much time off, based on our political activities outside of making music, that we kinda created our own versions and ideas of what a great record would sound like. When we got together we approached the record in a way that allowed tensions to become more a part of the process. But I think that's part of every band's experience, ultimately it drives it. I remember going into making that record and hearing the sounds that were coming out and hating it, despising it. Being a great artist is a form of great frustration and I'm not sure I'll ever be completely satisfied. But that keeps me going, even though at the time we were considering calling it a day. The other thing that kept us going was the knowledge that we could raise awareness and address issues, and engage young people politically."

"We're four strong-willed, driven individuals who take a lot of pride in what we do, but we're also a unit, and the band comes first," added Commerford. "So no matter how strongly you feel about this riff you wrote or whatever, if the band doesn't dig it, you've got to swallow your pride and move on. That can be discouraging, it can piss you off, but in the end the band comes out the better for it."

Ever the diplomat, Morello was more upbeat about the traumas that delayed Rage's second album, recalling: "I think it's been a positive progression. When we wrote the songs for our self-titled debut, we wrote most of them in only the first month we had known each other. It was like a creative explosion. [The second album] was far more meticulously put together. We were trying to find a path to accommodate what had become divergent musical tastes into a record that would be cohesive... a musical path that formed all of our different individual visions into a seamless whole, to make a record that we could all agree on."

"It's just that so many tensions arose when we made [the album] that we had to adopt a different approach," said de la Rocha. "A lot of tensions emanated from the conceptions that each of us developed after the first album about what a great record would sound like. Having not continuously written due to our political engagements, we came back with different ideas... It's not about self-aggrandisement or money. I just wanted recognition."

Although it seemed for a while that Rage Against The Machine might follow the Sex Pistols into a one-album blaze of glory instead of a lengthy career, the saving grace came in the form of album sessions helmed by Brendan O'Brien, the producer who had earned his stripes with Stone Temple Pilots and Pearl Jam among other alternative rock bands. The recording dates, scheduled for the three-month period beginning December 1995, would make things easier on the members of Rage by taking place at their own practice space at Cole Rehearsal Studios, Hollywood.

In mid-1995, though, this was still some months away. It seemed for the time being that de la Rocha had other things on his mind – namely, a struggle in his homeland compared to which, writing lyrics was a less urgent task. In many ways, the mid-nineties struggle of the Zapatistas would come to define much of his personal struggle at this stage in his career, so let's see what that struggle is all about, with the aid of some expert help.

BOMBTRACK 2

Mexican Freedom: The Zapatistas And The EZLA

When most Westerners consider Mexico, if they do at all, it is unlikely that they associate the country with the revolutionary struggle of the Zapatistas. Followers of geopolitics and late 20th century history will, however, immediately point to this movement as one of the most unexpectedly successful mass initiatives to take place in recent decades anywhere in the world.

On January 1, 1994, a brief war erupted between the Mexican government and a new group, the Zapatista Army of National Liberation (Ejército Zapatista de Liberación Nacional, or EZLN), who occupied five towns on the state of Chiapas. After 12 days of jungle combat, the Mexican army easily defeated the EZLN: according to historical precedent, that should have been that for the Zapatistas. Another revolution, another quick putdown. However, while the rebels lacked military force they excelled in negotiation skills, and a dialogue opened between the EZLN and the government, leading to a three-year period of uneasy truce in which the uprising gradually gained what it wanted. What did it want, and how are these objectives relevant to Rage Against The Machine?

Young, indignant and ready to rock: Rage Against the Machine in 1992. Clockwise from top left, Rage is Tim Commerford (bass), Tom Morello (guitar), Brad Wilk (drums) and Zack de la Rocha (vocals). PHOTOSHOT/DALLE

Above left and right: Tom and Zack in their yearbook photos. Who would have predicted that these cheerful-looking kids would grow up to be harbingers of doom?

Hardcore punks Inside Out, featuring Zack on vocals, tearing it up. Guitarist Vic DiCara is on the right.
VIC DICARA

Lock Up, with Tom second from right, were way ahead of the alternative rock curve and released only one album, *Something Bitchin' This Way Comes*. ROCKY SCHENCK@ROCKYSCHENCK.COM

In Rage's early days, Brad Wilk played drums with his back to the crowd. Why? Only he knows.
LINDSAY BRICE/MICHAEL OCHS ARCHIVES/GETTY IMAGES

No, not an early version of Slipknot. This was an early visual metaphor about censorship: a concern which grew more sophisticated in years to come. LINDSAY BRICE/MICHAEL OCHS ARCHIVES/GETTY IMAGES

The brand-new Rage Against The Machine performing at Lollapalooza at the Irvine Meadows Amphitheatre in Irvine, California on September 12, 1992. KEVIN ESTRADA/RETNA

June 1993, Mountain View, California: whatever book that is, it's bound to be a heavyweight read in line with Zack's political convictions. TIM MOSENFELDER/CORBIS

Tom with Fishbone singer Angelo Moore in July 1993. Rage quickly found their place among the wave of alternative rock and metal bands of the early 1990s. FRANK WHITE PHOTO AGENCY

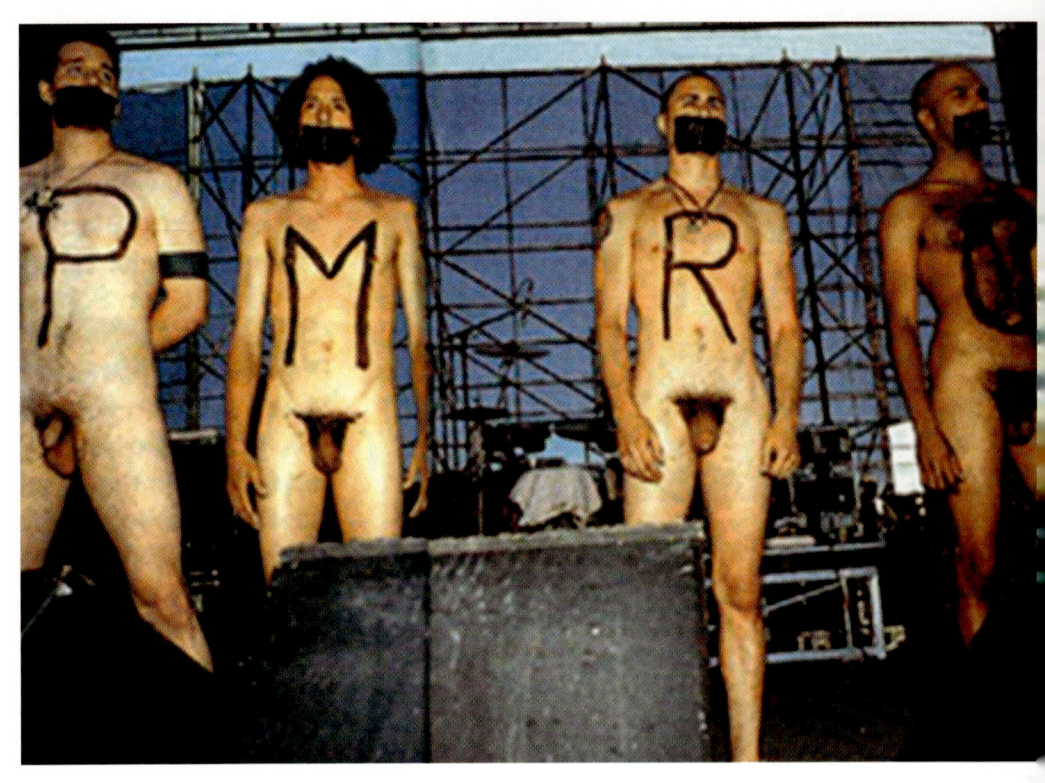

Rage's infamous naked protest at Lollapalooza. Would you have this much courage?

Rage in concert at Wetlands in 1992, a world away. STEVE EICHNER/WIREIMAGE

The power, the conviction, the on-stage aggression. There really is no performance like a Rage Against The Machine set. FRANK WHITE PHOTO AGENCY

Four kids and an upside-down American flag, signalling a national state of emergency. NIELS VAN IPEREN//CORBIS

Tom Morello, the mastermind behind Rage, guitarist extraordinaire and the only member of the group still in the public eye all these years later. GEORGE DE SOTA/REDFERNS

Mexican Freedom: The Zapatistas And The EZLA

Alex Khasnabish is an associate Professor of Anthropology at the Department of Sociology and Anthropology at Mount Saint Vincent University in Halifax in Nova Scotia, Canada. He has worked with and about social movements of various kinds for over a decade. "I come at my work as an engaged and political scholar: I refer to myself as a scholar-activist of sorts," he says. "My most recent work has to do with what we call 'the radical imagination', which is about the imagination of political possibility that animates the most powerful social movements. I'm the author of books about the Zapatistas and the North Americans who act in solidarity with and are inspired by Zapatismo. More recently, my work and writing has focused on the radical imagination, globalisation, capitalism, anarchism, and radical social change."

Who are the Zapatistas?

There are two different things to understand. On the one hand you have the EZLN, which is a Spanish acronym for the Zapatista Army Of National Liberation. It is an armed insurrectionary force made up of several different Mayan language groups, mainly organised in the jungles and canyons in the far southeast state of Chiapas in Mexico. The EZLN is the armed wing of the movement which began its uprising on January 1, 1994, coinciding with the first day that the North American Free Trade Agreement came into effect, although the Zapatistas were always very clear from the beginning that the insurgency was intended to mark 500 years of genocide against indigenous peoples following the colonisation of the so-called 'New World'. On the other hand you have the broad Zapatista movement, made up of the civilian bases in Chiapas but also of people in solidarity with those bases, both inside and outside Mexico. It's this movement which is the real revolutionary force.

What did the Zapatistas want?

What Subcomandante Marcos and the other Zapatista leaders offered was a passionate critique of the status quo, and an open-ended commitment to an ongoing revolutionary struggle. It was about people being able to live their lives with dignity and in connection with one another, on terms established by the communities themselves, rather than a top-down, one-model-fits-all method of revolution. When it comes down to it, that is the enduring legacy of Zapatismo – that it gave the lie to the old notion of power which states that we have no alternative but to march in line with somebody else's narrowly-defined definition of revolution or to resign ourselves to acquiescing to the interests of the powers-that-be.

What practical steps did they want to take?
They wanted to build different ways of governing themselves and organising themselves democratically. It was a struggle for autonomy, justice and liberty, not only for their own communities but for all Mexicans. The key objective, if it can be summed up in one concept, is autonomy: self-rule. They didn't want to secede from Mexico. Their initial demands included land, food, democracy, peace, justice: a basic list of revolutionary demands. Later the struggle became about forming a popular, non-sectarian, non-dogmatic movement for an alternative form of globalization on an international scale. Rather than insisting that you support them, they want you to struggle in your own way in your own place, with your own commitment to dignity in a revolution that makes sense to you and the people around you – and that really is the cornerstone to Zapatismo in terms of their vision of why you don't need to be enslaved to the one percent.

How did you become interested in the Zapatistas?
I started my undergraduate studies at McMaster University in Hamilton, Ontario, in 1995, which was the year after the Zapatista uprising began in Chiapas in Mexico. I was dimly aware of the Zapatistas at the time, and I was passionately aware of Rage Against The Machine. Like many middle-class Canadian kids, I wasn't particularly politicised, although I was certainly aware that there were things going on in the world that were wrong, wrapped up in systems of power. Coming to Rage's music when I was in high school, their songs were a soundtrack for that early period of discovery, and at university I took a couple of classes which provoked me to do some research on things in the world that I found interesting. That same year, Evil Empire came out. Many of

the songs on that album had to do with the Zapatista uprising, and I listened to that album again and again, and in doing so became really interested in this movement that Rage was talking about.

What form did your initial research take?
When I decided to study anthropology at grad school, I knew that I wanted my work to be connected somehow with that struggle, so for my master's degree in anthropology I worked on the connection between independent labour organising in Mexico City and the alliances they were building with the Zapatista struggle in Chiapas. I thought that was important for various reasons, mainly because a class-based struggle like the labour movement linking up with an indigenous struggle for self-determination is something that we don't see happening in a place like Canada and yet it's a potentially revolutionary alliance.

What was the angle of your dissertation?
When it came time to do my PhD, I realised that I didn't need to write another dissertation about the Zapatistas because so much had already been written on the subject, much of which was coming from Mexican scholars. I didn't want to be another imperialist anthropologist, going to Mexico to do the radical tourism and then coming home to write about it, so I took the opportunity to figure out what it was that fascinated academics such as myself throughout the global north, specifically in Canada and the United States.

How did the Zapatista movement tie in with the general political climate of 1994?
I was doing my dissertation right at the time when a dynamic new cycle of struggle was beginning on a global scale. The Zapatistas were such a central point of reference for so many people at the time, and many of the icons of the new, altered globalisation movement were based around the Zapatista struggle. I wanted to understand how far this radical reimagination of political possibilities that the Zapatistas were expressing resonated among people who had never been to Mexico, let alone Chiapas. That became the basis for my doctoral research

and then my first book, *Zapatismo Beyond Borders*. I spent over a year travelling around Canada and the US, talking to different organisers and activists, some of whom described themselves as 'Zapatistas in the north'. They had a direct connection with the movement. This was the basis for my second book about the Zapatistas, which was really about the Zapatistas as a revolutionary movement with global significance.

Who were these activists?
They were diverse: from anti-poverty activists to human rights observers to internet "hacktivists" and direct action anti-capitalist activists. There were radical film-makers, for instance, using the language of digital media to circulate revolutionary stories, in the same way that the Zapatistas were using storytelling in their communiqués to construct different notions of what is possible. In some ways, people who sent support directly to the Zapatistas were the least resonant examples of the connection. Instead, I saw a lot of people taking the Zapatismo inspiration – just as Rage Against The Machine were doing in their songwriting – and making sense out of it in terms of where they were located.

What profile does the Zapatista movement enjoy in the minds of mainstream America?
The cachet that Zapatismo once carried has faded among the mainstream, although that is not the case among radicals who very much see them as significant to the struggle. That has a lot to do with the nature of media spectacle and the difficulty that any social movement has when it comes to maintaining a presence in the public eye, because it needs to innovate and be constantly dynamic. The work of changing the world is slow and steady, however: as the Zapatistas have demonstrated, you need literally decades – if not centuries – to forge robust and powerful movements of resistance and alternative-building.

How could Zapatista thinking inspire the rest of us?
From their uprising in 1994 until the early millennium, they were an amazing force that really pried open the lie that many of us were being sold, particularly in the global north, by political and economic elites, that

capitalist globalisation was the only possible future. The lie is that there is no alternative, as Margaret Thatcher told us. They also pried open the notion that revolutionary politics needed to be conducted by a privileged cabal which sets the agenda for everybody else to march in line to. They moved beyond those awful notions of tyrannical, despotic socialism which people reacted so strongly against. These were real inspirations.

How have Rage Against The Machine helped to publicise the Zapatistas?

The extent to which Rage have been important to the struggle can't be overstated. The band were such an important, countercultural, revolutionary icon. They had a sophisticated and nuanced analysis, not only of systematic injustice but also of the Zapatistas movement itself, which made their songs a really listenable soundtrack to these revolutionary moments.

Do Rage Against The Machine's listeners understand the political references?

I remember seeing Rage play and there were people there who were clearly connecting with what they perceive to be angry music rather than the lyrics. It's always a struggle. You could say the same thing about The Clash or any other band that integrated politics into their lyrics. But for a generation of people like myself who were enmeshed in that musical scene, who were coming to political awareness at a time when communism was supposedly over and the Berlin Wall had fallen, for a band like Rage to be articulating those things in a language that people could listen to, understand and connect with, rather than the dry and dusty political language, was incredibly important. It's hard to quantify, of course, but it's difficult to imagine the resonance that Zapatismo had without the amplification provided by Rage.

How well do Rage express the objectives of the Zapatistas in their songs?

Better than in most academic writing, and certainly in the mainstream media. I say that sincerely. Everybody was jumping on the Zapatista bandwagon back then. You had major commercial media outlets going down there to rub elbows with Marcos and the other leaders, in order to present a snapshot of the movement which was almost inevitably inaccurate, usually grossly so. There was this awful quote that floated around about the Zapatistas being the first so-called 'post-modern' rebellion, which nobody really understood. It didn't make any sense, because it was just this little culture meme. Rage had an amazing capacity to articulate the truth in a super-catchy song that had a great guitar riff behind it. That's why they were so potent. They never got it wrong. They never misrepresented the movement for a second, and in fact they did it a great service by foregrounding the most important points for the benefit of people who weren't indigenous to Chiapas. It wasn't just a simple notion of charity, like 'Hey, go down there and be a revolutionary Zapatista!' – it was really about connecting the struggle with other struggles, historical or ongoing.

What's the bigger picture here?
What the Zapatistas were trying to do was much more important than simply seizing power: it was about transforming the way that power operates. It was about taking seriously the intersection between different kinds of oppressions and exploitation, and talking about indigenous rights alongside women's rights and other issues, such as domestic violence and imperialism and militarism and the military-industrial complex.

Tell us about the Shining Path.
The Shining Path in Peru is a traditionally Marxist-oriented revolutionary movement. They were very important for a lot of reasons when it came to struggling against the Peruvian oligarchy, but they're also well-known for their use of terror tactics, including the terrorisation of civilians in villages which weren't aligned with their aims. I think any revolutionary movement worth its salt that wants to create a better world can't do it on the basis of terror, and expect to produce anything other than terror. That was also what the Zapatistas said: they were always clear on that point.

Have the Zapatistas used force in their struggle?
No movement is perfect, and human rights organisations documented some abuse of human rights perpetrated by Zapatista soldiers in the first days of the insurgency, but it's remarkable to look at the history of the EZLN as an armed force and see that they never targeted civilians and they never engaged in terror tactics of any kind. In fact, since the early days in 1994 their weapons have only been used in self-defence. They continue to arm themselves because they are well aware of what would happen should they disarm. They are still defending land and their existence in the face of a totally genocidal machine bent on their destruction, but at the same time, they refuse to hold other people hostage to their own goals.

Have they succeeded in their aims?
They succeeded in building real autonomy for their communities in the early 2000s, and they continue to do so today. We're talking about several hundred thousand people on the ground in Chiapas, which is an amazing achievement. In many places where state governments still exist, they have a parallel government structure that people – through no coercion – are turning to because it works better, it's more just, and it's more responsible. In that sense, the Zapatistas have already won. It's impossible to think of Occupy, and the alter-globalisation movement, without considering the Zapatistas, and accompanying them with their music, Rage Against The Machine.

Despite their successes, be under no illusion that life was easy for the Zapatistas back in 1995 and '96, when Zack de la Rocha visited them on four separate occasions. The pressure of life down there in the communities, during the period when the cause was still being negotiated with the Mexican government, made the visits stressful – so much so that they turned the singer into a cigarette smoker.

"We'd wake up in the morning and as part of our project for the day, we'd meet with the *campesinos* and cook for them," de la Rocha later recalled. "And one of the ways to initiate conversations was to pick up a cigarette. I'd never smoked before, but I'd have one and communicate a bit. I thought, 'This is nasty, but I'm gonna do it'. Within two weeks, I was smoking like a regular. But to experience what the *campesinos* experience every day, surrounded by the military, you need something to appease the fear... if you're not used to it."

What did he actually do in Chiapas? In true Rage style, de la Rocha organised groups of visitors and got involved, driven – we can safely assume – by a sense of his heritage. Speaking to a couple of Spanish-language American newspapers, he explained: "This is the fourth time I have come to Chiapas. I have had a different experience each time. I was in San Andres during the second round of peace negotiations. It was in May 1995, just after the military offensive in February. This was when the San Andres sessions were starting. In the history of the negotiations there has always been, in one way or another, a failure... And this ended up being the same thing because the government has not complied with the signed accords. At that time, the Zapatista delegates were protected by more than 5,000 indigenous people from all over Mexico... they formed a peace cordon around the site of the dialogue in order to defend the Zapatistas and give them political support. I got a lot from that experience. It was impressive for me to be able to live that emotion and then be able to communicate to the people in the United States the resistance of the people and the testimonies of the peasants."

He continued: "In February 1996, I visited civil camps for peace, in La Garrucha. There, I experienced the terror the people felt: the intimidation by the soldiers, the isolation in which the communities had to subsist, the military camps located between the houses and the fields. I understood then that one of the great missions of a low-intensity war is to wear out the people through hunger and to create lack of goods. That starvation practice against the people has the same effect as throwing bombs on the population, but is more comfortable for the rulers because it maintains Mexico as a stable place and as a suitable place for financial investments, and it doesn't place the Free Trade Agreement at risk. We were witnesses to that. We saw how the soldiers burned and razed the fields, threw the children out of schools, and turned the schools into barracks... And each time we became more familiar with the Zapatistas' form of organisation, communal work and co-operation. And I realised that the motives behind the militarisation were to break down the community, to keep the people from organising in an autonomous manner in order to overcome poverty and isolation. We saw the intimidation."

On his third visit, de la Rocha brought like-minded individuals with him. "Later, at the beginning of 1996, I organised a group of young people: students, artists, activists from East Los Angeles, to go to Chiapas. It was just before the first San Andres Accords were to be signed. We saw how militarisation had increased, we saw how the militarisation of more than 70,000 soldiers obligated the 70,000 families to face death through hunger. We also saw the threat and daily intimidation suffered by the communities. We became conscious of the importance of civil society creating a defence line, because one of the obstacles that we could create against the low-intensity war was to be in the communities, to be with the children while the men went to work in the fields, just to be there. We identified with them."

He concluded: "Later I was at La Realidad for the Continental Encounter for Humanity Against Neoliberalism. We realised the importance of dialogue between civil society and the Zapatistas, and we identified with them as a generation. We are a people without a party. We are for a different world where money is not the only exchange value. We are against racist politics in the United States. Given the crisis and the Free Trade Agreement, the people of the United States also feel like people 'without a face', that is, with no alternatives, without possibilities. Dialogue and the importance of the place given to us by the Zapatistas made us feel that we were a part of the Zapatista struggle, because we are students, workers, artists... and many of us are Mexican. It is important for me, as a popular artist, to make clear to the governments of the United States and Mexico that despite the strategy of fear and intimidation to foreigners, despite their weapons, despite their immigration laws and military reserves, they will never be able to isolate the Zapatista communities from the people in the United States."

In less serious terms, and also in words less prone to the vagaries of an online translation program, Morello explained: "The Zapatistas are a guerrilla army who represent the poor indigenous communities in southern Mexico, who for hundreds of years have been trodden upon and sort of cast aside, and which really are the lowest form on the economic social ladder in Mexico. In 1994 on New Year's Day, there was an uprising there and they were led by the very charismatic Subcomandante Marcos. It's a group which is tremendously supportive of the most objectively poor and continues to fight for dignity, for all people in Mexico... They made tremendous gains in regards to the material condition of those in southern Mexico, you know: they've done their best to organise the community to help them become more self-sufficient. Because in the wake of the North American Free Trade Agreement, the differences between rich and poor have grown that much greater in Mexico, and in the United States as well, not coincidentally, so they've done their best to organise and their key gain is to keep in front of their countrymen's eyes and the world's eyes the struggle for land and justice and dignity, which continues to go on."

Interviewed by Public Enemy rapper Chuck D in a remarkable meeting of minds, de la Rocha came across as single-minded to the point of obsession when he discussed his empathy for the people of Chiapas. When his interviewer said, "You're rolling deep in Mexico and seeing some shit, and you're coming on stage and motherfuckers can't really [handle] that kind of intensity," de la Rocha answered: "It is what it is, I can't help it. I've just got to feel it, what I see. Every time I come back from there I learn. I just try to channel it, all that fear. I remember one time we were sleeping in this little school house, me and a lot of the students I helped to organise to get down there. We were in this schoolhouse and the army was trying to run weapons through the village at night, and the dogs were barking – we were fucking terrified. I thought if I had to experience this every day, that would be life in hell. So I just come back here and try to let people know there's people out there that don't even have what you have, and trying to get something to survive."

He continued: "One hundred and fifty thousand people have died there from curable diseases. The people there are responsible for producing 63% of all Mexico's hydroelectric power, and only a third of the people have lights in their homes. There's one doctor for every thousand people – there are more veterinarians than there are doctors to help people, more veterinarians and rich hotel- and land-owners than there are doctors to help people. And that's where that struggle emanated from, so when that thing happened on January 1 1994, the people decided that there was no other option but to take up arms to try to acquire the basic necessities of their lives. What happened as a result of the North American Free Trade Agreement was as it was passed and implemented in Mexico, it nullified article 27 in the Mexican constitution. Article 27 is the article which guaranteed land rights to peasants, indigenous farmers, and to their families as a result of what happened in 1910. A million people died in Mexico in the revolution of 1910, and for this very reason, which was nullified by NAFTA, it was a death sentence for the people living down there. When I heard what jumped off, I decided 'Fuck, man, I'm not gonna rely on five or six intellectuals as a resource for what's going on down there... [I'll] find out for myself'."

As for the role of his band, de la Rocha explained that he intended Rage's music to be the connection between Mexican and American audiences. "We act as facilitators so that they can participate," he said. "We put them in contact with the organisations and Zapatista support committees here in the US. And the interest and involvement of the young people of the United States in the struggle of the Chiapan indigenous people is greater each day. For this reason our music has become a bridge."

Where did Rage's record company paymasters stand on all this? A fantastic rumour abounded for a while that Epic executives had been so keen to retrieve de la Rocha from Chiapas so that he could work on the new album that one of their execs had flown down there, with a suitcase full of cash, as a bribe. The singer laughed the story off, although he sobered up rapidly when asked about a teaching experience he had had in the communities.

"I couldn't really call it a classroom," he told *Spin*. "It was more like a boarded tomb. It had a dirt floor, and was very poorly constructed out of wood, very desolate in there. The classroom was stuffed with 40 children, all the way from kindergarten to sixth grade. We taught basic math to these kids. The supplies we had were minimal; we had to break pencils several times and sharpen them so everybody had something to write with. I realised that the Mexican government had been spending hundreds of thousands of dollars a week just to keep the military force in those communities, while there was nothing these kids had to write with. That shook me. It was a haunting reminder."

He emphasised the personal nature of the Zapatistas' struggle, saying: "At home, my father often reminded me about who we were as a people, that we were indigenous. My father helped me understand the devastation that the Mexican people felt under the Spanish conquest in the early 1500s. I began to draw a sense of how that particular struggle and resistance affected my life. The slaughter of it is just so amazing and hidden. Seeing it through my father, in his artwork, had a profound effect on me. So when the uprising happened in Chiapas and unmasked the conditions down there, I was drawn to it in a way that I can't fully explain."

He added: "Inside I feel spiritually related to the Zapatistas, I don't feel I can either be satisfied nor alive if I don't fight for the weakest in society. But I won't join any armed group if I don't feel the conditions are right. The most important thing right now is to educate, inform and make people aware until the time is ready for an armed fight... and Rage is part of that process."

It wasn't all plain sailing for de la Rocha: Rage's deal with Epic made some interviewers a little suspicious. For example, *Propaganda* magazine asked him: "We have heard rumours that said that your record company, the multinational record company Sony, produce

Mexican Freedom: The Zapatistas And The EZLA

parts for weapon factories that make nuclear weapons among other things." He replied: "Yeah, but I'm not sure about that, I don't know anything about it... I guarantee that there are a lot of companies that make a lot of shit, including stuff for the weapons industry. It became clear in the sixties that armed fighting had failed, at least temporarily. So what is the most important information tool in our time? That's information. To me, not using Sony or abusing them to tell people what's going on in the US and Europe, would be the same if the Zapatistas didn't use the guns they've stolen from the Mexican army... I was wondering today, why would anyone climb to the roof of the American Embassy with a banner that says 'Free Mumia Abu-Jamal', why do you do that? That's to get the international press attention. The international network that Sony has available, is the perfect tool."

The cause moved the Rage members so much, and de la Rocha in particular, that three songs on their second album – 'People Of The Sun', 'Wind Below' and 'Without A Face' – plus 'War Within A Breath' from their third, directly addressed the Zapatistas' struggle. The issue remained so close to Rage Against The Machine's collective sensibilities that the EZLN flag was later used as a stage backdrop.

According to one report, Zack de la Rocha also asked Epic Records for $30,000 to donate to the EZLN. Epic's response is not known.

CHAPTER 5

1996–1998

Five years into their career, Rage Against The Machine looked as if they might not make it to six. As if their own internal dissent wasn't enough of a threat to their continued existence, then the environment in which they operated was much worse.

The entertainment business, founded as it is on profit and compromise, was prepared to tolerate Rage's outspoken views to a certain extent, but when the band found themselves performing on NBC's prime-time comedy show *Saturday Night Live* on April 14, 1996, they found out exactly how far that extent was. Booked to perform a new song, 'Bulls On Parade', followed by 'Bullet In The Head', Rage arrived to set up and rehearse, hanging the American flag upside-down from their guitar and bass amplifiers. This was done as a symbolic gesture: the inverted Stars and Stripes indicates a state of danger or emergency, according to Section 8a of the United States Flag Code, which reads (thanks, Google): "The flag should never be displayed with the union [the panel of stars] down, except as a signal of dire distress in instances of extreme danger to life or property."

"Our contention is that American democracy is inverted when what passes for democracy is an electoral choice between two representatives of the privileged class," said Morello afterwards. "America's freedom of expression is inverted when you're free to say anything you want to say until it upsets a corporate sponsor. Finally, this was our way of expressing our opinion of the show's host, Steve Forbes."

Rage's targets were especially visible that night, in the form of SNL's host, Steve Forbes, and the owners of NBC, the mighty General Electric. Forbes, then 50, was and remains a leading member of America's business elite and, more to the point in this case, a previous Republican presidential candidate. Add all this together, and Rage were truly venturing into the belly of the beast – the evil empire after which their new album was named.

Unsurprisingly, someone on the production team wasn't prepared to have America tuning in to the sight of the nation's precious flag strung upside-down, and ordered stage hands to remove the flags before Rage began 'Bulls On Parade'. Moreover, the band were asked to leave the building before playing 'Bullet In The Head', which in any case was about to have its more robust language bleeped out to avoid offending anyone.

"*SNL* censored Rage, period," fumed Morello. "They could not have sucked up to the billionaire more. The thing that's ironic is *SNL* is supposedly this cutting-edge show, but they proved they're bootlickers to their corporate masters when it comes down to it. They're cowards. It should come to no surprise that GE, which owns NBC, would find 'Bullet' particularly offensive. GE is a major manufacturer of US planes used to commit war crimes in the Gulf War, and bombs from those jets destroyed hydroelectric dams which killed thousands of civilians in Iraq."

The actions of the *SNL* producers were ridiculous. Rage's combination of adult language and political commentary – subtle, at that – shouldn't have been deemed a threat to the audience of a show that goes out at 10pm and which is regarded as slightly subversive in its humour and delivery. But no, as ever, the powers that be overreacted, insulting their audience's intelligence in doing so, and the money won the day.

No matter. Rage Against The Machine were on the point of a huge wave of activity, commencing with the release of *Evil Empire* on April 16 and following up with a lengthy world tour that would continue until September 1997. If that didn't ensure the delivery of their message to the masses, then nothing would, although the relative lack of promotional activity by the band themselves after the album's release indicated that all might not be well internally.

On the face of it, *Evil Empire* continues the assault on the themes established by the debut album, although there's a notable emphasis on the Zapatista struggle. The cover is less shocking than its predecessor, depicting an all-American superhero kid, and if you didn't take the time to listen, you might be forgiven for thinking that *Evil Empire* is merely *Rage Against The Machine Volume 2*. Nothing could be further from the case, however. You can forget the feelgood, we're-all-in-this-together choruses designed for entire crowds to sing in songs like 'Killing In The Name' and 'Township Rebellion'. *Evil Empire* is more pessimistic, less dynamic and generally more live in feel, the latter element probably due to the recordings having taken place at Rage's own rehearsal room. This is not to say that the performances are loose: far from it. Morello and Commerford in particular deliver their parts with microsecond precision. It's just the big-studio sheen of the first album is entirely missing, making *Evil Empire* a less comfortable listen.

After its release, Brad Wilk observed, "*Evil Empire* was a really dark record, and it made our first record look almost like a pop record, in terms of song structures and choruses that had catchy hooks and whatnot... I don't know if people necessarily wanted to hear Rage Against The Machine making a completely dark record. And maybe they were expecting to hear 'Killing In The Name' over again. We just weren't at that spot. We were in a very dark spot, and it sounds like it."

The album's most commercial songs, in other words its catchiest, were both singles: 'People Of The Sun' and 'Bulls On Parade'. These kick off the album, with the former a reductive, less-is-more anthem aimed squarely at Zapatista territory, and the latter a more opaque but equally devastating deconstruction of the military mindset. Here de la Rocha lays squarely into the "rotten sore on the face of Mother Earth", the "five-sided Fistagon". 'Vietnow' is another attack, this time on the media and its agenda, with the singer barking "I'm a truth addict – oh shit, I got a headrush".

'Revolver' addresses domestic violence with a chilling list of metaphors, introduced by Morello's solo wade through his guitar effects rack. Like 'Fistful Of Steel' on the previous album, 'Revolver' retreats into near-silence and whispered invective before rising up once more to a terrifying peak.

Whatever the 'sweet, indulgent fluid' in a bottle is that de la Rocha introduces at the start of 'Snakecharmer', it's up to no good: he continues to refer to viruses, hell, vomit and false friendship in a sequence of images of the recurring type that give the album its nightmarish nature. Curiously, the musicians sound like they're having no end of fun in this song, bashing out a precision-engineered range of riffs that makes them sound endlessly inventive.

'Tire Me', which won a Grammy in early 1997 for Best Metal Performance (although it's not the most striking song on *Evil Empire* by any means), continues de la Rocha's focus on minorities repressed by the USA, notably 'the Laos frontiersmen', the Hmong tribe from Laos, whose territory the CIA used as a supply area (drugs being among the products supplied). 'Down Rodeo' refers to Rodeo Drive, an insanely expensive shopping street in Beverly Hills, and the murdered Black Panther activist Fred Hampton.

'Without A Face' marks Rage's second mention of the Sendero Luminoso ('Shining Path'), a revolutionary guerilla group in Peru. Although the band as a whole were reluctant to explicitly support the actions of this controversial group, the mentions of the organisation in their lyrics (not to mention the references in the 'Bombtrack' video, as we saw earlier) caused more than a few journalists to take them to task.

Let us remind ourselves of Alex Khasnabish's words: "The Shining Path in Peru is a traditionally Marxist-oriented revolutionary movement. They were very important for a lot of reasons when it came to struggling against the Peruvian oligarchy, but they're also well-known for their use of terror tactics, including the terrorisation of civilians in villages which weren't aligned with their aims. I think any revolutionary movement worth its salt that wants to create a better world can't do it on the basis of terror, and expect to produce anything other than terror. That was also what the Zapatistas said: they were always clear on that point."

Writing in *Spin*, the writer RJ Smith said: "Three years ago, Morello praised the Shining Path, the Maoist guerrillas who attempted a cultural revolution in rural Peru and have reportedly killed thousands of innocent peasants. Violence, he said, was sometimes necessary to overthrow an oppressive regime. That belief distinguishes liberalism and Marxism, and it's one that Rage has since broadcast less frequently."

Smith took Morello to task about the Shining Path, with the guitarist replying: "It's not uncommon that the US press will take a group which is so threatening to its interests and demonise them, vilify them. You see it happen every day. To use a Chomsky quote, 'The greatest acts of international terrorism are planned in Washington'... I'm not disputing the fact that in liberation struggles there's often an enormous amount of violence. The centuries of deprivation and brutality that have been heaped upon people sometimes has a boomerang effect. There's been insanely genocidal US-paid-for behaviour on the part of the Peruvian government. When the mostly indigenous rural poor finally stand up for themselves and take up arms against their oppressors, suddenly Uncle Sam starts whining 'Terrorist! Terrorist! Terrorist!'"

Zack de la Rocha was less keen to espouse the Peruvian guerillas, saying: "You should talk to Tom about that. I don't personally support them. I support some of the things they fight for. I don't think Fujimori [the president of Peru] should remain in power, I think they should wrestle themselves out of the US's clutches and get control over their own faith, like all the other countries in Central and South America. But I think that Shining Path repeat a lot of errors that they should have learned from throughout history.

I think that if Shining Path got control, it wouldn't change anything about the Peruvian people's situation. It would just be someone else in power."

De la Rocha's convictions about the EZLN and its struggles in Chiapas remained strong, however, judging by songs such as 'Wind Below' (its title taken from a book written by Zapatista leader Subcomandante Marcos), which laments the North American Free Trade Agreement, or NAFTA, which saw American businesses use cheap Mexican labour to reduce costs. He bewails the state of the planet from "Gaza to Tiananmen" in 'Roll Right' and winds *Evil Empire* up with 'Year Of Tha Boomerang', released the previous year.

Evil Empire may be dark in sentiment but it's musically uplifting, even if it lacks the stadium-filling dynamics of *Rage Against The Machine*. Its title would have caused more than a few Americans pause for thought, of course – but then, if Rage ever had to define their mission, the concept of forcing their countrymen into a bit of self-analysis would surely be a large part of it. "Towards the end of the Cold War," explained de la Rocha, "the Reagan administration constantly tried to breed this fear in the American public by referring to the Soviet Union as the Evil Empire. We've come to understand that you can pretty much flip that on its head to see that the US has been responsible for many of the atrocities in the late 20th century." No arguments there, and if you're reading this outside the UK, don't assume for a minute that I consider this country blameless. Sure, we didn't have our own Vietnam, but our hands are hardly clean when it comes to militaristic foreign policy.

The album even came with a recommended reading list in its booklet, a comprehensive library of left-wing and progressive thinking that would form an entire sociopolitical education of its own if you consumed it all. Can you think of any other chart-topping album – for *Evil Empire* entered the Billboard listing at number one – that attempts a similar feat? The list covered political thinkers and philosophers such as Marx, Engels, Malcolm X, artists and musicians like Miles Davis, Bob Marley, Salvador Dali and

Andy Warhol, prophets such as Che Guevera, Arthur Koestler and Noam Chomsky, literary heavyweights including James Joyce, John Steinbeck, Henry Miller and William Burroughs, plus a dash of humour in *The Lorax* by Dr. Seuss. What these books all had in common was they challenged the status quo in some way, whether it was James Joyce's attack on Ireland's rotten Catholic establishment or Miles Davis's scathing autobiographical depiction of American racism. It's quite a library of revolution.

Of the book list, Morello commented, "There's a recommended reading list printed on the inside foldout of *Evil Empire*. There's a bunch of books sort of thrown in there, and those were just the ones we could get approval for in time. On our website, www.ratm.com, is the more complete list. But if you had to start with one thing, if it is possible to just name one thing, it would be *The Chomsky Reader*. It's an excellent beginning point. It gives you sort of an overview of how [things work], from your media to your government to your educational system. That's an excellent tome in that it sort of takes the blinders off of what's really the internal workings of society; where the power is and how the pyramid structure of corporate power affects your life. That's a good start."

Were *Evil Empire* to be released nowadays, some of these books would probably accompany it as a free download. Back in 1996, a printed list was the best any band could do. At least, until the *Evil Empire* world tour kicked off. An Australian and New Zealand leg had been executed at the start of the year, and Europe was next, beginning just as the album was released and extending through festival season.

As the tour powered through Spain, France, Switzerland, the UK and then Denmark, fun and games at the hands of local law enforcement was always close at hand. On the May 16 show in Copenhagen, Rage narrowly avoided serious injury. Wilk recalled, "It was the most intense moment of my career. We were tear-gassed on our bus right before we were due to go onstage. I remember the police coming in and trying to incite a riot, even though the kids weren't doing anything. After it happened we got up and played the most intense show we've ever done. After being threatened like that, I have never felt so alive in my life."

It would be nice to think that the members of Rage grew closer as a result of this brotherly solidarity, but this appears not to have been the case, specifically in the case of de la Rocha, who told *Spin* that autumn: "I wish I could say there were a lot of positive things that came out of [*Evil Empire*], but there weren't. Look, I don't particularly care for Black Sabbath, and Tom doesn't particularly care for a lot of the hip-hop riffs that I come up with. But the two, when fused together, makes something unique... I think throughout the last few years we've all gone through a series of ego explosions, and it's been very difficult to resolve them. The band has gotten very big. It's often really difficult for me. I haven't fared very well with the band's popularity, with the position that I've found myself in. I'm at constant odds with it."

Nevertheless, Rage soldiered on, playing in Sweden, Norway, Germany, the Czech Republic, the Netherlands, Italy, Finland, Denmark, Russia and Belgium before heading to the USA. This occupied their time until October, although the cramped tour bus and plane quarters must have made the strained relationships inside the band even harder to bear. Add to this the constant energy which Rage were devoting to delivering an impassioned performance every night, both musically and in terms of their politics, and that's an exhausting schedule by anyone's standards.

By now it was assumed that Rage Against The Machine would appear at charitable events of all kinds. A major one was that year's Tibetan Freedom Concert at the Golden Gate Park in San Francisco on June 16, where they played alongside the Beastie Boys, the Smashing Pumpkins, the Fugees, the Red Hot Chili Peppers and others. The two-day concert pulled in over 100,000 gig-goers, making it the largest American benefit event since Live Aid's Philadelphia leg in 1985. Cash was raised for the Milarepa Fund, a San Francisco-based pro-Tibet group.

Asked how he summoned the energy to be so concerned with many causes, Morello explained: "The cornerstone of it is indignation when you see things that are wrong, whether it's in your home, your school, your workplace or your society. It's when your heroes are other than sports people – they're people who've had the courage to fight back in the civil rights movement or the workers' rights movement or the women's rights movement. You start looking at the time we live in now and realise it's not separate from the history of those struggles, but very much a part of them. The future is anything you want it to be, and there is no injustice that is insurmountable if you have the courage of your convictions and are willing to take a stand."

As always, cynics asked the guitarist if he thought that Rage's fans, at least the younger ones, understood what his band was singing about. "We get asked often in interviews, 'The kids don't get it, do they?'" he replied. "We get to see that they absolutely do. I think our audience is an intelligent one and journalists aren't willing to believe that [people] actually get it! They think that's threatening or something... I took my music dead seriously when I was growing up with bands like Kiss, where I loved the music and the rock power of it, and later with bands like The Clash and Public Enemy where the lyrics made sense in my own life. I felt passionately about the bands I liked and I think our fans are no different from that."

On January 20, 1997, President Bill Clinton was inaugurated, and to underline the pessimism that many left-wing thinkers felt about the new, supposedly progressive Democrat leadership, Morello hosted a two-hour radio show called Radio Free LA. Guests included Michael Moore, Leonard Peltier, Chuck D, Mumia Abu-Jamal, Noam Chomsky and – most surprisingly given his pseudonymous existence – Subcomandante Marcos of the Zapatistas. Musical performances came from Morello, de la Rocha, Red Hot Chili Peppers bassist Flea, Stephen Perkins of Jane's Addiction, Beck and Cypress Hill. "That election resulted in one of the lowest voter turnouts in the history of the country, as more and more Americans came to realise that their government was not in their hands, but in the hands of big business," commented Morello afterwards. "Radio Free LA provided a musical and political gathering point for the majority of Americans – and young people especially – who rightly felt left out of the 'democratic process'."

A whole new tranche of fans was about to come Rage Against The Machine's way. In 1997, a year in which Rage spent the second to fourth quarters almost entirely on the road, the Irish rock group U2 invited Rage to open for them on their PopMart tour, an immensely high-tech (and high-budget) production that broke records for the numbers it attracted. Although the slice of revenue that Rage would earn would presumably have been significant, the band chose to donate their profits to a range of organisations such as UNITE, Women Alive and the Zapatista Front For National Liberation. The next tour, for which Rage were supported by Wu-Tang Clan, went less smoothly, partly because Wu-Tang pulled out after only week citing internal dissent, to be replaced by neo-soul group The Roots, and partly because many of America's law enforcement officials had woken up to Rage's message by now and were actively trying to block their progress. In fact, you could sum up this portion of Rage's career as a more or less constant conflict with various police forces.

"The Wu-Tang tour was dramatic, to say the least," said Morello. "The combination of our politics and a rap group terrified the authorities. We managed to intercept a memorandum meant for a local sheriff's department in Colorado, and it talked about anti-police sentiments and the blackness of Wu-Tang. They then tried to file injunctions, but none of them were successful thanks to the First Amendment. It was very weird though. It's not like we're devil worshippers."

A September 13 date at the Gorge Amphitheatre in Portland, Oregon, was almost cancelled when the local county sheriff, William Weister, filed a complaint with the courts, attempting to block the show from taking place. The publically-available documents refer to Rage as "militant, radical and anti-establishment" (true) and list their allegedly "violent and anti-law enforcement" (not strictly true) themes. However, the ban was rejected and the show went ahead, reportedly with four times as many police officers in attendance as usual. De la Rocha expressed Rage's reaction perfectly when he said from the stage, "There ain't nothing more frightening than a pig with political aspirations. We take it as an insult that he calls us violent, because everybody knows the police are out of control." Rage rammed home their message, for anyone who hadn't grasped it yet, by beginning their set with a cover of NWA's 'Fuck Tha Police'.

1997 was a year of ups and downs for Rage Against The Machine, quite apart from their brushes with various local constabularies. Record sales were consistently astounding, at least by today's feeble standards: in the summer *Rage Against The Machine* was certified double platinum for sales of two million units, while *Evil Empire* also went double platinum after only a year on sale. A Japan-only B-sides compilation called *Live And Rare* helped to keep sales healthy in Asia, and a self-titled DVD appeared worldwide later in the year. This featured a cover of Bruce Springsteen's 'The Ghost Of Tom Joad', one of the most hard-hitting songs that Rage had recorded in some time: tuning down for a super-heavy sound, the band lent the original version the immense presence for which they had become famous.

As if there wasn't enough Rage product flying off the shelves, the Manifesto label licensed the now eight-year-old Lock Up album *Something Bitchin' This Way Comes* and released it on CD, causing a legal furore to erupt over their decision to place a sticker on the case which read, predictably, "Featuring Tom Morello from Rage Against The Machine".

In October, Morello attended a 'March Of Conscience' in Santa Monica, California which protested against the sweatshop labour practices of Guess, Inc., the clothes manufacturer. Rage had got on board with this cause, lending their image to anti-Guess posters in Las Vegas and New York with the slogan 'Rage Against Sweatshops: We Don't Wear Guess? A Message from Rage Against The Machine and UNITE (Union of Needletrades Industrial and Textile Employees)'. Morello's presence at the March was a high-profile event, and it's perhaps inevitable that he was arrested for civil disobedience. Let's ask someone who knows about the issue to define it...

"Sweatshops are a way of exploiting the have-nots in favour of those who have a lot. In doing so they dehumanise both groups by keeping alive and actively creating injustice, inequality and downright abuse. They are also a key link in a very wasteful and more often than not useless industry." These words come from Liesbeth Sluiter, a Dutch sociologist who works as a freelance journalist and photographer on a wide array of subjects, working conditions and labour organisation being one of her focus subjects. Apart from her work for magazines and organisations, she has published six books: *Clean Clothes: A Global Movement To End Sweatshops* (Pluto Press) was her fourth. Visit www.liesbethsluiter.nl for more information on Sluiter's work.

Asked how and when her interest in and research into sweatshop-related industries began, Sluiter explains: "I have been working for the Dutch trade union organisation FNV since the eighties, out of the conviction that labour organisation is vital for a decent society. When in 2006 somebody pointed out to me that the Clean Clothes Campaign (CCC), based in Amsterdam, was looking for someone to write its history, I applied and was accepted. Although I had some knowledge of labour struggles, I wasn't prepared for the raw reality of sweatshops in low-wage countries. In particular, the close resemblance of working conditions in sweatshops in the western world in 19th-century New York and London to the present-day ones was shocking. They match, even in the gruesome details of the factory fires."

The public is not generally aware of the sweatshop problem in Western Europe. What facts would most surprise people about sweatshops and how they operate? "Child labour is one of its features that generally arouses indignation – and is also well-known," Sluiter replies. "The recent wave of well-publicised factory fires in Asia also has an impact. But this focus on the worst also creates a kind of bias: it distracts from the fact that child labour is usually a consequence of adults being underpaid and working long hours, and not being able to raise their children well. I've found that when you tell people about women working for 16 hours on end with their children sleeping in the factory, about women who are not allowed to go to the toilet not even when they menstruate, about wages that don't even add up to the cost of living for one week – in the end people will sigh and would rather forget about it. They feel powerless, and the production chain has become so immensely complicated that it's hard to show the connections between our cheap clothes and abuse in Bangladesh. It's only the most crass and/or emotional events like child labour or factory fires that will pierce that barrier of 'I don't want to know/I can't do anything about it'."

Although information on the guilty parties changes regularly (visit the Clean Clothes Campaign at www.cleanclothes.org for up-to-date information), some well-known companies are still connected, remotely or otherwise, with sweatshop labour. "While more than 70 companies, among them large ones like Carrefour and Aldi, have signed the legally binding Accord On Fire And Building Safety in Bangladesh after the latest factory collapse," says Sluiter, "Walmart and Gap have refused to sign it, proposing instead the same self-regulatory approach that has led to the fires. Walmart, of course, has a history of creating and condoning bad working conditions, always pushing for the lowest price levels."

How does the CCC achieve its goals? "The CCC develops various campaign strategies," she continues. "First and foremost, it supports local labour organisations and NGOs in low-wage countries, not with financial support but by making available its resources in the field of expertise, information and communication. It takes part in the debate within and lobbying of European institutions for better international law on working conditions and global companies' responsibility. The Western clothes-buying public is asked to get involved in putting pressure on the big brands to mend their ways. The CCC does not publish a list of 'responsible' stores or brands, where you can buy 'clean' clothes: things change quickly in this respect, and many so-called ethical brands don't measure up to their own claims of integrity. Often they only score on a few environmental criteria while labour issues are left out completely."

1996–1998

Sluiter enjoyed working with the Clean Clothes Campaign, describing it as "a typical networking organisation – flexible, decentralised, and with very little overhead. It started out in 1988 as 50 women picketing the Dutch clothes multinational C&A after a case of worker abuse in the Philippines, and now consists of a global partner network of over 200 groups, with 17 platforms in European countries, of which the British Labour Behind The Label is one. Ongoing concerns and focus issues are the right to organise, wages, working hours, health and safety, gender – over 90 percent of textile workers are female – migrant work, precarious contracts, and international law."

Less dramatic than Morello's arrest, but with more onerous consequences, Brad Wilk was diagnosed with Type 1 diabetes in 1997 and was obliged to make some lifestyle changes as a result. For an athletic musician such as a metal drummer, maintaining safe levels of blood sugar is both more important and more difficult to do than it is for most people, but to his credit Wilk stepped up to the challenge and began to manage his disease.

"I was first diagnosed with Type 1 in 1997," he said. "One night on tour I went to bed and had to get up to urinate four or five times during the night – and I didn't drink anything before I went to sleep. When I woke up the next morning, my eyesight had diminished by about 40 percent. I could barely see 10 feet in front of me. Everything was a blur. I also felt seriously weighed down and sluggish."

After the diagnosis, he continued: "I became pretty depressed. I knew that it was going to be incredibly difficult for me to continue touring while trying to figure out this disease and how it affected my body. I wasn't sure if I could even do it. But then I just buckled down and tried to make the best of it. I had a huge backpack and carried my own food with me around the world. I had my wife, Selene – my girlfriend at the time – come with me for support. From Israel to Spain, Australia, then to Japan, I accepted the challenge and moved forward. I was not going to let diabetes control my life. I was going to instead control my diabetes and live my life with an open mind and accept this lifestyle change. It wasn't easy at first, but I persevered."

Wilk manages his condition with care, especially before a show, he explained. "It's true that my drumming can drastically change my blood sugar levels. Any time your heart rate gets that high through vigorous exercise, you're going to have to watch it," he said. "The tricky thing is that sometimes drumming can swing it high, but most times will swing it low... So I will usually eat a banana right before I go on because it's high in potassium and helps muscle fatigue and, more importantly, keeps me from going into a diabetic coma! Bananas aren't always readily available all over the world, so, if necessary, I will substitute something else that has a good amount of natural sugar. I also test myself sometimes between songs, and always before an encore, just to make sure. I have a blood glucose monitor that gives me a result in five seconds. It's very helpful, and I've become quite fast at it. I also have the help of my drum tech, who has been with me since the inception of the band. He always has my monitor by his side and is ready to hand me the tester if I need it. I also keep juice of some sort on my riser just in case. I like to cover my butt, and I'm not talking about a pair of shorts here."

The occasional emergency has come up, added Wilk. "I've had a few close calls. One night in France I was on stage and knew that my blood sugars were getting very low. I have a pretty good sense and pay attention to what my body is telling me, so I drank about two-thirds of a bottle of Powerade. Two songs later I felt even worse and started to get disoriented and very dizzy. I began to slightly panic and couldn't understand why I wasn't feeling stabilised. So immediately after the song I still had sense enough to grab the bottle – which was in French, to make matters more difficult – and realised that they had given me a drink sweetened with sucralose that had next to no sugar or carbs. My tech then had to make a mad dash back to the dressing rooms to find something else before it was too late. Luckily, he came through. I also have very understanding band members who threw out a jam with no drums while I got what I needed. So hey, because of my diabetes, the audience got a little something extra. The glass is half full, people!"

"Diabetes is no walk in the park, I know," he concluded. "But with the proper care and knowledge, it can be a manageable disease. The more accepting you are about the fact that you have this disease, the better you will begin to take care of yourself. And it's nothing to be embarrassed about or ashamed of. Be proud of who you are, and don't let this disease keep you from doing what you want to do – unless, of course, you want to be a professional pie-eating contestant."

Into 1998, and the spectre of a third album was raising its head. The massive success of *Evil Empire*, dark and pessimistic though it was, had given Rage a morale boost, and the proliferation of causes to which they had lent their collective and individual names had reminded them of their original mission. Around this time, de la Rocha helped to found a collective group of entertainers called the Spitfire Tour, whose remit was to lead conferences at colleges throughout America: well-known left-wing personalities such as Jello Biafra, Chuck D, the actor Woody Harrelson and Jane's Addiction/Porno For Pyros frontman Perry Farrell had also become involved. Once more, domestic issues were at the forefront of Rage's thinking; a factor which had a major impact on their next, and arguably most powerful, work.

CHAPTER 6

1999–2000

Times were changing in 1999, and thankfully for the better. The recording of Rage Against The Machine's third album was smoother – much smoother – than that of *Evil Empire*, for various reasons.

"It was a healthier, more fulfilling process than times past," said Zack de la Rocha. "Right now, we're taking it day by day. I don't see why we can't continue, primarily because we have overcome a lot of the tensions. I don't think that in our heart of hearts we were really ready to destroy this gift that we'd fought for. I mean, we could have sold two or three times the amount of our first album, but I think that would have been destructive."

One reason for Rage's renewed solidarity was undoubtedly their need to close ranks in the face of nu-metal, a now largely (but not wholly) outmoded wave of hip-hop-influenced heavy metal that ruled the airwaves between 1994 – when Korn's first album appeared – and 1999, when the movement peaked. Rage Against The Machine's involvement in the nu-metal sound absolutely has to be deconstructed if we're to understand where they found themselves after eight years in business. The following may not make for pleasant reading if you're a fan of thrash metal or hardcore, as nu-metal is now practically the most unfashionable music ever invented, but bear with me for a minute.

Looking back, the nu-metal movement came and went with such speed, and its image was so driven by fashion, that even at its peak there was massed resistance against it, let alone after it began to decline. Interviewers liked nothing better than to needle de la Rocha and the other Rage members about their responsibility, or otherwise, for the rise of the nu-metal sound. The singer usually diverted such accusations, saying: "To say that Rage Against The Machine were primarily responsible for that sound is a little misleading, and a little ignorant of musical history in the States. There were so many bands fusing hip-hop and punk rock, for instance, Michael Franti in San Francisco or Anthrax and Public Enemy, or KRS-One rhyming over an AC/DC remix, there's a very clear history. What makes us unique within the convergence of that music is the fact that we did it with live instrumentation, and that we drew upon the lessons that Bob Marley and Public Enemy and The Clash passed on in terms of seeing music as a weapon."

OK, he had a point. When he and Morello combined rapped lyrics with metal riffs back in 1991, they weren't the first musicians ever to do so. But nu-metal, as it was in 1999, wasn't merely a combination of rap and rock: it had grown to have its own, identifiable sound. The first successful example of a rap-metal tune came in September 1986, when Run-DMC and Aerosmith collaborated on a reworked version of the latter's classic 'Walk This Way' and topped the singles charts worldwide. Five months later came the Beastie Boys, who released a raft of singles including the puerile but influential '(You Gotta) Fight For Your Right (To Party)', which featured guitar riffs by Kerry King of Slayer. This was followed up by US rapper Tone Loc, whose February 1989 hit 'Wild Thing' contained a simple riff under Loc's famously laconic rap. Soon after this came Faith No More's 'Epic' in February 1990, and 'Bring The Noise' by Chuck D and Anthrax in July 1991. The rap-metal floodgates subsequently opened to allow dozens of rapping rockers out of the woodwork, and the movement was born.

A related but less prominent subgenre was funk-metal, a slightly clumsy term applied in the late eighties to any rock band whose bass player used a slapping style: the best-known funk-metallers were the Red Hot Chili Peppers (who later achieved global success with a more pop-oriented approach) and Living Colour (an impossibly talented group of players who were just too far ahead of their time to keep it together for long). Other funk-metallers ranged from the credible, such as Infectious Grooves (a side-project of hardcore punks Suicidal Tendencies: you will recall their mocking 'Do What I Tell Ya!'), to the relatively obscure, such as the Dan Reed Network.

When these new styles joined forces with grunge against the traditional metal bands, even mainstream rock acts were unable to sustain much impetus. For a metal band to survive, it had to be diverse (Faith No More, Primus), too big to touch (Metallica, Iron Maiden) or too small to count (the legions of black and death metal bands). Even apparent untouchables such as Motörhead and Mötley Crüe only survived by the skin of their teeth.

In late 1998, when Rage were recording their new album, Fear Factory, Godsmack, Korn and System Of A Down were spearheading this new sound right into the upper reaches of the charts – looking different, singing differently, tuning their guitars low, rapping and emoting about personal trauma or political commentary. On the sidelines, metal bands such as Pitchshifter – which weren't 'nu' as such but which approached the sound with an electronic spin – were coming to prominence. Marilyn Manson were doing their horrorshow version of glam. The ripple effect spread as far even as thrash metal stalwarts Slayer, whose 1998 album *Diabolus In Musica* was heavily influenced by Korn-style groove. At this exact point, the bands which we now associate most with nu-metal were on their first album (Limp Bizkit, Coal Chamber) or just about to break into the public eye (Slipknot, Linkin Park), after which point the battle for supremacy would be all over, won in nu-metal's favour, until approximately 2002.

Make no mistake, Rage Against The Machine knew what was happening in the field of popular heavy music, and viewed these developments with a jaundiced eye. As Rage didn't have a DJ – and Morello, despite his insistence to the contrary, never really replaced standard guitar sounds with a simulacrum of turntable scratching – and didn't employ super-low tuning or indeed seven-string guitars, the standard nu-metal weaponry, they never really qualified as a nu-metal band. However, their part in the scene's birth is undeniable. Which other rock frontmen rapped as insistently, or as well, as de la Rocha? Maybe Anthony Kiedis of the Red Hot Chili Peppers or Mike Patton of Faith No More, but those singers kept their flirtation with that delivery brief – and in any case, had moved onto better things years before.

Morello correctly analysed the differences between Rage and, say, Limp Bizkit by pointing to the differing origins of their influences. "When we came out in 1991 there was no-one like us," he explained, "but of course there's a whole genre now of rock/rap bands. A lot of the hard rock part of Rage comes from Led Zeppelin or Black Sabbath, whereas those newer bands draw more on Metallica or Pantera. I can't criticise bands for maybe stealing our sound. I mean, we've got influences too. I would hate Tony Iommi [of Black Sabbath] or Terminator X [of Public Enemy] to hold a grudge because Rage Against The Machine are guilty of a liberal borrowing of some of their sounds."

Given that Morello focused on the differences in sound between Rage and the newer bands, it's interesting to note that Wilk and Commerford had no qualms about claiming direct responsibility for the nu-metal explosion. Asked if he considered himself a major influence on the new music, Wilk said: "I really want to believe that I was. I just want to say it, because I don't think that I have gotten any recognition for that, and I think it's something I consciously wanted to do. There's bands before us that were kind of doing it in a different way – absolutely. It's been going on for a long time. Both metal and hip-hop are rebellious types of music, so I think they actually do work well together in spirit. When this band first started in 1992, I was listening to alternative, punk and hard rock records, and I was also listening to hip-hop. The three other guys in the band were, too, and [it] wasn't something that was really thought out too much. It was almost like we couldn't really control our influences or how they came out."

Commerford added, "We need to get out there so people remember who kicked off this music trend. I want people to realise we are the forefathers of this form of music. And sometimes I read articles about other bands, where they'll get into conversations about the hybrid of rock and hip-hop and we don't get mentioned. And that kind of gets to me."

"Who would have guessed when we were just starting out in our grimy studio out in North Hollywood that a genre would spring up around us?" mused Morello. "I remember how hard it was to find a manager. There was this one powerful manager we talked to. He didn't want to manage the band, but he liked us and he sat down and tried to give us some advice. He spelled it out just like I was a little kid or something. He said there's no future in this rap thing – 'it's got no melody, no hooks'. He said we put on an exciting show, but there is no way we are going to sell records or have a career. The funny thing is we are now looking for a new manager, and he's one of the people who is trying to meet with us. I can't wait to see him again – to see if he remembers the conversation."

The vacuous nature of some of the nu-metal bands' songs led to Rage's collective disdain, as you might imagine, although the musicians were quick to point out that modern hip-hop could be just as shallow. Morello put this diplomatically, saying "I'm a fan of bands like Korn, Limp Bizkit, Kid Rock, but clearly they're coming from a different philosophical standpoint. Each of those bands are a product of their influences and convictions, and our convictions just happen to be different."

De la Rocha put it more plainly, stating that many of the groups "aren't really screaming about anything. It's just this fabrication... It's a shame the way most popular hip-hop is so void of real commentary. I look at Puff Daddy or Jay-Z, and I think, 'If Ronald Reagan was a rapper, he'd be in Puff Daddy's crew – the materialism and individuality.'" Even Morello fired a barb at Limp Bizkit, and specifically their huge-selling single 'Nookie', when he observed, "We share some things musically. But Rage Against the Machine is something entirely different... not only from a musical standpoint but also from a philosophical one. From our first rehearsals we have been not just about making great music but about forging those songs with our convictions, which is somewhat different than doing it just for the nookie."

Of course, the members of Rage are human, and prone to taking time off from their activism. "Like everyone else I have my lazy lapses," said Morello, "when the Sony Playstation beckons." He added, in complete contrast to the band's public image, "Although our work is always deadly serious, on a day-to-day basis there's some funny motherfuckers within this band. It's not always a heavy political vibe. That's the side the public sees, as opposed to the dressing room high-jinks."

That appears to be the limit of the band's leisure pursuits, though – asked if he had any groupie tales to share, Morello explained: "Quite the opposite. On a few occasions, Zach or I had to stop the show because we saw abuse happening to women in the pits. We weren't about to let dudes think it was an excuse to touch women inappropriately. That's just not going to happen at a Rage show. We're not going to play, we're just going to leave the stage unless that stops right now. On more than one occasion we did that. And the lesson was learned."

Years later, Morello also gave the whole evolution of nineties rock a revealing perspective when he said that alternative music, as it was labelled at the start of the decade, had consumed its own creators when it became part and parcel of mainstream entertainment. "In some ways [success] screwed them up," he said. "Those bands – and you can list them, from Nine Inch Nails, Tool, Rage, Smashing Pumpkins, Jane's Addiction, to the Seattle bands – shared one thing: they all had a love of underground music and punk rock. They all loved 'no sell out' music. But then, suddenly, they found themselves able to play the same venues that bands like Poison were playing, and to be on MTV between videos of Backstreet Boys and those types of artists. It created a sort of 'arena rock' personal crisis. It clearly affected them... It's no accident that Nine Inch Nails albums and Tool albums and Rage Against The Machine albums came out only once every four or five years. There was none of that thing of putting out an album every six months to try to capitalise on momentum, and try and become the biggest band in the world. These bands were all vexed, and afraid of being seen in the same light as the bands they disparaged, or the bands their heroes had disparaged."

Once that slackening of motivation had occurred, Morello said, it was only a matter of time before the record industry suits came up with the idea of rent-a-clone 'alternative' bands. "Those bands from the first few years of Lollapalooza created an audience, and then they didn't serve it," he continued. "Inside every cigar-smoke-filled record-label boardroom in the country, executives were saying, 'If only we had a Rage Against The Machine that sang about girls, and would show up for a video shoot'. And those types of bands did show up. And then of course everything got diluted. They had the form but not the content. There were the nu-metal bands, the Pearl Jam wannabe bands – bands that sold millions of records, but who had nothing like the talent of the groups they were trying to emulate."

As if this wasn't made clear enough, de la Rocha summed it up simply: "For every Nirvana there were 10 or 15 Bushes or whoever, and with Rage Against The Machine there's been some not so great bands." True – and damning.

While chaos reigned in heavy metal and Rage's fans awaited their new record, the group had some serious business to conduct in early 1999. On January 28 they headlined a benefit concert at the Continental Airlines Arena in East Rutherford, New Jersey, with proceeds donated to the International Concerned Family And Friends Of Mumia Abu-Jamal. So far, so normal for this band, you might think, but the event raised no end of a furore among the media and certain police forces, who were incensed that the concert was intended to raise funds for the defence case of a man who had been sentenced to death for the killing of a cop.

The timing of the benefit show was crucial, said Morello. "The reason why there's focus on it now is because on October 30, 1998, the Pennsylvania Supreme Court denied Mumia's appeal, leaving the way open for the governor to sign a death warrant. That's why we organised the concert now, because we're trying to save a man's life. He's in mortal peril right now, that's why it's come to the surface... When we heard the appeal was denied and the death warrant was imminent, Zack called me up and said, 'It's time to do a show'. We're actually in the middle of making a record right now, so we had to put that on hold for a minute and begin soliciting bands... We're raising funds for the federal appeal and trying to raise awareness as well to counteract the lies and propaganda of the Pennsylvania Fraternal Order of Police."

Reactions came from all sides. Radio disc jockey Howard Stern, labelled a 'shock-jock' by the shallower type of observer, derided the Continental Airlines Arena show on air, while New Jersey governor Christine Todd Whitman described it as 'deplorable' and commentary came from the Fraternal Order Of Police (FOP), an influential organisation that helps serving and retired cops and their families. "They're obviously very misdirected," FOP president Gilbert Gallegos said of Rage Against The Machine. "It's incomprehensible to me how they can continue to think Abu-Jamal is innocent, because the facts don't show that."

Morello later told the *New York Times*: "It's not the first time that Rage Against The Machine has opened up a can of worms by standing up for what we believed in. We've had the Ku Klux Klan protest our shows, but I didn't expect this from the Governor of New Jersey's office."

Of the Attorney General's 'deplorable' statement, Morello explained: "She basically apologised to the people of New Jersey for the First Amendment. She said this concert is deplorable and [that she] would love nothing more than to shut it down. Unfortunately [for her], there's the constitutional guarantee of free speech. We apologise for that, so the concert's gonna have to go on. Secondly, she seemed ignorant of her state's own judicial history. In 1966, 'Hurricane' Carter was convicted of a triple murder. He was an outspoken critic of the police. There was a lot of shenanigans during his trial as well. In 1975 Bob Dylan did a sold-out benefit concert for Hurricane at Madison Square Garden. This helped to fund a federal appeal investigation. All of his state appeals had been denied. In 1985, almost 20 years after the conviction, a federal judge ordered him released due to the fact that racism had affected the trial, there were grave constitutional errors, there was concealment of evidence by the police. It's an exactly parallel case."

Putting their money where their mouths were, so to speak, Morello and Abu-Jamal's lead attorney Leonard Weinglass appeared on Howard Stern's radio show opposite Maureen Faulkner, the widow of the policeman allegedly slain by Abu-Jamal (de la Rocha referred to her as a 'widow pig puppet' in a later song, with typical directness) and Stern, who took the cops' side.

"I'm outraged," Faulkner told Stern's show. "I heard about this [concert] about a week and a half ago off the internet. I read it at 10 o'clock at night and I was awake the entire night. I was just so upset that this band... they've been duped. In a way, I feel sorry for them because they have been misled by [Abu-Jamal's] defence attorney once again, and I would be willing to talk to them. I would be willing to give them the facts, the evidence, the court transcriptions that prove that Mumia received a fair trial and he is guilty of first degree murder, of murdering my husband in cold blood." She added, with slightly skewed logic: "I, in my own eyes, believe that Mumia sells. His voice sells. His hair sells. Many of the anti-death penalty people have made him their poster boy."

Morello countered with "Jamal did not receive a fair trial. In the United States of America, you do not execute a man who did not have a fair trial. There's a word for that, and that word is lynching... The Philadelphia Police Department has a long and glorious history of framing suspects. He is simply innocent of the crime."

Calls to cancel the benefit show by local politicians and the FOP failed, largely because of a recent precedent in which a show by Marilyn Manson had been permitted to take place at the same venue, after a proposed ban had been struck down after being labelled a violation of the American constitution's First Amendment. Still, attempts continued to be made to mess things up for Rage: after Governor Whitman told people that they should boycott the concert, 2,000 gig-goers reportedly requested refunds – only for those tickets to be snapped up by others.

It didn't stop there. The Arena's management insisted that Rage were not permitted to distribute literature of any kind in or near the venue: the group disputed this and eventually brought in several thousand copies of a leaflet titled *Who Is Mumia Abu-Jamal?* These were distributed from tables staffed by the various benefit groups, although a petty victory was scored by the Arena security, who stopped any sales of political materials from taking place.

Anyone with a brain will be able to understand both sides of the argument, although perhaps not the actions taken by those with a vested interest in preventing the debate from occurring. On paper, Abu-Jamal was a convicted cop-killer, and whether or not he had received a fair trial was simply not a concern for most observers, making Rage's job an even tougher one. What was most surprising was the heights to which the controversy ascended. As de la Rocha put it at a press conference, "I found it very surprising that the attorney general and the governor of NJ would denounce musicians who are doing a benefit for someone we consider an innocent man. To me, it rang of them trying to create a climate in which they would try to scare kids from coming to the show and getting the information. The case against Mumia that they're presenting is so thin that now they have to come after the musicians [and] radio stations who play those musicians."

Morello summed up many of the flaws in the prosecution's case in an interview with *High Times*, saying: "Regardless of what one thinks of his innocence or guilt, or regardless of what one thinks of the death penalty, that is secondary to the fact that you just can't go lynching people legally. Clearly, there was gross prosecutorial misconduct. There was the intimidation of witnesses. The main prosecution's witnesses changed their story several times – they were threatened and then rewarded for changing their story.

"There was an unbelievable manufactured confession where 25 cops were standing in the emergency room with the attending physician. No one heard Mumia say anything, then two months later, after Mumia had filed police-brutality charges and after a prosecutor's strategy meeting, all of a sudden the prosecutor says to the cops who were in the emergency room: 'OK now, did any of you happen to hear a confession?' Hint, hint. There was a mass amnesia for two months and all of a sudden three of them decided they had heard a confession. That's absolutely ridiculous."

Morello continued: "The judge was hostile and biased throughout the proceedings. The jury was illegally purged of African-Americans. As you may have heard, the Philly DA's office had a training video on how to get blacks off a jury. The amount of evidence that was withheld is incredible and very significant... In all, there were 10 witnesses who claimed to have seen some or part of the whole incident. Five of those witnesses saw one or more men running away from the scene. The prosecution has absolutely denied this, despite five eyewitnesses... The list goes on. The inadequate defence. The defence attorney interviewed none of the defence witnesses before putting them on the stand. The defence investigator quit before the trial due to insufficient funds. This is a death-penalty case! It's a travesty of justice, this whole thing from beginning to end. What we find so appalling is, if the other side is so sure of his guilt, then why are they so afraid of a new trial?"

Strangely, and by definition unprofessionally, one of the FOP's most senior members wrote at this time that he hoped his fellow officers would "obey the traffic-light laws" if an emergency call for police assistance came from the Rage concert. In other words, he wanted police to deliberately drive slowly if they were needed. In still other words, he was placing his own agenda above the law – a poor PR move at the very least, and seriously damaging to his organisation's reputation.

"That's just incredible," marvelled Morello. "It's so clear that at least some police don't consider themselves public servants whatsoever. They're often an independent rogue organisation who obviously choose when to enforce the law and when not to – so if some kid breaks his leg at the concert, they're gonna take their time coming. That says a lot about where each of the parties stand on this. I would hope any decent cop would want there to be a new trial, would want there to be no ambiguity in regards to this man's innocence or guilt. That makes sense if you're truly in favour of law and order. If you have a new trial with an unbiased judge, [and] an unbiased jury, then you're not gonna hear a peep from Rage Against The Machine, you're not gonna hear a peep from Nelson Mandela, from the European Parliament, from mayors across the US and the millions of people who've been supporting Mumia, in large measure because it smacks of the same kind of political dissident railroading that goes on in China, that goes on in Iraq. We used this partially as an excuse for bombing Iraq. If the situation were reversed and this was a political dissident who had boldly stood up for his rights despite the railroading of police in a country like that, the Attorney General for New Jersey would be handing out medals."

The Abu-Jamal benefit made the FOP into a powerful enemy for Rage Against The Machine. Spurred on by its president Gallegos, who fumed: "This is a mediocre band, at best, whose real talent is marketing an anti-everything image. We should not have to sit idly by and allow a murderer to be celebrated," the FOP called for Rage to be pulled from a forthcoming appearance on NBC's *Late Night With Conan O'Brien*. The campaign bore fruit for the cops when the New Jersey legislature passed a bill which extracted $80,000 from the Sports and Exposition Authority's profits, to be given to a charity supporting police officers' families.

Not coincidentally, $80,000 was also the amount raised by the show for the Abu-Jamal fund, presented to his supporters by de la Rocha on April 24. As reporter Christopher O'Connor wrote on Sonicnet, "A year after Rage Against The Machine and the Beastie Boys headlined a New Jersey benefit concert for convicted cop-killer Mumia Abu-Jamal, Governor Christine Todd Whitman signed a bill Tuesday granting $80,000 of the state's profits from the show to the families of slain police officers. Pete Cammarano, the spokesperson for bill co-sponsor and state Senator Richard Codey, D-Middlesex, said the $80,000 payment was designed as a 'disincentive' for the New Jersey Sports and Exposition Authority to book similar shows in the future. 'I think [the officials who run the arena] understand why this was done,' Cammarano said from Senator Codey's Middlesex office... Steffanie Bell, a spokesperson for Whitman, said that under the bill, the Authority will give the money to the state attorney general's office, which will distribute it to groups that support the families of New Jersey officers killed in the line of duty... The New Jersey Sports and Exposition Authority operates the Continental Airlines Arena. The $80,000 represents the profit the Authority made from the sold-out show. Authority spokesperson John Samerjan said the organisation knew of the bill for some time. He said its passage did not come as a shock and added, 'We're fine with it'. But he said First Amendment considerations will keep the bill from preventing the Authority from green-lighting other such benefits. 'If we had to do it over again, we'd have to do it over again,' Samerjan said."

O'Connor continued: "Mike Lutz heads the Philadelphia-based Pennsylvania State Lodge of the Fraternal Order Of Police, which has adamantly opposed Abu-Jamal's efforts. He said he was glad to see New Jersey distribute the $80,000 to the families. He had particularly harsh words for Rage Against The Machine. 'They're a hate group,' Lutz said of Rage, who have used the term 'pigs' in their songs. 'They're no different than the Ku Klux Klan and the Neo-Nazi Party [sic]'. Spokespersons for Rage Against The Machine and other bands that performed at the show could not be reached for comment."

While the battle raged on between band and authorities, the record industry continued to give its implicit support to Rage Against The Machine, nominating a new song, 'No Shelter', for a Grammy at its 40th annual ceremony in January 1999. A song full of contradictions, 'No Shelter' was included on the soundtrack for that year's remake of *Godzilla*, a movie only notable for being inferior in many ways to the songs which accompanied it. Its video clip depicted a nightmarish industrial scene, with young men and women being brainwashed into servility by their stern-faced masters, interspersed with messages about Mumia Abu-Jamal, the theft of Mexican land by foreign interests and the Hiroshima attack of World War Two. The song's targets include Nike and Coca-Cola and, curiously, the *Godzilla* film series itself, at least if the line "*Godzilla*, pure motherfucking filler, get your eyes off the real killer" is interpreted as such. The movie's tagline 'Size does matter' is referenced in the images of Abu-Jamal's jail cell and the message 'Mumia Abu-Jamal's cell is this big... Justice does matter!'

The Abu-Jamal case continued to occupy Rage's collective attention throughout 1999, peaking on 12 April when de la Rocha flew to Geneva, Switzerland to speak about the issue before a full session of the International Commission Of Human Rights of the United Nations. His second brief was to discuss America's application of the death penalty with the ICHR, which had agreed to hear the vocalist after an application from the Humanitarian Law Project, a non-governmental group that consults the UN on compliance of human rights laws. How many other rock singers would do the same?

The conflict between police and band began to manifest itself seriously: as *Juice* magazine wrote in February 2000, "a show near Boston, Massachusetts, was disrupted when 400 off-duty police confronted Mumia supporters outside the sold-out venue. Those who refused to take anti-Abu-Jamal flyers were threatened, 35 concert goers arrested. The Boston Globe reported that one woman had her arm pulled out of its socket by police. Police spokesmen claimed that none of this harassment had anything to do with the police protest. De la Rocha defended the band's stance from the stage, saying, 'Cops have been following us around all over the country saying we support cop killers. Let's make it completely clear. We don't support killers, and especially not killer cops. We do support innocent brothers and sisters being framed up in prisons all over this country, people like Mumia Abu-Jamal'."

The writer continued: "At a RATM show in Nassau, Long Island, in December, fans spotted with Abu-Jamal flyers were kicked out of the venue and physically assaulted by uniformed cops. Elsewhere, the FOP shied from direct conflict over the issue. RATM offered to join the FOP on ABC TV news to debate the issue, but the FOP cancelled, also backing out of a radio debate with a... Mumia supporter in Nashville. In response, RATM took to ordering dozens of Dunkin' Donuts to be delivered to the protesting cops outside shows."

The media had played a key role when it came to misleading the public about Abu-Jamal, Morello added. "One of the things that gets obscured when mulling over the details of the sham trial and the New Jersey Attorney General's statements is who Mumia Abu-Jamal is, why is so many people are interested in this guy," he explained. "The other side has tried to portray him as this bloodthirsty criminal cop-killing menace. That simply is not true. He's an award-winning radio journalist. He's been a community activist since his mid-teens. He was the president of the National Association of Black Journalists in Philadelphia. He had a spotless police record at the time of the incident. The one thing he has always been guilty of is that he's been a leading critic of police violence against minority communities. His outspoken opposition to racism and police brutality is what we believe got him in trouble and made him a marked man. For 17 years on death row he continues to not beg for his life, but to courageously deliver scathing social criticism, like his book *Live From Death Row* and his commentaries on both domestic and international events. He's probably the most censored man in America... Like Mumia says, they don't want his death, they want his silence. That's why we're determined to see that the execution doesn't go through, that Mumia receives a new trial and he's eventually free."

We'll draw a line under the Mumia Abu-Jamal case for now, noting simply that Rage's support undoubtedly helped his fortunes by bringing huge amounts of attention to him. His lawyer Leonard Weinglass observed: "When I travel and speak, there is more recognition now of Mumia's name. I think they've had a major part in that." In any case, a partial victory was ultimately won when his death sentence was commuted to a life sentence without parole in 2012. Although justice has not yet been served, at least Abu-Jamal remains alive and his supporters can continue to rally for a retrial. Visit www.freemumia.com for more information.

On June 13 Rage played the Tibetan Freedom Concert at Alpine Valley in East Troy, Wisconsin, alongside various acts concerned about China's invasion of Tibet, and then a rather different event the following month: Woodstock 1999. Thirty years after the original Woodstock Festival, and five years after the largely peaceful reprise that was Woodstock 94, the show was expected to be a wholesome celebration of the original festival's values, although its location was some 200 miles away from that of the 1969 event.

Most of the show went smoothly, although various organisational factors created a build-up of tensions which soon led to serious repercussions. The oppressive heat, lack of natural shade, ridiculously high prices demanded by food and water sellers (concert-goers were frisked on entry to check they were not bringing their own supplies) and the lack of sufficient water fountains and toilets combined to make a large portion of the audience angry. Fuelled by music from Metallica, Limp Bizkit and many other bands as heavy or heavier than Rage Against The Machine, who burned an American flag on stage during 'Killing In The Name', many of the crowd began vandalising the fences and other structures. They used the wood to build huge bonfires, lit by candles which had been sold at the show, the idea being that they would be used to illuminate a peaceful midnight vigil. Hundreds of New York State Police troopers were called in to contain the aggression. As the violence escalated, MTV – who had been covering the event live, and whose footage is still available on YouTube – pulled their crew from the site. After the event, reports came of sexual assaults and rapes that had taken place in the crowd, giving Woodstock 1999 a negative reputation that continues to linger long after the event.

The experiences of the female victims are especially chilling. *Rolling Stone*'s rock writer Rob Sheffield was covering the event, and he later wrote of one particular group of morons: "They point out girls... and chant, 'Show your tits!' Goon accomplices on the ground find the girls and surround them. Other goons walking by join the huddle with their cameras. The goons on the trailer chant, 'Pick her up! Pick her up!' Two short girls with backpacks are surrounded by a mob of about 60 guys. As the 'Pick them up' chant gets louder, the girls undo their bra tops, the cameras flash, and the trailer guys spot another target... 'There was no way out,' the brunette tells me. 'It was either show 'em or you don't get out.' 'There was no choice,' the blonde says. When I ask whether they plan to report this to security, they look at me like I'm from Mars."

It got worse, much worse, the writer continued, particularly during a performance by Korn. Sheffield interviewed a crisis worker called Dave Schneider, of whom he wrote: "Suddenly, Schneider saw a crowd-surfing woman get swallowed up by the pit; when she re-emerged, two men had clamped her arms to her sides. 'She was giving a struggle,' said Schneider. 'Her clothes were physically and forcibly removed.' Yet no-one nearby seemed to react. Schneider said that the woman and one of the men fell to the ground for about 20 seconds; then, he said, she was passed to his friend, who raped her, standing from behind. 'The gentlemen's pants were down, her pants were down, and you could see there was clearly sexual activity,' he said. Finally, the woman was pulled from the pit by some audience members, who handed her to security."

Morello was asked to comment on the fiasco in a *New York Times* feature titled *The Pop Life: Raging At The Media*, authored by well-known rock hack Neil Strauss. "Hey man, leave the kids alone," he wrote. "I've had enough of the frenzied demonisation of young people surrounding Woodstock 99. Yes, there were fires and the kids danced around them in pagan glee. Yes, parts of the stage and scaffolding were torn down with great enthusiasm. But was this just senseless violence, or were these acts of sweet revenge against concert organisers who gouged the kids throughout the weekend with grossly overpriced water, beer and food? Maybe the crass commercialism of the event and the greedy exploitation of these youngsters caught up with the vendors and promoters. Or maybe it was just a good old-fashioned healthy riot. One with a killer soundtrack. And while some of the concertgoers were naked or painted or covered in tinfoil, perhaps they were just rejoicing in not having to wear their annoying school uniform for three days."

He continued: "Media coverage of the event and the accompanying political grandstanding have been grossly hypocritical. Indignant editorials and television broadcasts raving over the 'horrific violence' and 'terrifying blazes' were rampant. But, when US Tomahawk missiles set a children's hospital outside of Belgrade on fire, killing many inside, it was not chewed over to this extent. More incredulous attention was paid to kids setting fires at Woodstock. The truly inexcusable crime committed at Woodstock is the reported sexual assaults. During our set we didn't see anything of the kind taking place, and would have stopped the show immediately if we had. Rage Against The Machine has a great deal of respect for its audience and demands that they respect one another. We use our music not only to entertain, but to galvanise and inspire our fans to fight back against abuse and injustice wherever they rear their ugly heads – in the home, in the school, at work or in society at large. And while most of the other bands at Woodstock 99 have a more escapist bent, they certainly shouldn't be blamed for this thuggish behaviour. More members of the New York City Police Department have participated in, watched and laughed at a broomstick rape than anyone onstage at Woodstock."

Morello concluded: "Yes, Woodstock was filled with predators: the degenerate idiots who assaulted those women, the greedy promoters who wrung every cent out of thirsty concertgoers, and last but not least, the predator media that turned a blind eye to real violence and scapegoated the quarter of a million music fans at Woodstock 99, the vast majority of whom had the time of their lives. Perhaps we'll have to wait until these vandals and pyromaniacs grow up to become the CEOs of media conglomerates, like their predecessors at the original Woodstock who enshrined and mythologised that event, to see where this concert fits into our history."

For now, more obviously historic events were on the horizon in the form of Rage's third album, *The Battle Of Los Angeles*, released on November 2 two weeks after a lead-off single, 'Guerilla Radio'. Acknowledging that the album title was provocative, Morello explained: "We wouldn't have it any other way. It's intentionally ambiguous, but part of it speaks to the fact that there's an ongoing battle of LA boiling just underneath the surface. There's a tremendous amount of tension in the city, as evidenced in the wake of the Rodney King verdicts [in 1992], and it's still bubbling close to the surface. We're just one court verdict away from the whole place blowing up all over again. And it's something you notice here every day on the streets. On the Sunset Strip, for example, there are Bentleys and Rolls Royces driving by, and there are people at the same time who are so hungry that they're almost ready to attack you for spare change. And also in our music, you can hear the tension of the city: the aggression, the smog, the hip-hop, the desperation and the hope that's all part of LA."

Where *Rage Against The Machine* was anthemic and *Evil Empire* ponderous, *The Battle Of Los Angeles* is something else again. Sleek, adrenaline-packed and revitalised, it sounds as if Rage had conquered their mid-nineties demons and returned to complete the job which they had started back in 1991. All this is encapsulated in the opening track, 'Testify', which attacks America's then-deteriorating relationship with Iraq, which was beginning to spiral towards violence again, several years after Gulf War I and two years after America and the UK had bombed Iraq in late 1998. This is followed by the single 'Guerilla Radio', the most catchy tune that Rage had written for some time, anchored by a insistent funk groove and lyrics whose targets included George W. Bush, then merely the Governor of Texas and "the son of a drug lord" (a possible reference to his father George Bush's CIA and their alleged crack dealings).

'Calm Like A Bomb' follows, a litany of grim images in true Zack de la Rocha style, which evoke a menacing atmosphere as much as conjure specific references. "What ya say? What ya say? What ya say? What?" runs the chorus, gauged perfectly for moshpit inhabitants. 'Mic Check' is an unusual song, one of Rage's more experimental compositions. Referencing Bob Marley ("Come with the fire only Marley could catch"), the song's clearest message is "With this mic device I spit nonfiction / Who got tha power / This be my question". It's a perfect run-up to 'Sleep Now In The Fire', probably the most striking song on *The Battle Of Los Angeles*, partly because of the furore that accompanied its release (see the next chapter). Referring to the arrival of Christopher Columbus as an invasion ("I am the Nina, the Pinta, the Santa Maria" – Columbus' three ships) and "the agents of orange" (the military defoliant Agent Orange, used on civilians in the Vietnam War), the song concludes that the end of history has been reached, a concept cited by the writer Francis Fukuyama.

De la Rocha enters personal territory in 'Born Of A Broken Man', which contains what appear to be several veiled references to his father Beto's religious fervour and ultimate mental breakdown. 'Born As Ghosts' discusses the wealth divide between rich and poor families, apparently in Los Angeles (as de la Rocha refers to the "hills find peace / Locked armed guard posts"), and 'Maria' takes a detailed look at the fate of immigrants from Mexico, judging by the reference to a "rico [rich person] from Jalisco". The album switches focus to the Abu-Jamal case with 'Voice Of The Voiceless', complete with a nod towards the dystopian vision of George Orwell, while the most prophetic song on *The Battle Of Los Angeles* has to be 'New Millennium Homes'. While it doesn't predict the sub-prime mortgages crash and subsequent global recession which occurred nine years later, it specifically links poverty with the Dow-Jones index and how "a fire in the master's house is set"; a clear call to uprising.

'Ashes In The Fall' discusses the areas of America which suffer most greatly from poverty, namely with the line "Swollen stomachs in Appalachia", which refers to the eastern region with levels of deprivation that are among the worst in the world – even though they are located in Earth's richest country. What's more, "The priests that fuck you as they whisper holy things" is a fairly scathing sentiment by anyone's standards.

'War Within A Breath' completes *The Battle Of Los Angeles*, returning to the cause of the Zapatistas, whose mission had been so comprehensively detailed on *Evil Empire*. De la Rocha was clearly still concerned with the EZLN's struggles, referring to the Zapatista emblem ('Black flag and a red star') and 'la raza' (the race). References to the Intifada, the Palestinian youth uprising in the West Bank, and the January 1, 1994 beginning of the North American Free Trade Agreement make the subject matter clear.

Rage followed up the message of the album with powerful video clips: 'Testify' came with a Michael Moore-directed promo that highlighted the similarities between the 2000 presidential candidates Al Gore and George W. Bush (you will recall how close that election was: Rage had that part exactly right), while 'Guerilla Radio' painted a portrait of the mind-controlled, zombie masses following orders from their paymasters while allowing their freedom to be controlled and ultimately removed.

Note that there's plenty of humour in these grim clips – the enslaved, plastic workers playing racketball and their limbs falling off, the mutated presidents-to-be uttering the same stream of pre-rehearsed crap for no-one's benefit. As an entity in touch with its audience's needs, Rage were performing at their very best. A live performance on CBS's *Late Night With David Letterman* added to the weight of the campaign for *The Battle Of Los Angeles*.

Rage themselves seemed, from the outside at least, to be weathering the storm of celebrity that was enveloping them. Writer Rob Tannenbaum reported after an interview with Morello that the guitarist "shows up for an interview at a starched business hotel in Hollywood wearing shorts, a T-shirt, and sneakers. Often, when Morello drives his battered red Ford Astro van into the Sony Music parking lot in Santa Monica alongside rows of BMWs and Benzes, a guard surveys him and says, 'Pick up or delivery?'", while de la Rocha, Commerford and Wilk were, as always, the polar opposite of the falling-out-of-nightclubs rock star cliché.

But not all was tranquil beneath the surface. De la Rocha worried about his band's progress, that was clear. In an interview with Ben Myers at *Kerrang!*, he mused: "After our early tours with Public Enemy, then Pearl Jam, we discussed whether we should make videos as a way for people to assimilate information. At first I was very opposed to it, but ultimately it was the right decision. Would our actions have been perceived the same way if we'd sold seven million records straight away? I don't think so. That's where me and Tom don't agree. We have a different approach to the way our politics are addressed. But then again we agree on most of the other stuff too. Ultimately the contention has served us well."

He continued: "One of the things I wanted to ensure was protection of this band's integrity. That we were walking what we were talking, as opposed to just talking. We're dealing with a monstrous pop culture that has a tendency to commodify and pacify everything – it's happened to so many bands in the past. It's important that artists in my position set an example and there's a fine line between the promotion of a product and the promotion of an idea." Clearly, finding that line – between selling his soul for commerce and selling his beliefs to the people – was something of a struggle for the singer.

One thing was clear, though: Rage Against The Machine were still pissed off at the world. In fact, there's so much indignation seeping from the songs on *The Battle Of Los Angeles* that it's tempting to speculate how much more amplified its sentiments would have been in America's most politicised years for decades – the present era, post-9/11. Released two years before that seismic event, the album still manages to stuff a planet's worth of anger into its contents. This level of protest is exhausting, of course, and difficult to sustain as a consequence. How long could the rage go on?

CHAPTER 7

2000–2002

In 2000, everything came to a head for Rage Against The Machine – and then switched focus, abruptly and rapidly. After so much spectacular progress, what the hell happened?

On paper, things had been going according to plan for the previous few years. Rage had successfully taken on the cops and made them look like fools. They had supported the Zapatistas. They had brought global attention to the cases of Mumia Abu-Jamal and Leonard Peltier. Endless campaigns had been fought and won in and around the issues of sweatshop labour, union rights, domestic violence and many other causes consequential to the wonderful Western world in which we live.

It was time to take a step upwards, so in January 2000, Rage Against The Machine upped the ante by taking on the entire house of financial cards on which everything we know rests, in a splendid piece of street activism which, if successful, would get people to wonder what actually goes on in the minds of the shadowy elite who rule us all.

By now Tom Morello wasn't merely being asked about individual cases of justice. Like Noam Chomsky, the renowned political thinker whose prodigious grasp of global concepts matched his own,

Morello often spoke about challenging everything. Everything, with a capital E. The way we think, the way we live, the way we do business, the way we fight wars, raise our children, spend money... Here he is, talking to MTV in late 2000.

"The educational system in America is basically a system of control, where a child's spirit has to be broken to make them fit like a more obedient cog into society," he said. "As a result, all too rarely are we encouraged to think independently, encouraged to challenge authority, or to act in accordance with our own ideas and beliefs, if they run contrary to a 'superior'. The blueprint for our educational system actually stems from Prussia, from pre-World War I Prussia, where much of the economy was based on sending mercenary soldiers to fight in other people's wars. For a young teenager this is clearly a ridiculous idea, so they had to be stripped of their will and their independent thought in order to make them good and obedient hireling soldiers."

He added: "Things have not changed too much today; there is, however, a great opportunity within the educational system to form a different kind of education for yourself, and that is by using the proximity of friends and like-minded people to learn to organise against injustices, large and small. To take the silly things you're forced to memorise in physics, chemistry class, and find a way to adapt them to improving the environment in your community... one of the things I did as a high school student was to write an underground school newspaper with some friends, which criticised foreign, domestic, and local policies. In a way, that provided us within the school system a better education than we were receiving in class."

What better way to educate Rage's listeners than by taking the struggle directly to the heart of the machine, in this case the New York Stock Exchange, home of the financiers that shape America's (and thus the world's) economic futures? On January 26, the band-members, video director Michael Moore and 300 fans arrived on the steps of the NYSE to shoot a video clip for a new single, 'Sleep Now In The Fire', which, you will recall, refers to parts of America's history in scathing terms.

Why go to the Stock Exchange in particular, instead of the Pentagon, the White House or indeed the World Trade Center, then about a year and a half away from the 9/11 attacks? This conversation between Morello and Chomsky on the former's Radio Free LA broadcast illuminates Rage's choice of target.

Asked by Morello if the world's biggest financial institutions (he suggested the World Bank as an example, but we'll extrapolate that to include the NYSE) are up to no good, politically and sociologically speaking, Chomsky ruminated: "Well, we should be worried about them, but they're not so much the man behind the curtain as the agency that is carrying out certain actions. These international financial institutions which were set up after the end of the Second World War have changed their functions over the years, but in effect they are essentially the agency of the major transnationals and the great powers. So what's called the G7, the seven big states, and the big transnational corporations which are on the scale of states, and the financial institutions and so on, they are trying to organise a certain kind of world. The agency for carrying out those plans to a significant extent, not totally, is the World Bank and the International Monetary Fund."

Chomsky continued: "Sure, we should be worried [about] the kind of world that they are trying to create and hence about the institutions by which they are doing it. And also about something very crucial about the nature of all these institutions, [which is that] they are basically unaccountable. In order to know about what the IMF is doing, even, you would have to dedicate an awful lot of energy and effort to put into it. You have to be a specialist. For most people that's hopeless – you can barely know about their existence, let alone what they are doing, even when it's public, which it often isn't. And they are making decisions which have an enormous impact on people. Well, that itself is illegitimate... any unaccountable exercise of power is in itself illegitimate."

"If you look further at what they are doing," he went on, "I think there is good reason to be concerned about it, but they are not acting on their own. They express what in fact is called in the literature the 'Washington consensus', and it's the 'Washington consensus' because it's forged in Washington, which is not only the home of the World Bank and the IMF for the most part, but also of the world's most powerful state, and the representatives of the major sectors of corporate power which either congregate there or send their representatives there. It's not called the 'Washington consensus' for no reason."

These were big targets under discussion, and while no-one – least of all the members of Rage Against The Machine – were under any illusion that their video shoot in Manhattan would bring any of them down, raised awareness of their existence could only be a good thing. Director Michael Moore, later to rise to greater prominence through his movies *Bowling For Columbine* (2002) and *Fahrenheit 9/11* (2004), was an edgy, left-of-mainstream character at the time and perfect as a choice to helm 'Sleep Now In The Fire'.

"I've been a huge fan of Michael Moore," said Morello, "who I believe as a political satirist is a genius... anyone who has not seen his movies should rush out and rent them, and they are brilliant. He also has a weekly show, *The Awful Truth*, on Bravo, which is a kind of funny left-wing *60 Minutes*. He's never directed videos for any other band, and it's an honour to have worked with him."

Moore chose to shoot the video on the steps of the Federal Hall Building on Wall Street, directly opposite the New York Stock Exchange. A federal permit was given for the shoot, allowing it to take place during lunch hour, when traders and employees would be on the streets.

Watch the video: it's amazing. The street is heaving with people, many of them regular fans of Rage Against The Machine, but there are also several suits in attendance – presumably Wall Street workers – who can be seen moshing to the music, which was played through speakers while the band played muted instruments. All the activity attracted dozens, perhaps hundreds, of police officers, who wasted no time in trying to stop the shoot from taking place. At one point a cop attempted to take Commerford's bass from him: the bassist refused to stop playing. Later, a police sergeant unplugged

Morello's guitar, but was evidently confused when the music didn't stop, since it was being piped in for the shoot. "The look on his face was like the first time cavemen saw fire," Morello recalled. "It was like Rage had some magical power over the police." The *Huffington Post* wrote, "The sergeant looked at Morello in disgust and then at bass player Commerford, who is built like a superhero, and walked straight between them to throw handcuffs on Moore, arresting him and dragging him off."

After the shoot, the members of Rage plus their fans attempted to enter the NYSE, but were pushed out by security: the building then lowered its security barriers, effectively closing down business for a while. "I guess we stopped downsizing for a couple of hours," said Morello afterwards.

Let's be clear: this was an excellent bit of entertainment, especially when you saw the discomfiture of the cops and the NYSE security, but over and above that, the 'Sleep Now In The Fire' shoot had a real meaning. Even if it only amounted to cocking a snook at Wall Street rather than promoting actual change, TV and the nascent YouTube viewing audience would see it and consider its message.

Any ideological conflicts here? Well, that depended on your point of view. After three albums and numerous world tours, a contrary issue that often came up was that of the personal wealth of the Rage members, an ironic factor given that they presumably used investment mechanisms (overseen by institutions such as the NYSE) to preserve said wealth.

As we saw earlier, Morello was relaxed about this ("I don't have any guilt about it, quite frankly" he told writer Rob Tannenbaum), but de la Rocha found it harder to reconcile ("Having money affects my art. There have been times when I've felt removed from the community I'm struggling for" he told the same writer). Tannenbaum took the argument even further, to his credit, asking Morello what he thought would happen to him if the revolution ever happened and he was taken to task for his material gains. "I look forward to standing before that tribunal," said the guitarist. "That's the kind of problem I wish I had."

The 'Sleep Now In The Fire' clip was among the nominees for that year's MTV Video Music Awards for Best Rock Video, although it lost out to Limp Bizkit's amusing but ultimately insignificant 'Break Stuff'. Unusually for him, Tim Commerford decided to protest at the award by causing some havoc on stage: walking on stage, he climbed a set prop in the shape of a 20-foot plastic palm tree and attempted to bring it down by rocking it back and forth. While Limp Bizkit singer Fred Durst offered amused commentary such as "Now that guy is rock and roll – he should be getting the award!" security goons climbed the tree and tried to bring Commerford down. Eventually he acquiesced and jumped to the stage, where he was borne away, visibly struggling. He was arrested for disorderly conduct and served a night in jail. "I'm a huge fan of Rage," added Durst afterwards, reasoning, "I guess that really was raging against the machine."

Although Commerford remained unrepentant, laughing the stunt off as an act of "personal politics", de la Rocha took a more serious position, telling the media that he needed to take a long walk to recover from the incident and that "I was so humiliated that I left."

"I don't think the band as a whole had a unified opinion about Timmy's scaffold climbing and subsequent fall at the VMAs," reasoned Morello, as always the diplomat. "Frankly all four of us have never sat down together and talked about it... I've known Timmy for a long time, so when he leapt onto the stage, climbed on the scaffold, and then beat the crap out of a couple of 300-pound cops, it didn't really surprise me, because I'm familiar with his work. But I think the rest of America got to meet him through this worldwide broadcast!"

Reporter Maureen Herman wrote in *Rolling Stone* that the idea of disrupting the stage had been on Commerford's mind before the show. The band members had joked the night before with Michael Moore, also present, that they would ask Fidel Castro (in New York for the United Nations Millennium Conference) to accept on their behalf if they won.

"I didn't expect an evening of Tim versus the NYPD," said Morello. "Earlier, Tim had mentioned something about toppling the podium if we won, for no particular reason, which seemed like a silly idea to me. Right before the award we were up for was announced, Tim asked Zack and me if he should do it. We both said no."

As Commerford approached the stage, Morello yelled, "Tim, no! Don't!" He recalled, "I was cowering in my seat while he climbed up there, squatted on the MTV precipice and started rocking back and forth, seemingly trying to make it fall over and on the two sexiest people in the industry, Jennifer Lopez and D'Angelo... [Limp Bizkit] had no idea there was a gargoyle up there giving the rock and roll sign and saying, 'This is bullshit'."

Moore, who had told Commerford beforehand, "I'm not going to tell you what to do, just don't hurt anybody," later said, "Maybe I should have talked to him more like a teenager and told him not to do it. But hey, this is rock and roll — stuff happens. That shouldn't be a surprise... Rock and roll used to be about playing music that stood for something. Now it's background music for Burger King and McDonald's commercials. I think the bass player of this band is against really bad MTV props."

Sure, it was all a bit of fun. In some ways, though, Commerford is an unusual character. He had been fooling around with stage names for some time — Timmy C here, y.Tim.k. there — and even posted a strange message at the www.ratm.com bulletin board that read "I am changing. I am trying to get a grip. My tastes are different (I actually like onions). But I'm not content, so in other words, I feel the need to rock fools." Elsewhere he admitted, "My job is to deal with my insecurities. I do worry about feeling good about myself. Before the band, there was a point where I didn't think that I was cut out for music. I nearly left it behind to be a carpenter. With Rage, everything is a sporting event and all other bands are competition, friend or foe. Onstage or on the bus playing Playstation, it's on."

Although the bassist rationalised his earlier online message, saying "That was just me dicking around. It was letting people know that I'm out there. I've always shied away because my anonymity is important. I sit at home like a regular guy getting psyched thinking about playing shows. It's a great thing," perhaps the members of the band – de la Rocha serious and brooding, Commerford extrovert, the other two somewhere in between – were beginning to diverge just a little too much for comfort.

In retrospect, it's possible that too much band activity and too much compromise was getting in the way of the various members, in particular Zack de la Rocha. Side projects were frequent but fun, including his vocals on a Roni Size/Reprazent album and Wilk's drumming with Cypress Hill – both out that year – but with a new album to promote, another one on the way plus a live DVD scheduled for 2001, *and* the VMA meldown, perhaps it was all too much. Maybe Rage had peaked. Perhaps de la Rocha had reached his breaking point. Either way, something had to happen.

One more key event lay ahead before the impending implosion: a free concert which Rage were scheduled to play in mid-August at the Democratic National Convention, the point being to protest against the two-party political system that was about to be exercised in that year's presidential elections. Predictably, the Los Angeles Police Department ramped up their security measures at the venue, the Staples Center in LA, building a 12-foot fence around the concert area and staffing the event with 2,000 riot gear-equipped cops. Police horses, motorbikes, squad cars and even helicopters patrolled the perimeter, lending the show an atmosphere of total overkill. What were they expecting to happen – World War III?

By now, Rage Against The Machine and their fans were accustomed to this kind of overreaction, especially when de la Rocha made the point from the stage that "Brothers and sisters, our democracy has been hijacked... we have a right to oppose these motherfuckers!" A group of concertgoers then began throwing rocks at the police, who promptly turned off the electricity and shut down the gig, warning the crowd to disperse or face arrest.

This would have a been a familiar case of crowd control, had not the cops then turned to using pepper spray to neutralise two male protesters who were guilty of the heinous crime of waving flags in their faces. Tear gas and rubber bullets were then deployed to get rid of the rest of the crowd, and all in all, it was yet another irritating example of American law enforcement going way, way over the top when it came to use of violence.

An American Civil Liberties Union spokesperson later said that the event was "nothing less than an orchestrated police riot", while de la Rocha stated, "I don't care what fucking television stations said, [that] the violence was caused by the people at the concert; those motherfuckers unloaded on this crowd. And I think it's ridiculous, considering, you know, none of us had rubber bullets, none of us had M16s, none of us had billy clubs, none of us had face shields." The official police response was that their actions had been "outstanding" and "clearly disciplined". Footage of the protest and response was included on a later DVD and is, as ever, now available on YouTube.

The last few months of 2000 were chaotic. Rage had been scheduled to open for the Beastie Boys on tour, only to have that taken away from them when Beastie Boys drummer Mike D suffered a cycling injury. Then dates at the Fillmore Auditorium in San Francisco at which Rage were supposed to record a live album, were postponed. The group also fired their managers, Gary Gersh and John Silva. That's a lot for any band to go through, especially when internal relationships were already fragile.

The most dramatic two years of Rage Against The Machine's career were over, with Woodstock, the *Battle Of Los Angeles* release, the 'Sleep Now In The Fire' controversy and the Mumia Abu-Jamal concert and confrontation with the FOP compressed into this short period. That's more stressful activity than most bands squeeze into decades of existence, and it takes stamina to maintain that level of presence.

After this, the stamina inevitably ran out. On October 18, Zack de la Rocha released a statement which announced that he was quitting the band. It read, "I feel that it is now necessary to leave Rage because our decision-making process has completely failed. It is no longer meeting the aspirations of all four of us collectively as a band, and from my perspective, has undermined our artistic and political ideal."

As *Rolling Stone*'s David Fricke reported, de la Rocha informed Morello on the morning of October 18 by phone of his decision, but was unable to contact Commerford and Wilk until later, instead releasing his statement later that same day. "Morello was not shocked by the suddenness of de la Rocha's action," wrote Fricke. "'I thought each record could be the last, each show could be the last,' Morello says, referring to the internal strife that has plagued Rage since their formation in Los Angeles in 1991. 'Also, the announcement came when Zack was taking a couple of years off. Zack was not planning on playing a Rage Against The Machine show or writing a Rage Against The Machine song until 2003.'"

This was all the more strange because it came just as Rage were about to release a covers album called *Renegades*, recorded once the idea of a live album had fallen through. The three remaining members did their normal quota of press interviews to push the record, a fine effort as covers albums go, although many of the questions they faced were inevitably to do with their future rather than the album itself. "There's always been this looming solo-record thing – Zack was vocal about what he wanted to do for a long time," said Commerford. "It's hard for me to get bummed out about it. I'm looking back on 10 years, thinking that was a great thing. But there is a lot more to be accomplished."

He, Morello and Wilk made it immediately clear that the band would be continuing, either under a new name or as Rage Against The Machine, once a new singer had been recruited (Morello mentioned "calls we have gotten from some amazing and interesting people"). Names such as rapper B-Real from Cypress Hill were mentioned, although whether these came from scoop-hungry hacks or the band themselves is not clear.

As for the threesome's relationship with de la Rocha, it seemed there would be little ongoing contact, although there appeared to be no outright acrimony. The band members were not in the habit of socialising with each other away from the tourbus in any case. Wilk explained: "Because we spend so much time together as a band when a tour ends, we tend to go our separate ways, just to preserve our sanity, so that we all want to come back to [Rage] again further down the line. Having to deal with the non-music aspects of the band can begin to interfere with friendships, so any time away from one another is pretty important... Even when I'm not touring, 75% of my time is spent working on music. I've been working with groove samplers with my [wife Selene] who used to sing in the band Seven Year Bitch and I also have a couple of friends who I get together with to jam on a telepathic level – no discussion goes into it. We just play and connect and see what happens. That to me is a pretty amazing thing to do. It's so different to writing traditional songs with a band and it provides a nice contrast."

Commerford had considered life after the band, he told writer Ben Myers: "I think about what it will be like once all this is over. My job has been to deal with the relationship between four people while going onstage and dealing with my own personal insecurities. That's it. That's my role. Hopefully there'll be something out there for me to do after the band, because I do worry about it. I don't worry about the money, but rather feeling good about myself and doing something I want to do. It's going to be hard after this to match everything we've achieved in Rage... As I become more of a veteran on the scene, I still ultimately have to deal with the level of insecurity which is always higher than the excitement level. I guess it's just human nature. I guess it's just the way that I am. If anyone tells you that they're secure with being on such a large stage in front of such a large audience, I say that they're talking bullshit."

Sadly, de la Rocha himself had been optimistic about his role in Rage as recently as the previous year. As he told Myers, "I don't think that in our heart of hearts we were ever ready to destroy this gift, you know? Right now we're taking this day by day, but I don't see any reason why we can't continue to do this, primarily because we've really overcome a lot of the tensions that existed within the band around the mid-nineties. There were definitely some very serious tensions back then, but now we're talking much more, discussing things and acting more as a collective than we ever have. Because of that I see no reason not to continue into the future."

Morello played his usual diplomatic role to the hilt, saying in December: "Timmy and Brad and I are currently concentrating on the release of *Renegades*. Rage Against The Machine has not broken up. Zack left the group on good terms, and we all wish him well. We want to give *Renegades* – an album we are very proud of – all the attention it deserves, and then figure out the future of Rage Against The Machine. I can guarantee you that we will continue to push the envelope musically and continue the fight for social justice, hopefully on an even greater level than in the past."

Renegades did a great job of saluting Rage's heroes and beefing up their songs to add excitement, particularly in the case of Bob Dylan's 'Maggie's Farm' and Cypress Hill's 'How I Could Just Kill A Man', whose acoustic and hip-hop roots are given Morello's trademark riffed-up rearrangement. Other songs are reproduced in a close manner to the original – see Minor Threat's 'In My Eyes' – or stripped back to their most essential components, as in The Rolling Stones' 'Street Fighting Man'. It's not all abrasive, with its subtle version of Devo's 'Beautiful World' and a gloriously funky take on EPMD's 'I'm Housin'' (already a massively groove-laden song), and there's a full range of dynamics to match any album of Rage originals.

"There were a couple of songs bandied about at rehearsal that didn't make the final cut," recalled Morello. "They included an amazing juxtaposition of Rush's 'Working Man' with Eazy-E's 'Ruthless Villain' as well as going around with Frankie Goes To Hollywood's 'Two Tribes'. We also tried and abandoned Gang Of Four's 'What We All Want' and the Gap Band's 'You Dropped A Bomb On Me'."

Looking back at the recording sessions, producer Rick Rubin – a man famous for getting bands into the right frame of mind for music-making at peak form – remembered that the band seemed to be getting on well. "You hear stories [such as] they don't show up and they hate each other," said Rubin, interviewed by David Fricke.

"It was not like that in the least. It was nothing but pleasant." Morello agreed, recalling that the three-night process of choosing which songs to cover – in which each musician chose three of the final 12 – was similar to "the atmosphere of spontaneity when we made the first Rage record. If we had been operating with business as usual – 'Hey, we're gonna do a new studio record' – *Renegades* would never have come out."

"Working with Rick Rubin was phenomenal," added Morello. "He is not only a great producer but a great collaborator as well. He has a great appreciation for many styles of music. He was at the early DC hardcore shows, as well as being the guy who made some of the first hip-hop records. He has a knowledgeable appreciation of heavy metal and folk music, and funk, that I've never seen in a producer before. He's also a very clever and funny guy... with an unruly beard!"

Commerford was enthusiastic about the new album too, telling *Juice* magazine: "We've got a great new record that I personally think is one of the best, if not the best record we've ever done. It's certainly the most mature album, and I'm really excited to get it out there. Right now that's my main focus... Rick Rubin is kind of a legendary guy, and ever since we've been a band, me and Zack used to drive to rehearsal and it was like, 'How cool would it be to work with Rick Rubin?' That was what we talked about all the time. Rick at that time had the Def American thing happening and we didn't have a record deal. It was like, 'Whoo, maybe we can get signed by Rick Rubin!' So it was just kinda crazy to work with him."

He added: "I'd developed an idea in my mind of what he would be like – and he was nothing like that. I thought he was like this hardcore biker guy, you know – that's the way he looked. But you can't judge a book by its cover, because he's a totally soft-spoken, kinda Zen sort of guy. You know, a nice sweet guy, really intelligent and really on top of his game – and he's a bomb producer. This was the first time I just laid back as far as my comments and what I was hearing goes. I thought, 'I'll just leave it to Rick, and Rick will

against huge odds, Rage used their platform effectively. The world has changed since those early days, though, and the battle rages on. STEPHEN STICKLER/CORBIS

The only other early-nineties band of equal significance as Rage when it came to musical dynamics was and remains Tool, whose singer Maynard James Keenan appeared on stage with RATM at Lollapalooza in July 1993. FRANK WHITE PHOTO AGENCY

On stage with fellow traveller RZA from the Wu Tang Clan. PHOTOSHOT/GEORGE DE SOTA

"There are some funny people in this band," said Tom, although few believed him. Photos like this demonstrated his point. PHOTOSHOT/GIE KNAEPS

y 1996 Rage were at their peak. Their live show was a *tour de force*, despite internal tensions that ultimately ecame intolerable. SHAWN MORTENSEN/CORBIS OUTLINE

At this photoshoot in '96, Zack made it clear where his allegiance lay when it came to the Mexican power struggle. "He identifies with the people in Chiapas," worried his father, Beto. PHOTOFEST NYC

A gang of misfits. Tom Morello never expected Rage to flourish for racial and political reasons. PHOTOFESTNYC

At the Rock Torhout Festival in 1994, Rage gave it everything they had in the days before internal strife tore them apart. PHOTOSHOT/GIE KNAEPS

Winning the battle, but still fighting the war: Rage at the 39th Grammy Awards in 1997. STEVE EICHNER/WIREIMAGE

Zack whipping up the crowd during a performance at the MTV Times Square studio in New York City.
FRANK MICELOTTA/GETTY IMAGES

Above left and right: Tearing it up at the Pukkelpop Festival. Note Tom, delivering his unique guitar skills.
PHOTOSHOT/GIE KNAEPS

On August 14, 2000, five thousand people gathered outside that year's Democratic National Convention in Los Angeles to see Rage Against The Machine play. GENE BLEVINS/SYGMA/CORBIS

All great performers expose their inner struggle on stage, and here's Zack de la Rocha doing just that.
ROB VERHORST/REDFERNS

sort it out'. And then, boom! I got the final CD and I just loved it... There's no pressure at the moment to get anything sorted. This record is the main priority at the moment. This is a record we wrote and recorded and did all this work on before Zack left the band. So I've just gotta go, 'OK, let's not lose focus on this because this other thing happened. Let's not lose sight of what's the most important thing.' And the most important thing is that I feel passionate about this record."

Despite this, the band members knew that a new singer would have to be found if a future for Rage was to be taken seriously. Rubin lent his weighty support, saying that with the right new vocalist, "It could turn into a Yardbirds-into-Led Zeppelin scenario. In many ways, Tom Morello is the Jimmy Page of today". Logistically, the band believed, the new line-up could hit the ground running: as Commerford explained, "Every song we ever wrote in Rage Against The Machine, we wrote the music first, and then the words got put on it. We will still be able to make those musical sculptures. I think it's a great opportunity for a singer who has a different style... like, 'Wow, what a great place to speak from'."

While this was going on, de la Rocha had vanished from view. Many years later, he looked back at this grim period, saying: "When I left Rage... first off, I was very heartbroken, and secondly, I became obsessed with completely reinventing my wheel. In an unhealthy way, to a degree. I kind of forgot that old way of allowing yourself to just be a conduit." As he went through this period of self-analysis, life went on for his old band mates: by now, Commerford, Wilk and Morello were all married and starting families.

Even so, the band continued to operate posthumously, as it were. On February 20, 2001, a DVD called *The Battle Of Mexico City* was released, chronicling the on- and off-stage experiences of Rage when they went south of the border back in 1999. "It was awesome!" enthused Morello, interviewed by Australian radio. "We had never played in Mexico City before, and the show was probably one of our best so far, in the history of the band. The audience was just crazy and MTV filmed the whole event, so I think it's going to be broadcast, and we have the rights to it so we get to share it with everybody... before the show there was a riot: the battle of Mexico City was being fought outside the venue. There were about six or seven thousand [people] inside, and then there was another three and a half thousand outside who broke down the barricades to get into the show, and the police riot group was called in and there was tear gas. It was pretty dramatic."

He added that Rage had reduced the ticket prices to allow the Mexican audience to attend the show: "Tickets for shows in Mexico City are normally tremendously expensive and... only the rich can afford to rock, and that's not in our way of thinking, so we lowered the prices for the show. All of the proceeds of the show were going to the Zapatista community in southern Mexico to a few poor communities down there [but] about two days before the show, we received a letter from Subcomandante Marcos, who is one of the leaders of the Zapatista movement, asking us to give the money not to the communities where his Zapatista fighters are, but rather to the flood victims from the recent flood there. So we thought 'Magnanimous gesture' and we were happy to do it."

It seemed that as many people were taking notice of Rage Against The Machine in this strange limbo period as they did when the band were in full flow. A Grammy award came their way for 'Guerilla Radio' in February, while Morello scooped Best Guitarist at the California Music Awards. Politically, they weren't slacking either, with all three members attending a protest against the Free Trade Area Of The Americas (FTAA) in San Ysidro, California and Morello taking messages from Rage fans with him when he visited Mumia Abu-Jamal in jail in Greene, Pennsylvania. Most of all, however, they used the spring of 2001 to hone their next musical endeavour, following up on a suggestion by Rubin that they jam with Chris Cornell, formerly of Soundgarden, to see if any chemistry existed.

The jam sessions, which took place in April, were immediately fruitful, recalled Morello. "Chris stepped to the microphone and sang the song, and I couldn't believe it. It didn't just sound good. It didn't sound great. It sounded transcendent. And... when there is an irreplaceable chemistry from the first moment, you can't deny it." With astonishing speed, the new group wrote 21 songs in a mere 19 days and began recording in May, with Rubin behind the desk. An early name for a new band was rumoured to be Civilian, although Morello later discounted this as exactly that – a rumour.

A couple of years later, Cornell looked back on the new band's genesis, explaining to interviewer Amy Freeborn: "[The press] looked at it as two bands with strong history and strong integrity and the possibility that [those things] would be compromised. But I was there in the room writing the songs and I knew no integrity was going to be tested." He'd had a dialogue going with Morello for some time, he added: "After Soundgarden broke up I just really wanted to do a solo record, for no other reason than I'd been in bands my whole life. I just wanted to make a record where every decision was mine. If it was good it was my fault, if it was bad it was my fault. During that time I had a lot of phone calls from different musicians wanting to work with me, but it just wasn't the right time for me. I did the solo record [*Euphoria Morning*, 1999] and toured it, and that was a lot of fun. When I was getting ready to go back in and start working on new solo material, I realised that I didn't really like it that much. It was a kind of lonely experience."

He continued: "Around that time I'd met Tom, a couple of times, and he'd been interested in working with me, but more as a Tom solo idea or a movie idea... That was before the last Rage album [*The Battle Of Los Angeles*] because they didn't even know if Zack was coming back to do the vocals. Tom called me up in regard to starting a band, and the memory of seeing Rage play live at Lollapalooza was one of the most impacting performances I've ever seen in my life. It just made sense right away. When we got together and started working together it was exactly what I thought it would be like – fun and fresh."

When the news broke that Rage and Cornell were jamming, fans' ears pricked up. While Soundgarden's grunge heritage was sufficiently different from Rage's rap/rock background that the new partnership was almost guaranteed to sound original, the two bands shared a fanbase and an attitude and on paper at least, the pairing sounded good. "Me being in the band and starting to write music straight away changed a lot the way they worked together," said Cornell. "It was the three of them – guitarist Tom Morello, drummer Brad Wilk and bassist Tim Commerford – working with me, when they were used to just writing with the three of them, and not Zack."

He added: "We didn't really worry about sounding like our previous bands. I'm not a rapper, I'm a singer, and I also write guitar parts and songs. Even if I took a Rage song and sang with my vocal on it, it wouldn't sound like Rage. When we first started writing... there were a couple of songs that were a little bit reminiscent of Rage, but that's them doing what they do. But me singing over it, that's what [the new band] sounds like. They – we all – wanted to see what doing it with vocals had to offer."

The musicians played on, while the two management teams representing both sides attempted to broker a deal between the two record companies – Cornell, with A&M; Rage, with Epic. This complex deal almost scuppered the new band, it was later revealed, and took several months to complete, only resolving in 2002. By then, a global reshifting of political perspective had occurred in the form of the World Trade Center attacks on September 11, 2001 – ironically the event most likely to incur some form of intelligent response from a band like Rage Against The Machine. Although the group commented on the tragedy, their role in the seismic events of the period revolved more round the wholesale banning of their songs from radio after the event by the owner of several stations, the giant Clear Channel.

"There's only been a few times in my history as a musician and an activist where I've ever felt 'the Man' push back," Morello told *The Progressive*. "One of them was the immediate aftermath of 9/11. Clear Channel banned all Rage Against The Machine songs from all their radio stations. They faxed this memorandum to all the stations which listed specific songs that could not be played, including John Lennon's

'Imagine' and the Gap Band's 'You Dropped A Bomb On Me'. The only artist whose entire catalogue was singled out was Rage Against The Machine."

As we'll see in the next chapter, protest music of all kinds was off the menu for most unthinking people in the wake of 9/11. How strange, in retrospect, that Rage themselves were busy on different, and decidedly non-political, projects as the dust settled. Into 2002, and ideas were bandied around for a name for the new band, while side projects abounded – Wilk playing drums on the soundtrack to *The Dangerous Lives Of Altar Boys*, for example – and fans waited impatiently for concrete news.

This came on March 19, when the still-unnamed band announced that they had been booked for a slot on that year's Ozzfest, the travelling American rock concert helmed by Sharon and Ozzy Osbourne, plus Ozzy's sporadically active band Black Sabbath. Literally days later, a second announcement came saying that Cornell had left the group. You can imagine the businesslike Morello tearing his hair out in frustration over the lack of a professional image which this presented to the public...

"Coming together as a band was not so simple because of a lot of business reasons," lamented Cornell, long after the fact. "We had separate record companies, managers, lawyers, separate everything. It was two separate record companies fighting over some kind of ownership. They were approaching us as two separate entities. It became awful and we didn't see a clear road to the future. Everyone was fighting, literally, right in front of us."

"There was a tremendous amount of drama and unnecessary conflict, which was generated by our managerial situation," Morello told *Launch*. "Timmy and Brad and I had a management company, and Chris had a separate manager, and there was not enough room in the picture for both of them, and it created an enormous amount of conflict, which for a while undermined the band's solidarity."

Cornell's temporary departure appeared to be due to a combination of frustration over the failed business dealings behind the scenes, and a struggle with his own personal demons. He endured a spell in rehab around this time, explaining that he'd undergone a "horrible personal crisis", which he attributed to alcohol addiction and other unnamed causes, but also to the managerial shenanigans behind the scenes which had left him close to despair.

"I just needed a hiatus," he told Freeborn. "All the fighting – it wasn't what I agreed to do. It was a very terrible part of my life, personally. We've all been in situations that are volatile and not very good. But by leaving, I realised that I didn't want to be feeling like this any more and that it was the music that came first – I wanted to be in a band, but I wanted to enjoy it. And I found out that we all felt the same way. So that set a different tone. We thought then: this is serious. We want to allow ourselves to try this band out."

Recordings for a debut album took place once all the musicians were back on their feet, and an album release was scheduled for November. In May, 13 rehearsal tracks were leaked onto peer-to-peer filesharing networks, another blood-pressure-raising event for Morello, who fumed: "I'm mad. So mad. Some jackass intern at Bad Animal Studios in Seattle stole some demos and put them on the internet without the band's permission. I'm so mad. They sound nothing like the record, and I can't wait for people to hear the real thing."

By the summer, however, things were running relatively smoothly once more, with a new management company, The Firm, on board and a deal in place between Epic and A&M's Interscope label, allowing each company to release the new band's albums, one after the other. All that was needed was the name, and in September, the announcement finally came.

As Morello later recalled, the band's name came out of the blue. "That was Chris's suggestion, [which] came to him in a vision," he said. "We're all on the two-way pagers, and Chris one night said, 'I got it. It's Audioslave'."

BOMBTRACK 3

Music And Protest: Who Cares?

I wonder how you're feeling at this point. Are you sick of hearing about Rage Against The Machine's political protest songs yet? Maybe you are, maybe you're not. As it happens, we've come to a point in the story where Tom Morello stops writing about politics and social issues for a while to concentrate on his new band, although a year afterwards he re-enters the arena more energetically than ever before.

If you're getting a bit bored by the protest stuff, I understand that fully. It takes energy to give a damn, especially across the length of an entire book. Try doing it for an entire lifetime, like Morello and Zack de la Rocha. Then try doing it at a period in time when people generally don't have an appetite for revolution, as it is now, in late 2013, as I write this. Not easy.

Why should people's interest in fist-aloft protest anthems ebb and flow so? After all, the same old problems pervade our lives just as perniciously as they ever did. We still need solutions to the same old questions. To answer this, I've drafted in the eminent Dorian Lynskey, a freelance music writer who has written for publications including *The Guardian, The Observer, Q, MOJO, GQ* and *Spin*. His book, *33 Revolutions Per Minute: A History Of Protest Songs* (Faber & Faber, 2011) is a wide-ranging examination of protest music of the last 100 years and was praised for its analytical depth. Let's see what he has to say about Rage Against The Machine, shall we?

Why did you choose to include Rage Against The Machine's 'Sleep Now In The Fire' in your book *33 Revolutions Per Minute*?
Narrative reasons. Every song in the book needed to tell a story about a particular moment in the history of the protest song. When Rage first emerged there was still quite a lot of political music around, including Riot Grrrl and post-Public Enemy radical hip-hop, but by the end of the nineties Rage were in a tiny minority and I wanted to explore that decline. Also, in 1999 you had a new outbreak of activism in the form of the anti-globalisation movement, with Naomi Klein's bestseller *No Logo* and the World Trade Organisation protests in Seattle. In light of that I wanted to contrast Rage's classic approach – direct and confrontational in the tradition of punk and hip-hop – with the more opaque, impotent discontent of Radiohead between *OK Computer* and *Kid A*. And the video, directed by Michael Moore on Wall Street, was the perfect way in to that story. Not forgetting the fact that 'Sleep Now In The Fire' is one of Rage's best, most lyrically intriguing songs.

What was the wider impact of the 'Sleep Now In The Fire' shoot?
The video was a fantastic bit of guerrilla street theatre, but these things are always difficult to quantify at the time. You need hindsight to make that kind of judgment. For instance, you can only measure the long-term impact of The Clash when you learn that Billy Bragg started making music because of them, or that Public Enemy wanted to be The Clash meeting Run-DMC. That's the kind of way in which Rage's actions would have had an effect: a lot of different people would have been alerted to the issues raised by the video. That's what protest songs do: they highlight an issue and inspire at least some listeners to think about the world in a different way.

What subjects do Rage address in 'Sleep Now In The Fire'?
Zack is representing the worst of America in his lyrics: that song reminds me a lot of Jello Biafra of the Dead Kennedys, whose writing is very

influenced by theatre and who often inhabits hateful characters in his songs. There's a lot of history in the song – Vietnam, Hiroshima, lynch mobs and Columbus. Zack is saying 'I am the Nina and the Pinta', referring to Columbus' arrival in America not as a discovery but as a rapacious invasion, which is a powerfully controversial position to take. He also uses Francis Fukuyama's famous line from the end of the Cold War about how we've reached 'the end of history': the great ideological battles are over and capitalism is now the only game in town. By putting that line in the mouth of his murderous narrator, Zack is challenging that idea. His implication is that America may have won the Cold War but it still has to reckon with its own history of violence and exploitation.

In any collection of protest songs, Rage are presumably a no-brainer inclusion?
Well, Rage are one of the few bands – Public Enemy being another – from whose catalogue you could choose pretty much any song. I didn't have to zoom in on a particular song or album, like I had to with Bob Dylan or Green Day. They were the last globally successful rock band to put radical politics front and centre in their music, and to show that you can be big in spite of that. If you want to illustrate to somebody that you can express political opinions – in some cases, unpopular opinions – and still be huge, assuming that your music is good enough, Rage are a peerless example. There was no other band at that time that could have filled that space: it was a very particular combination of personalities and upbringings. What made it work was their sound, and particularly Tom's guitar. It was so potent and innovative that it gave them licence to say anything. You could say the same about Public Enemy: their music was so good that no matter what they were rapping about, it would have worked. Bands like that represent the zenith of protest music. The sound itself is radical and rebellious, so it makes the lyrics twice as impactful.

Can you define the appeal of 'Killing In The Name' for kids who might not appreciate the song's political message?
Rage were always good at keeping their lyrics relatively simple, and not overexplaining. The old joke was that Rage's teenage fans liked

that song because they didn't want to tidy their rooms – but that's what's so good about it. The line 'Fuck you, I won't do what you tell me' addresses a kind of adolescent stroppiness which is the essence of resistance. You don't have to be left-wing to appreciate it: I'm sure even Tea Party libertarians would utter similar sentiments about the US government. And anyone can say that about their parents, of course: it's such a primal thing. By taking that spirit and relating it to other people and bigger issues, Rage made politics seem a very natural extension of the adolescent desire to forge your own identity, ask questions and not buckle to what everyone else wants. It's protest as instinct, as an emotional eruption.

Protest music always runs the risk of being too preachy or dense or distant or self-righteous, but none of those criticisms apply to a song like 'Killing In The Name'. The way that Rage structured the song, like 'Bullet In The Head', was like a burning fuse: the tension builds and builds, and finally explodes. If you match the right words to that structure, political sentiments seem incredibly thrilling and natural.

Why is there less protest in rock music in 2013 than there was 20 years ago?
There's no single reason. Generally, there's less of an appetite for it. Once 9/11 happened, the West became much more defensive and much less in the mood for internal dissent and questioning itself, and so the spirit of protest was muted – with the notable exception of the Iraq war demonstrations in 2003 – until the financial crisis of 2008 and the Occupy movement which followed it. It's not that the issues are any less relevant. Rage are not specifically of their time, lyrically: a lot of these things still matter, whether it's militarism or police brutality or American hypocrisy or whatever. Those problems endure.

But there are times in history when the circumstances are more generous towards political expression and there's a concomitant craving for political lyrics, for example during the civil rights movement and the war in Vietnam. Or look at British punk or seventies reggae: these were responses to a widespread sense of emergency. You didn't have that sense during most of the nineties, which was a relatively cosy period for most Westerners. Currently you have the opposite problem: the world's problems seem so vast and suffocating that they're more likely to inspire the kind of neurosis and malaise you find in Radiohead or Arcade Fire than the empowering 'get up, stand up' attitude represented by Rage. Among bands and their fans, there's a general 'what's the point?' attitude towards protest music that can only be shaken up by a sudden outburst of anger – the kind that inspired Green Day's *American Idiot* or Plan B's *Ill Manors*.

Why is it difficult to adopt a protest stance if you have a neutral background?
The metaphor I use is the broken chain: whenever I interviewed people for my book, they always had a foot in a previous era of protest songs. Rage appeared in 1992, when hip-hop had been very political since Public Enemy's second album. Tom Morello had grown up on protest songs in an activist household, Zack had been in a hardcore band and attuned to Mexican-American politics via his dad, so between them they had so much experience and music to draw on. It wasn't a giant leap into political music; it was a natural evolution. It's the same all the way back. Chuck D of Public Enemy could remember the Black Panthers, Vietnam, Martin Luther King being shot, James Brown singing 'Say It Loud, I'm Black And I'm Proud'. Joe Strummer could remember seeing the anti-war protests of 1968 on TV as a teenager. There is a natural chain. But if you're 20 now, you have to look back a long way, basically skipping a generation, to find inspirational, politically alert musicians. Where are your reference points? It would almost feel like a throwback now.

Can't new bands protest as effectively these days?
A surprising number of artists continue to release protest songs now and then: I make a list of them every year. But Rage's entire mission – the band name, the cover of the first album, every single lyric and interview – was about their politics. I think young bands would find

that very weird, and the bands that try to do it, like the King Blues for example, don't seem to get beyond a core fanbase of people who like the message. It's not because the evil industry is shutting them out, although it's certainly more conservative than it was in the eighties: it's because they're not brilliant enough to break through regardless. How do you become an emphatically political band in 2013 with no cultural momentum to help you along? How good would you have to be, and how perfect would your timing have to be? I still believe that it's possible, but it's dauntingly hard.

To what extent is Rage an unorthodox band?
These are very unusual people. I know from my dealings with Tom that he is a dogged person who is quite willing to let go of fame and money for long spells, and go and play the tiniest little demos that you never hear about, because he doesn't get any publicity for them and he certainly doesn't get paid. He does them because he wants to. He's got this huge passion, sincerity and intellect mixed with a kind of amiable charm. He's one of the only musicians I've met who seems like he could handle the job of an elected official if he wanted. Zack, who I haven't met, always seems coiled with rage and not equipped for that role of roving spokesman, but that's what makes him so hair-raising on record. It's such an unlikely combination of individuals and, of course, that's why it didn't last. So perhaps the question is not 'Why aren't more people doing this?', it's more 'How did it ever happen in the first place?' What a miracle that this happened: Tom Morello meeting Zack de la Rocha is like Morrissey meeting Marr.

Perhaps there are more, and more relevant, outlets for protest than music these days?
Clearly, many young people are really upset about various issues, but they don't necessarily feel that music is the best way to express those feelings. The internet gives us so many outlets that people who might have been craving a Clash or Rage song now have blogs to visit or Tumblr posts to write. That's where political catharsis happens now. Twenty years ago they'd have been writing to the music papers and

going to Riot Grrrl shows. So it's not that people don't care about the issues, it's that music doesn't have the central cultural role that it used to have. The downside of internet debate is that if a political song is released now, you instantly get people picking apart contradictions in the lyrics, or pointing out that the band had a sponsorship deal with a footwear company or whatever. The late writer Steven Wells once complained that Riot Grrrl's ideology had been 'combed over, examined, misinterpreted, rewritten and kicked to death a hundred times'. And that was before the internet. It's so much worse now, hence a certain wariness on the part of musicians.

Maybe politics just isn't cool any more?
When Mumford & Sons were asked by Q magazine if they were Tories, they responded that they couldn't remember a single political discussion in the band. It was horrifying. There was no way that would not have been considered absolutely freakish in a previous generation: in the eighties, even Wham! and Spandau Ballet talked about politics. I'd honestly prefer someone like Frank Turner. I don't share his politics but at least he has some. He's not blithely admitting that he doesn't give a shit either way.

So yes, I do think it's easy and safe to be apolitical now, but of course not every Rage fan in the nineties was reading Chomsky and listening to Crass. To some extent the band shaped its audience and made fans more inclined to investigate politics for themselves, and it would be hard to do something like that again – but not impossible. Great bands don't just cater to a need, they create that need.

CHAPTER 8

2002–2006

This chapter is effectively the story of Audioslave, a band whose role in retrospect was basically to occupy some talented musicians while they waited for their earlier, and better, bands to reunite. Fans of the group won't thank me for saying that, but at the same time, Audioslave also spurred Tom Morello into some of his finest work outside the band. It is a tale of two halves, so to speak.

Let's be clear. Audioslave's first salvo was amazing – 'Cochise', an epic song and video that dominated the rock media for the rest of 2002 and into 2003. Based on a huge, hypnotic groove riff straight from the Led Zeppelin school and featuring Chris Cornell's awe-inspiring wails, the single was an instant demonstration of how Rage Against The Machine's sound could function with a singer rather than a rapper. Any doubters were silenced.

Check out the 'Cochise' video. With much emphasis placed on visual drama and filmic (and literal) pyrotechnics, plus the muscled torsos of Wilk and Commerford – the latter of whom had expanded his body tattoo to an eye-opening extent – 'Cochise' is a feast for the eyes and ears, and couldn't be a better introduction to the new band. If any new group of musicians needs an object lesson in how to get the attention of a jaded fanbase, this is that lesson.

While the media burbled its appreciation, and fans of both Soundgarden and Rage tuned into this new phenomenon, details emerged of the deals that had enabled the group to make their debut. For starters, a British group also called Audioslave had been paid a sum not unadjacent to $30,000 to agree to share the name with Cornell and crew. As the *NME* wrote on October 23, "The group were approached by US lawyers when the American Audioslave were worried they might be confused with their English namesakes, who are more used to playing low key gigs around the North-West. The Liverpool Audioslave, whose rock songs include 'Every Day's A Hangover', 'We're All Fucked Now' and 'Enemy In Me', have now come to an 'amicable settlement' with Cornell and Co."

The article continued: "Singer Christopher Price, who works as a nurse in the A&E Department of the Royal University Hospital in Liverpool, said: 'We'd had a few messages posted on our website from fans telling us that an American band was trying to steal our name – but we didn't take them seriously at first. Then, one day, our manager got a call from the US to say they were interested in negotiating a deal – and it was then we decided we should get a solicitor involved. But we're all big fans of the American rock scene anyway, and we felt quite chuffed they wanted our name." And that, readers, is the last you'll ever hear of the former British Audioslave, who renamed themselves The Most Terrifying Thing and vanished into obscurity.

When a self-titled debut album appeared on November 19, 2002, it entered the Billboard chart at number seven after selling over 160,000 copies in its first week on sale – numbers which, a decade later with the music industry in tatters, sound astounding. It went gold after a month and triple platinum within four years, which represents popularity only slightly less than that of Rage Against The Machine, given that record sales were sliding rapidly towards their present-day slump at the time.

Audioslave has many memorable moments, for sure, although whether it is as essential as the musicians' previous work – on both sides – is open to debate. Take the song 'Gasoline' for example, and I choose this song because in many ways it encapsulates the tone of the album. Cornell's vocals soar above Morello's muscular riff and the groove of the rhythm section, with the arrangement of the song rising and falling dynamically: you can almost predict the movement of a stadium crowd as the song progresses. It's this that makes *Audioslave* ever so slightly less attention-grabbing than, say, *The Battle Of Los Angeles*: there is an element of predictability surrounding a large portion of the songwriting. Maybe this is due to its allegiance to the tropes of classic rock – the loud chorus, the midsection-plus-solo, the spiralling vocal melody – or maybe, just maybe, some of the edge that defined Rage Against The Machine was missing.

One thing that *Audioslave* was definitely not was political, in the sense that we have come to define it in this book. Asked why this was the case, given his previous work, Morello reasoned: "There are many overtly political bands that do not sell 14 million records like Rage Against The Machine, because the first thing they have to take care of is the musical chemistry. You can have all of your politics lined up and all of your analyses together, but it's got to be a great rock and roll band. And the way great rock and roll bands happen is organically. The convergence of those four musicians made a band called Rage Against The Machine that had a political content. Had we started out saying it must be A, B, C, D, trying to shoehorn ideas and music into a little box, it wouldn't have worked. When bands do that, it's either derivative or it's not compelling."

He added: "With Audioslave, the four of us got in a room and we said, what's this going to be? We're not going to try to be Rage Against The Machine; we're not going to try to be Soundgarden; we're going to see what develops. It developed musically, very successfully for us, in a way that felt just great in the room. For me, Audioslave didn't have political content."

Then again, the band didn't need to have such a thing. Musically and lyrically, the *Audioslave* album found itself a comfortable home among lovers of stadium rock. Cornell and the other musicians had expected at least some complaints from listeners who had hoped for some of the vitriol of Rage's previous albums, but if any came, they were muted at best. Audioslave debuted as a live act on November 25 on the *Late Show With David Letterman* and followed up a week later at KROQ's Almost Acoustic Christmas event, during which Cornell told the audience "These guys saved my life this year".

Talking of bands with balls, in early 2003 Morello introduced The Clash when they were entered in the Rock And Roll Hall Of Fame. As he recalled, "Rage Against The Machine had played shows in front of a quarter of a million people, and I was far less nervous than in that room of a couple of hundred. It was right after [Clash frontman] Joe Strummer's passing, as well, so it was an emotionally charged evening. One review of my speech said that it was probably the most overthought speech of that night, perhaps in the history of the Rock And Roll Hall Of Fame. Absolutely – I wrote about 80 drafts of it... Growing up, alternative media was not part of my life. It wasn't where I got my news. I got my news from Clash albums, frankly. I thought the *Sandinista!* [triple album, 1980] had more accurate and vivid portrayals of US policy in Central America than [NBC presenter] Tom Brokaw was giving on the news. And it fired my imagination as well."

In the meantime Zack de la Rocha had emerged from the 18 months or so of obscurity that he'd undergone after quitting the band. DJ Shadow, the American producer, had recruited him for vocals on an anti-Iraq War song, 'March Of Death', which was released for free online – a pretty advanced idea in 2003, several years before artists began to do this on a regular basis. The track, essentially a slab of distorted bass and drums overlaid with de la Rocha's passionate barks, was hardly the finest work either man had ever completed, but still, it signalled that de la Rocha was still around and as full of fire as ever.

Before the single's release, de la Rocha released a statement which ran: "Lies, sanctions, and cruise missiles have never created a free and just society. Only everyday people can do that, which is why I'm joining the millions worldwide who have stood up to oppose the Bush administration's attempt to expand the US empire at the expense of human rights at home and abroad. In this spirit I'm releasing this song for anyone who is willing to listen. I hope it not only makes us think, but also inspires us to act and raise our voices."

He also revealed that his long-mooted solo album was on its way, reportedly with the help of DJ Shadow and The Roots' drummer Questlove, although this never appeared, for reasons unknown. "After our session, the results of which I was extremely happy with, Zack was supposed to finish the rest of the album with another producer," shrugged Shadow. "He apparently never showed up to those sessions, and to my knowledge, never attempted to reschedule. Why? No-one seems to know."

Meanwhile, Audioslave began the process of rushing out material. A second single, 'Like A Stone', topped the American charts and went gold not long after its release. A third song, 'Show Me How To Live', was banned from MTV, supposedly – and predictably – because its scenes of a high-speed car chase were too extreme for viewers. A self-titled DVD was released in July and the band continued to hit the road, presenting the eminently digestible Audioslave sound to the masses with great acclaim. A slot at the returned Lollapalooza tour helped spread the message further. Not to be outdone, the ghost of Rage Against The Machine was still present in a new in-concert album, *Live At The Grand Olympic Auditorium*, which consisted of sections from Rage's final concerts in Los Angeles in September 2000.

Life in a gold-selling rock band must have been fun, but in retrospect, the politics-free period in which Tom Morello – always the most active of the band in that area – found himself at this point was never likely to last long. In between Audioslave commitments, he had begun to play the occasional solo show on acoustic guitar, appearing as an alter ego, the Nightwatchman. At these events, he played and sang his own songs, which were concerned with social issues as much as or more than any composition by Rage Against The Machine.

He recalled the Nightwatchman's origins, saying: "It was a Thanksgiving event at a teen homeless shelter called Covenant

House, in Hollywood. Each year they have a talent show and a dinner, and I would go there and MC. There was a 19-year-old kid there who was really down and out, with a troubled past and a potentially troubled future. He didn't have a great voice, but he stepped up to the mic and sang as if the soul of everyone in the room was at stake. He obviously just thought, 'I've got some ideas in my head, and I can put three or four chords together'. What he was doing felt important in a way that a lot of music on the radio doesn't. I thought, 'Man, I really want to get involved in something like that'. It made me want to go out and do this in front of people."

The new project's introduction came when Morello appeared on the Tell Us The Truth tour, a 13-date jaunt around America which also featured Billy Bragg, Mike Mills of R.E.M., Steve Earle and other artists. Its focus was purely on activism for a range of unions, environmental and reform groups for the media, in particular the last of these. Morello explained, "Media consolidation needs smashing and globalisation needs unmasking. When presidents and politicians lie, it is the job of the press to expose those lies. When the press fails, the gangsters come out from hiding. The lie becomes the law. The point of the Tell Us The Truth Tour is to help others make connections, and to show them that activism can change the policies of this country."

Asked about the Nightwatchman's inspirations, Morello referred to his idol Joe Hill, a Swedish singer-songwriter who had been executed in Utah in 1914 on false murder charges. The night before his death, Hill sent a message to a fellow labour leader which read: 'Don't waste time in mourning. Organise'. Hill's attitude remained an inspiration close to a century later, Morello explained: "He was a poet laureate of the labour movement. He put revolutionary lyrics to very simple tunes and helped unite workers of different backgrounds and ethnicities. He helped them see their common interests through music."

Morello knew, of course, that his previous work with Rage and Audioslave was the primary reason why kids showed up to see him play as the Nightwatchman, and was careful to negotiate this in publicity. "I began playing at open mic nights in 2002, sometimes even on nights off during the Audioslave arena tours," he said. "I'd go and sign up as the Nightwatchman because I didn't want people screaming out [for] 'Bulls On Parade'. I just wanted to play my songs. Even at those very early shows, when I was a fledgling singer-songwriter, it felt like that might be what I was put here to do... Every time I write a song, record a song or step on any stage, I play as if everyone's soul in the room is at stake. I feel if you're honest in your music, and you're able to weave your convictions and your point of view in the music you're making, then every show you play matters, in that regard. The connection with the crowd and my belief in the material was pretty strong, even at the start. However, I've had to win over every crowd that I've performed in front of."

Morello made it clear that the Nightwatchman and Audioslave were polar opposites in terms of their mission, saying: "It was spawned to act as an antidote for the arena rock of Audioslave. I greatly [enjoy] playing and being in that band, but there was one itch that it didn't scratch. The worldview of that band and my worldview were two very different things. So I just began writing songs on my own, with really no agenda other than to have an artistic outlet... There will be kids there who are fans of my electric guitar playing, and you see them there scratching their heads. But it's something that I enjoy doing. I look at it more as an extension of my politics. Then again, some of the songs are not explicitly political. It really helped me grow as an artist and songwriter. Once you prick the vein, you never know what is going to come out. You could aim for all union songs and you find yourself in other territory."

The labour unions and their welfare were dear to Morello's heart, he explained. "I come from a coal-mining family in central Illinois, and unions were always a big part of the life and fabric of the town. It was always ingrained in me from the time I was a little kid that it's the solidarity of workers that is a crucial counterbalance to corporate greed. And if we don't stand up together, we will certainly be taken advantage of individually. I've been a member of

Los Angeles [musicians' union] Local 47 since 1989 and a member of Industrial Workers Of The World as well. I think in a time when the working class and unions are being assailed in the United States, I do my best to fight back with my music."

He added: "I think as workers we need to stand together in these tough times. I've been a part of the Coalition Of Immokolee Workers to the janitors here in Los Angeles. My music has been a part of some historic labour victories in this country. I don't want to paint too rosy a picture, because we are under a dire attack. But in times like these, the key thing is solidarity. We have to remember that we're all in this together. We also need to stand by our principles. One thing I see a lot is, in the name of getting the right Democratic congressman in office, we'll sometimes compromise our core values. Just look at the example of Wisconsin. The last thing in the world either political party wanted was a working-class uprising in Wisconsin, and they did everything they could to head it off. One thing I want is a working-class uprising on a national scale – on a global scale. That's what my songs are about. So I don't think we should sell ourselves short. We should aim high and shoot for the moon."

Morello had also lent his weight to an American taxation initiative called the Robin Hood Tax, a phrase which also referred briefly to a similar idea in the UK before the coalition government shot it down in 2013. As he explained, "The National Nurses Union, they're friends of mine, we've done great shows for them before and they're spearheading this Robin Hood Tax, which is basically a small tax on the wealthiest financial trading. A small tax on that would generate billions of dollars for the National Treasury and would help tremendously. Basically, what we have now is a system that is a kind of Robin Hood in reverse: we're stealing from the poor to pay the rich, and this tax would address that."

And so, after only a short year or two away from Rage Against The Machine, Morello was once more as deeply involved in awareness-raising as he had ever been. There was no holding the man down, it seemed, although he admitted that the pressures of family life had reduced the amount of time he had available for the various causes which approached him for support. "The parameters have narrowed pretty dramatically, since I have two small children under three years old, so the bar just got higher!" he said. "The issues that have always been near and dear to my heart are labour issues, issues that deal with the crime of poverty, anti-racist issues.... I performed at the NATO protest in Chicago, the Nurses' action in favor of the Robin Hood Tax, the resurgence of the Occupy movement on May Day, the Guitarmy in New York City, and the anti-Wal-Mart protest here in Los Angeles... for me the music is a form of expression and I feel compelled to wield my guitar in the name of justice, and so wherever injustice rears its ugly head you gotta be careful, because you might get flattened by the Nightwatchman."

In 2004, Morello contributed a Nightwatchman track called 'No One Left' to the *Songs And Artists That Inspired Fahrenheit 9/11* soundtrack. The album also featured a song called 'We Want It All', a collaboration between Zack de la Rocha and Nine Inch Nails frontman Trent Reznor. The two songs were totally different in tone, with Morello's haunted, Johnny Cash-alike ballad the polar opposite of the driving, powerful punk anthem that de la Rocha had contributed, but what was reassuring was that the sentiments were expressed with equal power in each case.

It didn't stop there, as you might have come to expect by now. While Audioslave continued to work, receiving a Grammy nomination for 'Like A Stone' and preparing for a second album, Morello teamed up with System Of A Down singer Serj Tankian to form an activist movement with a difference. Axis Of Justice, with its stentorian title, evoked stern images of protest and sacrifice, but in fact its method was subtle. A coalition of musicians, with Tool's Maynard James Keenan, Wayne Kramer of the MC5, the hip-hop group Jurassic 5, and Michael 'Flea' Balzary of the Red Hot Chili Peppers stepping up to join Morello and Tankian, the Axis Of Justice did its work by organising booths at music festivals and other events, allowing local activists to get involved in regional cells. The fact that other hugely famous rock musicians got involved

– sometime Guns N' Roses and then-Velvet Revolver guitarist Slash and Slipknot/Stone Sour frontman Corey Taylor among them – says much for the power of its political message, not to mention the contents of Morello's address book.

Promoting the cause with an album called *The Axis Of Justice Concert Series Volume 1*, the musicians took their inspiration from a worrying experience which Morello had had a few years before. As he explained, "At Ozzfest a few years ago in San Bernardino, I was appalled at the number of white power and Nazi tattoos that people were just flying, like it was OK to do. Every band on the main stage was multi-ethnic, from Ozzy Osbourne's band to System Of A Down. I thought, you know what? This is my music, too. I think we should have some representation at the show. When we set up Axis Of Justice at Ozzfest, it was a tremendous success. The only problem we had was that the organisations didn't have enough literature to give away."

He added: "We formed the organisation a little over two years ago to build a bridge between progressive-minded musicians, fans of rock and rap music, and local grassroots organisations. For 10 years in Rage Against The Machine, kids were asking me, 'I love your band. I feel motivated. How do I get involved?' We formed this organisation to answer that question for the kids who were basically like I was. I grew up in a small, conservative Midwestern town. I had these ideas in my head but there was nothing to connect to. I wouldn't have known if there was an anti-nukes rally happening in the next town over. So we send an Axis Of Justice tent on anybody's tour that asks, free of charge. We organise the booths at the shows. We invite local grassroots groups and speakers. We play videos. And kids come. At Ozzfest two years ago and Lollapalooza last year, we had the most educationally intense 20-by-20 [feet] space ever in a rock and roll show."

Axis Of Justice booths subsequently became a regular fixture at both Audioslave and System Of A Down gigs, of which there were many as both bands were peaking in popularity at the time. The organisation also recorded a monthly radio show broadcast on the LA station KPFK, archived online for later consultation. All in all, with the Axis literature and message available on- and offline, plus Morello's Nightwatchman performances, there was no excuse for any follower of his music to remain uninformed.

And still Audioslave worked – and worked. Perhaps in response to the tortuous writing and recording processes that had made making albums such a drag in the Rage Against The Machine days, the new band was prolific, bringing a second album into play as early as 2003 and scheduling a release in May 2005. Some of this speed in getting things done was down to the volume of leftover music the group had in the vault from the debut album recording sessions: as Morello observed, Audioslave had "almost another album's worth of stuff [already done]".

Tim Commerford, for one, was excited about the new songs, while making it clear that his old band still retained a place in his affections. "I'm still really proud of Rage as much as I am of Audioslave," he enthused. "I still love it when I turn on the radio and I hear a Rage song. I love that. I love that Rage Against The Machine is my other band, or was my other band, [but] I'm just really proud of the fact that with Audioslave, our sound is based on a completely different thing than Rage. With Rage, we wrote riff rock and had rap vocals, so we didn't really concern ourselves with melody for the most part. With Audioslave, it's all about melody and chord progressions. It feels like this is the right direction to go."

Brad Wilk agreed, saying: "I'm very proud of Rage Against The Machine. And with Audioslave, I don't really want to say it's better or worse, it's just completely different. With Zack, it was very percussive and rap-oriented. With Chris, he is a true singer, and he says a lot without using a lot of words, and it's a much more open, spacious feel. It completely changed the chemistry."

Announcing the run-up to album number two, Audioslave made cultural history – ironically, in the most 'Rage-like' way – by becoming the first American rock band to play a show in Cuba. The free gig, which took place in front of a crowd of 50,000 Cubans, was held at La Tribuna Antiimperialista José Martí and filmed for a DVD, released later that year: before the show, the band members toured historic areas and met Cuban musicians. As Wilk recalled, "We went to a music school that was once a high falutin country club before [the 1959 revolution]. They turned it into a free school of music, and we went in and watched these kids who couldn't have been more than 19 or 20 years old just do these jazz improvisations, and it was both humbling and inspiring. It just blew my mind. The people and the culture there are incredible. What they don't have as far as materialistic goods that we have in America, they just make up for it tenfold in their spirit and in the arts and in their music."

Unusually, Audioslave included a few Rage and Soundgarden songs in their set, and continued to do so in American shows after their return. Explaining this, Wilk said: "We both come from bands that had pretty important histories. But we felt like we had succeeded on that level as our own entity, and we didn't use our other bands as crutches to prop up Audioslave. When we started playing old Rage and Soundgarden songs and actually embracing our past, we got a very warm response to that. It makes it great every night, we have so much music to choose from."

The Cuba trip might reasonably be interpreted as a political statement, but the band members played this down, insisting that the show was a cultural exchange. In order to make it happen, permission had to be granted both by United States Department Of The Treasury and the equivalent Cuban body, the Instituto Cubano De La Musica, and in fact this proved so hard to organise that US dates had to be moved as the various red tape moved back and forth. "At the end of the day, we had to get Dick Cheney's signature and Fidel Castro's signature, and it was not an easy thing to do," remarked Morello. "But it feels pretty good to say we were the first American rock band to put a stop to the rock'n'roll embargo."

Despite the Cuba show, it's interesting to note that Chris Cornell had never represented himself as particularly interested in the political issues espoused by Rage, and indeed his fellow musicians took care not to represent him that way. As Wilk explained, "The three of us never wanted Chris to join the band to be in a political band. We wanted Chris in his own right. He's an amazing lyricist.

He's not joining Rage Against The Machine; it's an entirely new band."

This disparity in the musicians' viewpoints fuelled the occasional rumour to the effect that Audioslave were about to split up. This was obviously an irritant to the band members, as it was to Wilk in more than one instance. On one occasion he explained: "The honest-to-God truth is that you have four guys in a room creating music. We're not worried about [those rumours] or answering to that. We have one thing, and that's making music that we love and being true to our fans. All that stuff is how rumours and speculation start. And there's not much you can do about that, really. I pay no attention to that stuff. But if I allowed myself to get involved with it on that level, I'd be basically reading what other people may be speculating about the truth."

He added: "I already know the truth. I already know what happened. So for me to spend my time reading about that stuff seems really counter productive. I don't know what's being said, but, man, there's better things to spend my time on. We have Axis Of Justice. We work with charities and giving money from our ticket sales to charity. That's all stuff that you'll know about, or you won't. The important thing isn't that you know about it or that it's in the press. The important thing is that the money is getting to the people who need it and the music is getting to the people who want it."

Commerford revealed that Rage Against The Machine had actually tried to play a show in Cuba before, but had failed to agree – for undisclosed reasons – on the logistics. "In Rage, we tried to go to Cuba and play, and we were not able to get on the same page as a band to do it," he said. "I feel like we dropped the ball big time in Rage Against The Machine. And here we are with Audioslave, maybe not as overtly political as Rage, but we are doing things. We're playing Cuba, we're playing Live 8, we're playing the Katrina benefit, and that's a great feeling."

In May Audioslave's second album, *Out Of Exile*, was released after a brief club tour. Interest in the album had been boosted by the appearance of two singles, 'Be Yourself' and 'Your Time Has Come', the second of which was released after a timed-out internet link which allowed the first million people who clicked on it to download it. This was one of the first examples of a band giving away their product, in recognition that in the internet age, music was effectively valueless.

For the first time, Audioslave's music began to feel slightly pedestrian. Sure, the riffs were big and the vocal melodies expansive, but to some critics, there was a slight feeling that the approach which Audioslave had debuted on their first album had not evolved. But what did they know? *Out Of Exile* debuted at the top of the American charts, after all, and the band received a Grammy nomination, their third, later the same year. As if there wasn't enough material on the shelves, a second DVD appeared in October, chronicling the Cuba show from April. Astonishingly, Audioslave planned to record a third album as soon as they came off the road in early 2006: whatever creative substances the musicians were taking, we could all do with some.

By this time reports were coming in that promoters were offering the sometime members of Rage Against The Machine large sums of money to reform. However, as the musicians had so much other stuff to think about, few observers took the idea of a reformation seriously. Even Zack de la Rocha was busy making music: the reclusive singer was seen in October 2005 singing and playing the jarana huasteca, a guitar-like five-string instrument, with a collective of musicians called Son De Madera. The group performed various shows to raise money for a charity called the South Central Farmers, a group of urban vegetable and fruit growers from Los Angeles. Morello also worked with this organisation, and it was a chance meeting at one of their events that kindled the idea between the two men of working together once more.

Another milestone for Morello came in 2006 when he visited his long-estranged father in Kenya. The trip was sparked after one of his half-brothers, Seleni, visited Morello while studying at Georgetown University in Washington, DC. The two struck up a friendship and the Kenya trip followed, with – it was reported – a positive outcome, unlike a previous visit in 1994 which had ended badly. This time Morello's dad apologised for "41 years of not being a father".

Back in America, Morello plunged once more into activism, receiving the Eleanor Roosevelt Human Rights Award for his support of workers' rights in 2006 and, as an experience that must have been diametrically opposed in terms of how much fun it involved, being arrested at a Los Angeles demo in support of the same cause. The event was labelled "the largest act of civil disobedience in the history of Los Angeles" by its organisers; afterwards, Morello commented: "In these political dark ages, it's important for us to stand up for one another. These hotel workers by the airport make 20% less wages than the hotel workers around the rest of Los Angeles. We are here to express our solidarity with them, to help them unionise and help them close the gap between their sub-poverty wages and the millions and millions of dollars the people who own these hotels make."

In the meantime, there was plenty to do. Audioslave did indeed start working on their third album after their spring tour finished. As Commerford explained, "There's always something that impedes you from being able to go into the studio right after you've been on tour and make a record, because that, ideally, would be the best time to do it. So, we did it. We knew we had a lot of songs that we had started to work on and gotten some rough recordings of." However, more tour dates behind the new record – titled *Revelations* – would not be forthcoming for a while, he added: "A break is kind of due. This is the first little bit of time in months where I've been able to just relax and enjoy my family and that sort of thing."

In retrospect, perhaps the haste to get back into the studio didn't serve the album well. Commerford revealed some initial uncertainty when he told *Launch*, "I'm pretty fearless after this whole thing, because I really felt like, 'I don't think we have enough ideas to warrant going into the studio' – that's how I kind of felt going into this. And then we did it, and I'm really happy with the record and how it came out and the songs and all that, and yeah, I would love to keep that whole vibe happening and keep that going."

"We just try to be better on every record," he added defiantly. "The next record will be a challenge to make a better record. I do believe this record is a perfect third record. I love the way it sounds. I love how we made it and I love the people we worked with. It's all good."

It wasn't, though – far from it. In July 2006 rumours spread that Cornell was about to quit Audioslave. Although he denied them, the singer did admit that he was about to record a solo album, often a euphemism that precedes a parting of the ways. This may have hindered the progress of *Revelations*, released on September 5 and, sadly, not a patch on the previous album and nowhere near the quality of *Audioslave*. Songs such as the title track and 'Original Fire' had some memorable qualities, not least because Morello was on his most inventive form when it came to coaxing bizarre sounds from his guitar, but critical reviews were average and interest in the album short-lived, although it sold well in its first week.

In any case, bigger things lay ahead. Two major announcements came hot on each other's heels in early 2007. On January 22, the annual Coachella Valley Music And Arts Festival, scheduled for April 29 that year, stated that Rage Against The Machine would be reforming for the headline slot, for one show and one show only. Three weeks later, Chris Cornell announced that he was leaving Audioslave. Surely these announcements came the wrong way round?

CHAPTER 9

2007–2009

One band ended, another reformed, all in the space of a few short weeks. It's hard to say why this happened. The writing must have been on the wall for Audioslave towards the end of 2006, and given that Zack de la Rocha and Tom Morello were back on good terms after Rage's hiatus, it made sense to resurrect the old band. It certainly seemed that way, judging by the statement which Chris Cornell issued at the time.

"Due to irresolvable personality conflicts as well as musical differences, I am permanently leaving the band Audioslave. I wish the other three members nothing but the best in all of their future endeavours," he huffed. Later he implied that a greatest hits album would be released to satisfy label commitments, while 'a friend' (there's always one) told the *New York Times*: "Chris was unhappy with the financial arrangement within the group – he wrote all the music, yet the other three bandmates took an equal share in the multimillion-dollar publishing rights." Multimillions? Unlikely, unless Disney chose to use only Audioslave songs on the next few *Star Wars* movie soundtracks...

It seemed also that Cornell's planned solo album (a collaboration with producer Timbaland which turned out to be horrendously bad, although that's another story) had got in the way of Audioslave's business, which itself had never run smoothly. The singer added, "Tom and I did have communications about the fact that I was gonna go make a record, and that I was tired of what ended up seeming like political negotiations toward how we were gonna do Audioslave business and getting nowhere with it."

He added, "Getting along as people is one thing. Getting along as a group of people that can work together in a band situation... We weren't particularly getting along well, no. Bands work in a way where everyone at some point has to have a similar idea of how you do things... Three albums into it, it started to seem like our interests weren't as conjoined any more."

So it was goodbye, Audioslave, at least for now. While the Rage Against The Machine fanbase girded its collective loins for the reappearance of Rage in April, Morello had a new album out under his Nightwatchman alter ego. *One Man Revolution* was released on April 24, 2007 and was followed up by a solo tour in support of singer-songwriter Ben Harper. A thoughtful, understated suite of songs, the album was the polar opposite of the electric storms of guitar which he'd unleashed on pretty much every other record he'd released, showcasing his deep, impassioned vocal and command of subtle, acoustic dynamics. In fact, this was Morello at his most open: stripped of the pyrotechnic guitar playing that had made him famous, he laid himself bare. "The lyrics that resonated, and the ones I felt compelled to craft into song," he commented, "were the ones that mined the deeply personal vein of suburban angst and its machinations. So, I've never been afraid of the truth on my records, be it political or personal."

Don't think for a minute that the Nightwatchman is a mere foible or side project on Morello's part. He takes it seriously, and with good reason: after all, when bands fall apart and stadium-sized audiences drift away, what greater vehicle is there for a message than one guy with one guitar?

That said, the Rage reunion – a full-production, bells-and-whistles affair – was on its way, prefaced on April 14 by a set at a benefit show for the Coalition of Immokalee Workers in Chicago. Morello and de la Rocha played a few songs on acoustic instruments, a perfect way in to the fully-fledged Rage show which took place at Coachella on the 29th of that month. It was not without controversy, as you'd expect, and indeed as many had hoped. Announcing the group's return as a necessary measure in the face of the many evils of George W. Bush's current administration, de la Rocha paraphrased from the stage a quote from Noam Chomsky to the effect that, like all American presidents since World War II, Bush could and should be arrested and tried under war crimes laws for his military actions while in power.

Chomsky's original quote is worth revisiting in full, as it contains within it a clear explanation of everything about the US administration that fuelled protest bands such as Rage. Morello had always supported Chomsky's thinking, saying as far back as 2000: "Chomsky is one of the greatest thinkers of our time. Anyone not familiar with his writings should rush out to the library or bookstore and get familiar. He has been described as the greatest intellectual dissident of the 20th century, and that is not an overstatement. A good starting point for Chomsky's ideas would be *The Chomsky Reader* or several books of interviews he has given to [broadcaster] David Barsamian. He is someone definitely worth checking out."

In the Radio Free LA radio broadcast from 1996 which he'd given to Morello, the learned professor savaged the White House's history of war crimes, with accusations levelled at the Truman, Eisenhower, Kennedy, Johnson, Nixon, Carter, Reagan, Bush, and Clinton administrations. "Every single one of them, every last rich white one of them from Truman on, would have been hung to death and shot," he said, "and this current administration is no exception. They should be hung, and tried, and shot. As any war criminal should be..."

A clip of this speech ran on Fox News, accompanied by an on-screen headline which read: 'Rock group Rage Against The Machine says Bush admin should be shot'. Conservative commentator Ann Coulter made the classic authoritarian error on the show of saying in response, "They're losers, their fans are losers, and there's a lot of violence coming from the left wing." With these words she made the issue more visible to a whole demographic of rock fans who might otherwise have ignored it.

On July 28 and 29, Rage played at a hip-hop festival called Rock The Bells, where de la Rocha responded in detail to the Fox story: "A couple of months ago, those fascist motherfuckers at the Fox News Network attempted to pin this band into a corner by suggesting that we said that the president should be assassinated. Nah, what we said was that he should be brought to trial as a war criminal and hung and shot. That's what we said. And we don't back away from the position, because the real assassinator is Bush, and [vice-president Dick] Cheney, and the whole administration, for the lives they have destroyed here and in Iraq. They're the ones. And what they refused to air, which was far more provocative in my mind and in the minds of my bandmates, is this: that this system has become so brutal and vicious and cruel that it needs to start wars and profit from the destruction around the world in order to survive as a world power. That's what we said. And we refuse not to stand up, we refuse to back down from that position."

On August 24, de la Rocha made his position even clearer at a show in Alpine Valley, Wisconsin. During 'Wake Up', he explained: "We played this show at Coachella Pavilion. It was our first show back. I said a few things from the stage, and the next day Fox News ran this whole piece about us saying that the presidents should be assassinated. But those fascists always get it wrong when they just want to pin a band in the corner for standing up. What we said was that the whole Bush administration should be put on trial for war crimes and then hung and then shot, that's what we said."

This time he added: "But besides that, it made me think about something. It made me think, what are they so afraid of? It made me think about what scares them. Is it really four musicians from Los Angeles who've got a point of view? Is it really just this music and these rhythms and these words? Is that what they're scared of? I thought I'd think about it, and you know what? My conclusion is this: nah, they ain't scared of us, they're scared of you! They're scared that you might come election time and throw Bush and Cheney and all them fascists out of power. That's what they're scared of. And let me say this: the Democrats are scared of you too. They know that you see through their bullshit too. Because when Bush was wiretapping, spying on citizens, torturing innocent people — they were supposed to be the people to defend us from them, and they didn't do shit! So the Democrats are scared of you too. Why? Because they know they're coming to power and they're taking it all for granted, but they're scared, because they know that if they don't start fucking pulling troops from Iraq that you're going to go and burn down every office of every Senator that doesn't do the job."

He concluded: "Well I will say this, that the world is watching us now. The whole world is watching us. The brothers and sisters in South America who are dealing with this imperialist violence have got their eyes on us. Our brothers and sisters in Iraq got their eyes on us. Because we are the ones that are prepared to, and [are] going to, put an end to this nonsense. So wake up. Come on, wake up! Wake up!"

Once the band were back doing press, endless questions came in that largely fell into two categories. Firstly, how the band were getting on these days — it being subtly understood that de la Rocha had been the outsider among the Rage members, and that his dissatisfaction with internal matters had caused the split in the first place. Secondly, interviewers asked — and still ask, six years later as I write this — if a new Rage album would be appearing at some point.

Responding to the former query, de la Rocha admitted: "So much has changed. When you get older, you look back on tensions and grievances and have another perspective on it. I think our relationship now is better than it's ever been. I would even describe it as great. We're going to keep playing shows — we have a couple of big ones happening in front of both [Democrat and Republican] conventions. There was this interesting thing that happened during the Clinton administration; people were looking inward and not outward, and not addressing what was going on. Rage set the political foreground for things that would come very shortly thereafter. I think people might see that what we are saying has more relevance now than when the band first came out."

Of a possible new album, Morello neatly deflected most questions. "That's a whole other ball of wax right there," he said. "Writing and recording albums is a whole different thing than getting back on the bike, you know, and playing these songs. But I think that the one thing about the Rage catalogue is that to me none of it feels dated. You know, it doesn't feel at all like a nostalgia show. It feels like these are songs that were born and bred to be played now."

Now, here's the thing. Although Rage continued a regular gigging schedule into 2008 and also performed shows in 2011, they are now – perhaps sadly, now I come to think of it – not the main focus of this story, apart from a mighty last-ditch shock to us all that you'll read about in Chapter 10 and Bombtrack 4. All the members were also occupied in side activities – Wilk and Commerford played in Maynard James Keenan's Puscifer project in 2007, for example – and Morello himself was embarking on more Nightwatchman activity. He played in support of the Dave Matthews Band when the group played in Europe that spring, playing on stage with them most nights, and when at home in LA he played a regular residency at the Hotel Café, where he was joined by a list of guests including Serj Tankian, Perry Farrell, Nuno Bettencourt of Extreme (a guitar hero to match Morello, if from a rather different genre of music) and Sen Dog of Cypress Hill. Over the years he has played on several major movie soundtracks – *Talladega Nights*, *Spider-Man*, *The A-Team*, *Iron Man*, you name it – and even played a cameo role in the movie *Star Trek: Insurrection*. This is a man with no time to waste.

In 2008, Morello released the second Nightwatchman album, *The Fabled City*. This time, the sound was more or less split evenly between the acoustic sombreness of *One Man Revolution* and a full-band, electric sound that Rage fans would recognise, at least in part. "The template is half Dylan and half Hendrix," he said. "It's going to be half acoustic and half electric. Not only will there be the no-sell-out, acoustic, three-chords-and-the-truth part of the show, but also, with the band I put together called the Freedom Fighter Orchestra, there will be more insane electric playing than I've ever done with Rage or Audioslave, because it's not confined to a three-and-a-half minute song."

The songs were also a little more inward-looking than those of the debut album, Morello explained. "I felt both musically and lyrically the themes have been expanded... Over the course of the last couple of years there was a lot of personal loss: family members passed away, some very close friends, even my dog died, and so that has a way of seeping into the lyrics. While the *One Man Revolution* record was kind of a call to arms, this record was a way of dealing with loss and trying to find hope and redemption through music."

As for the album's increased rock content, he added: "The first time around I wanted there to be a clear distinction between what I'm doing with my solo stuff and my rock work, because otherwise, if I put out a solo record just under the name Tom Morello, people would expect it to be a jazz-metal instrumental odyssey, and that's not what I was doing. But with this one I feel much more comfortable blurring the distinction between the two."

"I wanted to bring in some of my rock music roots and elements into this project," he continued. "Even though the record has electric instrumentation, I'm still just using an acoustic guitar. I brought some of my electric guitar effects pedals, added some riff rock, soloing, and even introduced my Django Reinhardt impersonation, which is evident in the song 'The Lights Are On In Spidertown'... I like the idea of combining all the elements of my playing and not restricting any of it. Even in Rage and Audioslave, while I love playing electric guitar in those bands, the solos are contained to eight bars within those three-and-a-half minute songs. There'll be no such constraints on this upcoming tour. We've already played a few shows and it's been really exciting."

He backed up the album with an 18-date tour of America, promoting it with an appearance on *The Late Late Show* with Craig

Ferguson and on *Late Night With Conan O'Brien* – which, for non-American readers, represent pretty much the peak of US prime-time entertainment exposure. Not bad for a protest singer.

It's important to point out here that while Rage Against The Machine's music might have been superseded by their other activities, the band continued to be an immensely powerful force at any and all of the shows they played, in 2008 as in 1992. Levelling their crowds with a classic catalogue of songs, updated to represent today's problems as much as those of the last century and delivered with as much, if not more commitment than ever, Rage were still a vast force to reckon with.

Evidence of this came on August 27 and September 2, 2008, when the band protested against both the Democrats and Republicans at the annual conventions of each party. The former was one of the most dramatic moments of Rage's career, Morello recalled. "We performed a show for the Iraq Veterans Against the War," he said. "Like political Pied Pipers, we led the 10,000 kids out of the venue... Originally our path was blocked. Just imagine it: 60 veterans in full military uniform like on the Marines [TV] commercial, with the gold buttons and the white hats and the camouflage fatigues, marching in formation with 10,000 people through Denver. We were stopped by the riot police who said, 'You're welcome to protest, but you have to do it in the free speech zone', which was an empty parking lot surrounded by a chain-link fence. It was known as the freedom cage."

He added: "The veterans, who have seen horrors beyond our imagination, are not going to be intimidated by these police, so they decided to change the route of the march and march straight to the door of the Pepsi Center, where they were blocked by 700 police in riot gear. After a long and heated negotiation the police said they were going to arrest the veterans and everybody else, tear-gas them and take everybody off to the jail. At that point five of the officers walked off duty rather than raise a hand against the veterans. The veterans decided that they were not going to go quietly, and decided that they were going to march straight into the police line before the police had a chance to arrest them.

"At this point, very dramatically, someone sent from the Obama campaign came out and avoided the whole police-versus-veterans bloodbath at the door of the Pepsi Center, and acceded to all their demands, to meet with Obama's veterans liaison, which is what they wanted... So it was a pretty huge victory. It was pretty crazy, and it was a not uncommon theme throughout both conventions, with all of the riots in the streets. I guess one of the things that surprises me, given the economic crimes at home and the war crimes abroad, is why there's not more rioting in the streets when there's no conventions going on, but we'll see."

A week later, at the equivalent Republican event, Rage received a similarly negative reception, if without the air of genuine danger which they had experienced at the hands of America's 'caring' party. In Morello's words, "They [the cops] showed up at exactly the time we were scheduled to perform, and as soon as we got out of our vehicle we were immediately surrounded by riot police, who told us if we approached the stage we'd be arrested for playing music. They said that we were not on a permit for the day's show. We produced the permit and showed them that none of the artists that had already been playing for the previous four hours, including Anti-Flag and Michael Franti, none of the artists were listed on the permits. They just tried to use that as an excuse to stop us from playing. We were there right on time to play, and they physically barred us from getting onto the stage because they were afraid of the music we were going to play."

He continued: "Imagine if in Beijing during the Olympics, a Chinese band whose songs were critical of the government was told they'd be arrested if they attempted to sing those songs in a public forum – there would have been an international human rights outcry. But that's exactly what happened in Minnesota. But this is a band that has made a living singing a song that goes 'Fuck you, I won't do what you tell me', so we weren't about to go back to the hotel with our tails between our legs. So we outflanked the police line and went into the middle of the crowd, and played a couple of songs passing a bullhorn back and forth, and it seemed to go over pretty well."

The protests continued, with festival gigs played in the UK and Holland that year introduced by the sight of the band standing silently on stage (fully dressed this time), with orange Guantanamo Bay-like prisoner suits with black hoods over their heads. Clearly, wherever Rage Against The Machine were headed, it wasn't in the direction of compromise.

The side activities continued. Morello lent his guitar playing and an animated avatar version of himself to *Guitar Hero III: Legends Of Rock* as a 'guitar boss' on a song written by him for the game, before a playable version of 'Bulls On Parade' could be unlocked. More seriously, he also played on stage from time to time with Bruce Springsteen and the E Street Band on a version of 'The Ghost Of Tom Joad': as he confided in one interviewer, this required serious courage. "I have to have one or two sips of [whiskey] before I step on a stage with Bruce," he said. "[He has] always been very gracious with his arrangement – he leaves space for a 60-bar guitar solo! So I try to weave some melody through it, but I also try to tap into the angry ghost in that song, the historical ghosts, and give them flight."

Morello and Springsteen played the song at a concert the following year to celebrate the 90th birthday of veteran folk singer Pete Seeger, after which Morello said: "I came late to the genre of folk music. I was a fan of heavy music – first metal, then punk, then hip-hop. Then about 12 years ago it dawned on me that folk music – the music of Woody Guthrie and Phil Ochs, early Bob Dylan, Johnny Cash, Pete Seeger – could be as heavy as anything that comes through a Marshall stack. The combination of three chords and the right lyrical couplet can be as heavy as anything in the Metallica catalogue."

He added: "I discovered Woody Guthrie primarily through Dylan and Springsteen, and now after digging into his music, you'd have to put him in the top five artists of the 20th century. He's certainly the first punk rocker. There is a certain amount of chaos in his personal life that I do not aspire to. He really did put his music and politics and whims before everything else. He had much greater responsibility to humanity than his family. But nothing was going to restrain him, neither the government nor corporate-sanctioned no-trespassing signs, not even the mother of his children, from doing what he felt was right, which was to reflect the stories of the 99 percent back to them in beautiful poetry."

Meanwhile, Zack de la Rocha had launched a new band called One Day As A Lion, a duo with drummer Jon Theodore, sometime of The Mars Volta. Their self-titled EP, released in the summer, was a surprising piece of work. The singer played keyboards instead of a guitar, delivering distorted, processed sound samples, making the overall tone gritty and stripped-down. "I've known Jon for several years now," he said, "and I saw some of his first performances as a member of The Mars Volta. He comes from Baltimore and had been in some underground bands there, so I'd heard of him. When I did see him, it was clear that music in LA was never going be the same now that he was here. I've worked with some great drummers, and have seen people try to execute those kinds of things before, but never as effortlessly and with as much feel. He exists in this realm between John Bonham and Elvin Jones. I haven't seen drumming like that in a long time. So I immediately felt compelled to get to know the guy and pick his brain and find out what kind of music he was interested in. We had a lot in common. We met in jams a couple of summers ago, without the intention of making an album."

Of his unorthodox keyboard playing, he added: "Jon had a friend named Troy Zeigler, who now plays with Serj Tankian, and Troy had this very small rehearsal space where he would teach drum lessons. The room was filled with random instruments – there was percussive stuff, these old eighties metal amps that hadn't been used in ages, and a dusty Rhodes keyboard with some broken keys. I plugged in through a metal amp and ran it through this messed-up delay pedal that had a trigger on it, and we immediately started playing. It felt like two people having a conversation using whatever phrases were at our disposal. We had to document it. We're still using that keyboard. We had to [get] an old number two pencil and jam it into the side to keep the top on... I've always wanted to experiment with sounds that could provide a kind of tension, something you can't avoid. With this new music, it wasn't a choice not to use guitars so much as the spontaneity of that moment when Jon and I got together, regardless of the instrumentation. We wanted to produce a sound that was much larger than what you'd think it could be."

Although, five years later, no more One Day As A Lion material has been released, at the time de la Rocha apparently believed that it was a long-term project. Asked if the EP would be a one-off, he insisted: "No! This is not simply a burst of energy. We are going to be making records and writing songs. We're still in the process of forming as a band – we need a keyboard player, I'm not good enough to do it all myself – so that will be rectified soon. The name speaks about a generation of people, a kind of development that I feel. It's an intuition about people who aren't going to be so concerned about elections to get what they need. And whose politics aren't going to revolve around a bourgeois morality. Their interests are going to be focused on food and housing and justice and revenge. And without going too far into that, that's an intuition that I had."

Election fever gripped America, at least the percentage of its citizens who gave a damn, in late 2008. The prospective election of Barack Obama, the first African-American president, made the process more exciting than usual, without a doubt, but the Rage members had fundamental issues with the structure of the two-party system – and expressed those issues with their usual forwardness. Morello in particular made a stand, performing at the Open The Debates rally as the Nightwatchman and endorsing the independent candidate Ralph Nader.

Of the election process, he explained: "Now more than ever, there's a more fertile ground for artists to try to reveal the nature of both parties, who are mainly the public relations team for transnational corporations. Barack is clearly the most viable candidate, the most intelligent, the one with the most forward-thinking position, but I would hate to see the flames of discontent be watered down by rhetorical visions of hope and change, when historically those things have only come from immigrant workers or people fighting against segregation, or against the second-class position of women. History has taught us that when it comes to ending war, it's always been the people on the ground who've led the movement. Veterans who have come home and fought against the war. Iraqi kids. And artists and musicians."

It was refreshing to see Morello kick back against the popular, and wrong-headed, view by many of the populace that the Democrats were a socialist, or even left-wing, body. "I laugh when people describe Barack Obama as a socialist president," he chuckled. "As a socialist musician, I'll tell you when we have a socialist president... I think they're all in the same corporate bag. I was the scheduling secretary for US Senator Alan Cranston for two years and I got to see first-hand the internal workings of a senatorial office and how beholden it is to big money... He had a more progressive reputation than Barack Obama had, and still, he spent most of the time on the phone asking rich guys for money. None of that money comes for free."

For Brad Wilk, the anti-election impetus was strengthened by the ongoing war in Afghanistan. "I think people are finally realising that George Bush is a fucking scam," he seethed. "I feel like Middle America is finally realising, especially after these disasters [such as Hurricane Katrina] and watching how they were handled, that they're getting the message. We're at the 2,000 mark for people killed in Iraq, and what's coming of it? Did we find weapons? No. Did we find there's lots of oil? Yes. All of the things that people who were against the war, the reasons they had, there they are for anyone to stare at."

Wilk was optimistic about the chances of the population to alter things for the better, however. He explained: "The simplest answer is that people do have the power to change. People have power in numbers. When the war started and I was out protesting on Hollywood Boulevard, I realised that the number of people there was so much more than they were saying on television, which is controlled by the right-wing people who don't want you to see this. The odds are stacked up against us and it's more important than ever to realise you have a voice and you need to speak up. It can be very depressing. But you can run away from it or you can use your voice to try and make it better."

Morello had encapsulated some of this view of the world in his new Nightwatchman album, explaining: "That's what the song 'The Fabled City' is about. It's about the fact that for millions, around the globe for billions, people are unable to become the people they were meant to be, and do the things that they were born to do, because of poverty. There's this consumerist idea of 'The Fabled City', this consumer paradise, but there's an iron gate that runs around 'The Fabled City' and the iron gate is closed."

He continued: "It's a joke that the elections that we have here are basically run by public relations firms, and that every word that comes out of each candidate's mouth is choreographed by a billion-dollar corporation to hit a particular demographic and tickle their electoral funny bone in a particular way. One party's in favour of freedom and opposed to evil, and the other party's opposed to evil and in favour of freedom. It's just a joke... It's not apathy why many Americans stay home on Election Day, it's because they don't have a candidate on Election Day."

More than a few interviewers pointed out to Morello the similarities between him and Barack Obama. Both were half-Kenyan, raised in Illinois, educated at Harvard and left of centre politically, although Obama was clearly more of a centrist thinker, and only three years in age separated them. Morello acknowledged that Obama's election would be the best outcome, although he clearly retained some reservations, saying: "Since racism is the great curse of America, it would certainly be a step in the direction of civilisation, if, given our horrifically racist history, we were able to elect a semi-progressive African-American to the highest office in the land. That would be historically significant.

"However, there's a certain number of filters: in order to rise that high, inevitable compromises have to be made. You have to talk about the use of force against Iran, you have to say we have to up the war in Afghanistan, you take these hawkish positions [on] the death penalty, and things like that, things that I don't frankly know if Barack Obama, in his heart of hearts, believes in. But you certainly can't run for president and not say them, the way the system is currently set up. The gatekeepers are the ones that hold the purse strings at the end of the day, and in order for anyone to rise that high there are inevitable compromises which I find distasteful."

He went on: "When I was watching the conventions on TV, the thing that made me most sceptical about the possibility of Obama becoming elected was when his wife was giving a speech. I grew up in small-town Illinois, and I was trying to watch her speech through the eyes of the neighbours who I grew up with and the parents I grew up around, and I don't know that America has the ability to vote for a candidate whose wife is African-American and smarter than they are. I hope that I'm wrong, it would mean that it's a different country than the one I grew up in, but we'll see."

As 2008 ended, Morello explained that Rage shows in '09 were possible, but that a new album remained a remote possibility. In fact, he reiterated what everyone knew at this point: that his priorities lay elsewhere, quite understandably. When asked by *Billboard* whether the band planned to head to the studio in 2009, Morello stated that: "We've had a wonderful year and a half of playing shows, and I don't see any reason to not play more shows. The thing is there's only so many hours in the musical day, and mine are very occupied right now." He added that the Nightwatchman is now "my principal musical focus, as I see it, for the remainder of my life. From the earliest days of playing open-mike nights at coffee houses, it was apparent to me that this music was as important to me as any music I've ever been involved in. It really encapsulates everything I want to do as an artist."

One more project awaited him, this time a band called Street Sweeper Social Club, a duo (plus session and live musicians) with rapper Boots Riley of a hip-hop trio from California called The Coup. Friends since 2003, when they had both been guests on Billy

Bragg's Tell Us The Truth tour, the two supported Nine Inch Nails and Jane's Addiction in spring 2009. Attention came rapidly their way thanks to an appearance in June on *Late Night With Jimmy Fallon* and a slot with Public Enemy at a VH1 awards ceremony, all of which led up to the release of a self-titled album in June.

Street Sweeper Social Club is a powerful set of songs, comprising potent rock riffs with Riley's smooth flow of lyrics. No change there from Rage Against The Machine, you might think, but in fact SSSC was no Rage clone, largely thanks to the huge difference between the rapping styles of de la Rocha and Riley and several melodic choruses that were worlds away from Morello's mothership band. Heavy funk influences abounded, too, notably on 'Clap For The Killers' and, although the riffs were recognisably 'Morello-esque', there was no whiff of repetition.

In October, Rage lent their name and presence to a campaign which sought to close the American Guantanamo prison facility in Cuba, after it was revealed that aggressive music from rock bands – including their own – was being used in interrogation of the prisoners. "The fact that music I helped create was used in crimes against humanity sickens me – we need to end torture and close Guantanamo now," declared Morello. "Guantanamo is known around the world as one of the places where human beings have been tortured – from waterboarding, to stripping, hooding and forcing detainees into humiliating sexual acts – playing music for 72 hours in a row at volumes just below that [which can] shatter the eardrums. Guantanamo may be Dick Cheney's idea of America, but it's not mine."

Want to hear something truly surreal? In December 2009, Brad Wilk got long-awaited approval from US Food And Drug Administration to manufacture his diabetes-friendly lemonade, Olade, which used the sweet herb stevia instead of sugar. Now, as well as a celebrity drummer and protestor for a variety of causes, Wilk was a beverages maker. You really couldn't make this up.

CHAPTER 10

2009 to date

You will no doubt be aware of *The X Factor*, the popular prime-time talent show that is broadcast every year in the UK, US and probably elsewhere to millions of slack-jawed viewers. The brainchild of the A&R suit-turned-celebrity Simon Cowell, the show pits a succession of singers against each other, whittled down by public vote to a single winner whose first song is released just before Christmas every year, virtually guaranteeing a Yuletide chart-topper, if that means anything anymore.

It's a strange phenomenon by any standards, as the music is rarely better than mildly diverting and often as weak as dishwater. However, the occasional musician with a bit of edge comes through, and one such is the singer-songwriter Matt Cardle, who won the 2010 competition. He happens to be a huge fan of Rage Against The Machine and agreed to be interviewed for this book.

"I got into Rage when I was about 11," says Cardle, who scored a major hit after winning *The X Factor* with a cover of Biffy Clyro's 'Many Of Horror', retitled 'When We Collide'. "Tom Morello comes up with some of the sickest, funkiest, hardest riffs, again and again and again. I can't think how the guy does it. Some of his songs have so many amazing riffs, you think 'Where the hell is he getting them from?' Some of them are so simple as well, you can't believe how easy he makes it sound. The other thing is that he plays a DJ role at times, because there's so much hip-hop in Rage, and he creates sounds that only computers and turntables can normally do. He doesn't have a space shuttle in front of him either: it's just about six effects pedals. It's insane what he can do just with a Stratocaster or a Telecaster. The guy's an absolute genius. I watched an interview with him where he was talking about the main riff on 'Bulls On Parade' and he wanted it to be as threatening as possible, so he keeps his wah pedal on mid sweep. It's the most horrible, dirty, disgusting sound, and no-one else would ever use it, but he does and he plays single notes on it, which sound brilliant. His riffs are all about less is more."

Asked why it's so important to hit the number one spot if you're an *X Factor* winner, Cardle explains: "It's like the space race! You come off the show and you've got the super hype and you want to get it. I didn't go on *The X Factor* wanting to win it – I was just like 'Let's see how this goes' – but by the end, you get so close, you want to fucking win it. You're like, 'I haven't come all this way for nothing'. You're running around promoting your arse off, of course you want to get to number one."

In late 2009, it looked like business as usual for *The X Factor*, which had nabbed the Christmas number one for the previous four years. As December approached, the eventual winner, a kid from Tyneside named Joe McElderry, demolished his opposition one by one. Non-fans of the show, of which there were and remain many millions, felt their will to live seeping away as the inevitable result loomed.

It fell to a marketing consultant called Jon Morter and his wife Tracy to find a solution to *The X Factor*'s pitiless annual domination of the public's ear canals. Morter, who was experienced when it came to building groups of like-minded supporters of various causes through social media, decided to form a Facebook group in support of 'Killing In The Name' for that year's Christmas number one. The perfect antidote to the vacuous bullshit pushed in the public's faces each year courtesy of Cowell and his production team, the song would make a huge statement about what could be achieved in the face of apparently unsurpassable odds when sufficient people united in action. The essence of Rage Against The Machine's almost two-decade-long message, in fact.

Morter provides a long and detailed account of what happened in the 'Rage Factor' campaign, as some wit dubbed it, in this book's final chapter. Rage did indeed go on to beat *The X Factor* to the Christmas 2009 number one spot, announced on December 20, in a coup which left many observers speechless but many more full of celebratory glee. The size of the Cowell organisation, backed up by the giant Sony empire (yes, Rage's label: the irony was not lost), made the victory all the sweeter.

After the 950,000-strong campaign, which had grown exponentially before the result thanks to the added support of musicians such as John Lydon, Dave Grohl, Paul McCartney, The Prodigy and even the stiff-upper-lip old BBC, Rage thanked the UK audience in a statement which ran: "We're very, very ecstatic and excited about the song reaching the number one spot. We want to thank everyone that participated in this incredible, organic, grass-roots campaign. It says more about the spontaneous action taken by young people throughout the UK to topple this very sterile pop monopoly. When young people decide to take action they can make what's seemingly impossible, possible."

Matt Cardle, a man with a unique perspective on the event from both sides, as he is surely the only winner of *The X Factor* who is also a Rage Against The Machine fan, says: "When I heard Zack de la Rocha come on Radio 1 and say that he was the singer in the band which was number one the year before I did *The X Factor*, I was so happy because it was so unlikely. For a song that is so full of hate, it made me chuckle. I did feel for Joe McElderry, but then again the campaign wasn't anything to do with his song, it was just bad timing where people had had enough of this guaranteed number one and went for another option instead."

Let's be in no doubt that Joe McElderry is far from the villain of the plot: he seems to be nothing more than another wide-eyed teenager with a good voice, spat out by the Sony machine for a brief moment of glory and destined for obscurity in a few years. A point worth bearing in mind is that while McElderry, and the many other pop pawns like him, are at the top, they have to work extremely hard. Just ask Cardle, who says: "There's a stigma which comes with winning: there's a stigma if you're a male winner and a stigma if you're a female winner. The whole thing is surrounded by this crowded comparison, but you can't compare James Morrison with Paolo Nutini. They're both different and they're both doing really well. I can only do what I do, to the best of my ability. You can't help the opinions that people have about your career."

To win the show takes application, he warns. "You've got to really want it: you can't just do it on a whim and hope for the best. You have to know that this is what you want to do for the rest of your life. It's fucking hard work, before, during and after – especially after. You have to sustain it, so be prepared to work really hard. I know people who say 'It's an easy option, it's a cop-out'. It fucking isn't! It nearly killed me. Real working musicians know how hard it is."

The same goes for Simon Cowell, who is merely an astute businessman who saw an opportunity to make money and rode it for all it was worth: he's not the one at fault, not really. The people responsible for the dominance of *The X Factor* and the many terrible, terrible programmes like it are you and me, the ones who watch the bloody thing year in year out. Thank God for Rage Against The Machine, and supporters like Jon and Tracy Morter, who showed millions of people that it doesn't have to be this way.

Quite apart from the windfall of cash from sales of 'Killing In The Name', which Rage donated to charity, plus the record they had set for the most downloaded song ever, another benefit of the Rage Factor was that the band promised to play a free show in the UK in the summer of 2010 as a thank-you to their supporters. Scheduled for June 6 at London's Finsbury Park, ticketing was managed cleverly, with members of the public entering an online lottery in February – backed up with photo registration, so the tickets couldn't be resold at inflated prices – with the one downside being that demand far outstripped supply.

The show itself was electric. De la Rocha used the stage to denounce Israel's blockade of Gaza, ongoing at the time, and introduced the Morters on stage. As for the band's performance, the opening notes of 'Killing In The Name' were perhaps the most adrenaline-packed moments I have ever experienced at a rock show. This came after the main set, when the band had retired for a break before the encore and the huge screens at either side of the stage showed the details of the Christmas chart battle six months previously. At one point McElderry, innocent fool that he was, was shown declaring that 'Killing In The Name' was nonsense, or words to that effect – as was Cowell, labelling the Morters' Facebook campaign as 'cynical'. Both statements were received with roars of anger, which switched to righteous pandemonium when the final sales figures for both songs were flashed up on screen – the Rage total some 50,000 downloads higher than McElderry's vacuous ditty.

It was a mighty event, by anyone's standards. As Rock critic Ian Gittins wrote in *The Guardian* the following day, "Close to 40,000 people flocked to north London – and the event could have been far bigger; more than 180,000 had applied for tickets via an online lottery, and several hundred ticketless fans scaled the fence. Inside the park, the mood was one of militant triumphalism, with no contest over the fashion item *du jour*: the many T-shirts proclaiming 'Rage 1, Cowell 0'. The polemic of 'Bullet In The Head' confirmed that Rage remain a sledgehammer of a band... As 40,000 throats joined de la Rocha in bellowing 'Fuck you, I won't do what you tell me!', Mr Cowell could consider himself well and truly told."

Rage were on a roll, passing through Europe for more festivals before returning to Los Angeles for a July 23 show that was their first in their home town for a decade, curiously. A benefit gig for Arizona organisations fighting the SB1070 immigration law – also known as the Support Our Law Enforcement And Safe Neighborhoods Act, a draconian piece of anti-immigration legislation – the show raised $300,000. A South American tour followed, with the first ever Rage gigs in Brazil, Chile and Argentina: at the first of these, Morello wore a cap on stage marked with MST, the acronym of a Brazilian group called the Landless Workers' Movement. Rumours of a conspiracy abounded after the TV channel Multishow, which had stated that it would broadcast the entire show, cut to a programme with the laughable title of *Sexytime* instead. As a result, stage announcements by de la Rocha about the MST movement were not broadcast, causing Morello to tweet: "I understand the network cut away when I put on the MST hat. That means we're winning."

Frenetic activity followed, with a Street Sweeper Social Club release called *The Ghetto Blaster EP* issued via the Cooking Vinyl label, plus a one-off single between sometime Blink-182 drummer Travis Barker and Morello, plus Wu-Tang Clan rappers RZA and Raekwon, called 'Carry It'. What people were more interested in for obvious reasons was new Rage Against The Machine material, and at this time de la Rocha indicated that a new album might well come to pass. "We're all bigger and more mature and we do not fall into the problems we faced 10 or 15 years ago," he is said to have told a Chilean newspaper called *La Tercera*. "We're working on a new album due out next year, perhaps summer, for the northern hemisphere." While this report may or may not have been apocryphal, he definitely told the *NME*: "I think it's a genuine possibility. We have to get our heads around what we're going to do towards the end of the year and finish up on some other projects, and we'll take it from there."

However, fans have had to be happy with more Nightwatchman material in the meantime, as a new Rage album doesn't appear to be forthcoming. Morello's third album appeared in August 2011 after a handful of Rage festival dates, which are the most recent to date. Titled *World Wide Rebel Songs*, the album came out on the New West label and was another vituperative but thoughtful set, including among its many themes the issue of union rights which had always enthused its maker. By late 2011 the Occupy movement was taking up much of Morello's time and attention: he made a point of playing at several locations where protesters were gathered, inviting Wayne Kramer of the MC5 to record with him in support of the movement on his new album.

An EP, *Union Town*, raised money for the America Votes Labor Unity Fund, but as with *The Fabled City*, Morello wasn't only looking outwards for inspiration: some of his songs came from private sources too. "There is a great deal of personal experience woven into all of the Nightwatchman records," he said, "but because I am among a handful of 'political' artists, that tends to be what the media focuses on. On *World Wide Rebel Songs*, some songs, in particular 'Facing Mount Kenya' and 'The Whirlwind', deal very explicitly with my Kenyan heritage and coming to grips with its role in my art."

The Occupy movement, based as it is on so many of Rage's historic targets – the finance world, the military and its role in government policy, the unregulated antics of those who create and keep wealth – was a natural home for Morello. He was quick to define his involvement as a working man, however, rather than a celebrity dropping by for a quick sing-song. "The Occupy movement is not waiting to be blessed by rock stars," he said, accurately. "I don't go there as a leader, but as a participant. The movement has injected into mainstream discourse the dirty, unspoken five-letter word 'class'. The way corporate media likes to portray America is as a homogenous whole that high-fives each other at the Super Bowl. But what we have is a grotesque disparity between the rich and poor that is only getting wider. Every successful progressive or radical movement needs a great soundtrack. And it just so happens that many of them have been provided by people with an acoustic guitar."

Talking to writer Jason Leopold at *Truth Out*, Morello explained: "While I've been involved in a myriad of social justice causes over the course of the last decade, the Occupy movement on a global scale is really the first movement that concisely expresses what I believe is the core problem facing our society, which is class inequality... Despite the police repression that removed the Occupy encampments from the courthouse steps and parks around the country, the idea

[is] that this grotesque and relentless economic inequality that is just hammering the globe right now is not OK, and that it's not an accident, there are criminals responsible who walk freely among us.

"One bit of evidence of [the] ideological success of the Occupy movement is, when in memory have we had a Republican presidential candidate who's had his feet held to the fire because he's too rich?" he continued. "People are taking a harder look at economic inequality in response to the success of Occupy. With regards to criticism about the movement having no focus, I think that the Occupy movement does represent the 99%, and in that 99% there are a wide variety of opinions on all sorts of matters, from politics and economics to sports and music. It's not a homogenous bowl and can't be put into a box, and that's one thing that separates the Occupy movement from previous left-leaning movements that are often divided by ethos factions."

The man was everywhere in 2011, performing an acoustic benefit show in Madison, Wisconsin and writing about it in *Rolling Stone*, jamming with Bruce Springsteen on three separate occasions through the year, visiting Occupy zones in the US, Canada and the UK, appearing on screen in films such as *Iron Maiden: Flight 666* (a documentary of Maiden's ongoing *Somewhere Back In Time* world tour), *Chevolution* (a Che Guevara documentary) and *Let Fury Have The Hour*, a documentary about countercultures. He also exercised his artistic skills by writing a 12-issue comic-book series for Dark Horse Comics, titled *Orchid*, each issue of which was accompanied by a song which he had written.

Little wonder that as this book came up to date, no new Rage album was on the horizon. Although Commerford is said to have talked about nebulous plans being made for 2014 and beyond, nothing has been confirmed. The news page at www.ratm.com has not been updated for a year, although the latest news piece was a tasty one – concerning the release of a 20th anniversary box set of their first, and best, album.

The three-disc box set, titled *Rage Against The Machine: XX*, was pretty lavish, containing the 2010 Finsbury Park show and film footage from the early days, as well as B-sides and the original demo tape, released on CD for the first time and sounding surprisingly good. The remastering job on the album tracks wasn't particularly noticeable unless you were a genuine audiophile, which is a tribute to the skills of original producer Garth Richardson.

Asked by a writer from MTV Hive if the 1992 Tom Morello would have approved of a 2012 super-deluxe box set of his record, Morello mused: "We had limited commercial ambitions when we formed Rage Against The Machine. We didn't think that we'd be able to book a club show due to the genre mixing of the music, the ethnic composition of the band, and the lyrical contents of the songs. There was no precedent for those three things on a stage in Los Angeles or certainly on a radio station or in record stores." Elsewhere, he added: "In some ways it feels like it's been 200 years since the album came out and in other ways, it's gone by in a flash. I'm still processing it myself. We wanted it to be very inclusive. We wanted every video. We wanted the most recently filmed, action-packed, Finsbury Park victory show to the very first ever public performance at Cal State Northridge of a lunchtime concert. We wanted the original demos to be a part of it. Then [producer Rick Rubin] waded through a mountain of videos and stuff like that, and put together something that I think is really pretty great."

Looking back, Morello was amazed at how brightly Rage burned in those early days, saying: "I'll tell you, it's a band that came out of the box pretty hot. We wrote and recorded that demo tape before we started playing shows. While we didn't have any expectation of ever getting a record deal or even being able to book a club show, we were pretty honed in our rehearsal studio. Listening to those demos, we were pretty damn good! We rehearsed in a friend's recording studio and so it was convenient to record the songs there, but I have a very vivid memory of the first couple of shows that we played and how people immediately responded in a way that was certainly not the case with any other band that I've been in."

He added: "We wanted to give [the fans] a lot in this, and not something to just go, 'It's the 20th anniversary, here's a remaster of the record', but to really give them a career's worth of Rage Against The Machine. Great stuff for them to enjoy because, just speaking for myself, the relationship that I have with Rage Against The Machine fans is one of the most important relationships in my life. They've been so great to me and to us; it's long past due that we really put their needs first, and that's one of the things that this box set does. It says, 'Thank you very much. Here ya go'."

Perhaps with a touch of sadness, Morello confirmed: "There's no real plan at all beyond this box set. The reason why we wanted to mark the 20th anniversary with this was to do something that was very clearly and explicitly for the fans. I think Rage Against The Machine fans are probably the most dedicated, intense, and patient fans in the history of rock music. And this will be the first official Rage Against The Machine release in 12 years, so we really wanted to mark the auspicious occasion... the 20-year anniversary of the first record coming out was something that was a real career retrospective."

At the end of 2012, Barack Obama was seeking election for a second term, and in the run-up to this event a politician called Paul Ryan – the Republican nominee for Vice President – caused a certain amount of amusement in an interview by nominating his favourite composers as Beethoven, Led Zeppelin and Rage Against The Machine. Morello wasted no time, replying in another *Rolling Stone* editorial: "Paul Ryan's love of Rage Against The Machine is amusing, because he is the embodiment of the machine that our music has been raging against for two decades. Charles Manson loved The Beatles but didn't understand them... and Paul Ryan is clueless about his favourite band, Rage Against The Machine. Ryan claims that he likes Rage's sound, but not the lyrics. Well, I don't care for Paul Ryan's sound or his lyrics. He can like whatever bands he wants, but his guiding vision of shifting revenue more radically to the one percent is antithetical to the message of Rage.

"I wonder what Ryan's favourite Rage song is? Is it the one where we condemn the genocide of Native Americans? The one lambasting American imperialism? Our cover of [NWA's] 'Fuck

Tha Police'? Or is it the one where we call on the people to seize the means of production? So many excellent choices to jam out to at Young Republican meetings! Don't mistake me, I clearly see that Ryan has a whole lotta 'rage' in him: a rage against women, a rage against immigrants, a rage against workers, a rage against gays, a rage against the poor, a rage against the environment. Basically the only thing he's not raging against is the privileged elite he's grovelling in front of for campaign contributions."

He concluded: "My hope is that maybe Paul Ryan is a mole. Maybe Rage did plant some sensible ideas in this extreme fringe right-wing nutjob. Maybe if elected, he'll pardon Leonard Peltier. Maybe he'll throw US military support behind the Zapatistas. Maybe he'll fill Guantanamo Bay with the corporate criminals that are funding his campaign – and then torture them with Rage music, 24/7. That's one possibility. But I'm not betting on it."

Ryan's allegiance to the Republicans was not the problem here, Morello stressed elsewhere. "That was never the issue. Everyone is welcome, regardless of their political affiliation, to enjoy Rage Against The Machine. The power of the music speaks to people regardless of their ideological bent. The difference with Paul Ryan is, if you're going to put yourself forward as someone who's going to enact policy that's going to harm 99.9% of Rage Against The Machine fans, then I'm going to have something to say about it. Especially if in multiple interviews you're trying to act cool by saying Rage is one of your favourite bands, I'm sorry, you just put the golf ball on the tee, I'm going to swing at it."

With Obama back in office, the world moved on, and in 2013 Brad Wilk and Tim Commerford emerged into the public eye with performances on Foo Fighter Dave Grohl's *Sound City* movie soundtrack. The former stuck around longer, thanks to his expert drumming on the most anticipated heavy metal album of the year: Black Sabbath's *13*. The veteran heavy metal quartet – Ozzy Osbourne, Tony Iommi, Geezer Butler and Bill Ward – had been reduced to a trio when Ward had refused to rejoin the sporadically-active band for their latest comeback, thanks to what he referred to as an 'unsignable' contract. Ward, a jazz-trained drummer whose unearthly ability to drag the beat for a more 'doomy' feel – contributing greatly to Sabbath's invention of metal back in 1970 in doing so – was no easy act to follow, but Wilk stepped up, delivering a solid, groove-laden performance that perfectly complemented the unexpectedly good songs on *13*.

As is typical in most band situations, Ozzy Osbourne was only informed of Wilk's recruitment at the last minute, or even later. Although the singer reported that Wilk "did a good job. I don't have anything bad to say. He's a very nice guy", he explained that he had initially expected his regular touring drummer Tommy Clufetos to do the job. "The way it was dealt with wasn't very fair on Tommy," Ozzy said. "[Producer] Rick Rubin just didn't want to work with him for reasons I don't know. He's a great drummer, and he's been with me for a while now and I just felt that nobody discussed the decision about Brad to me, and it's not fair to Tommy. Tommy was promised the album... It's not because he was my drummer and my ego wanted him. It was just the way it was dealt with. It just got me a bit, it got me pissed off about it. It's all right now. He's a great drummer. I don't know what the problem was." Geezer Butler added: "In the studio, Brad was more like a Bill kind of thing, like an old-school drummer – more jazzy and that kind of thing, which suited the new album."

Rubin himself explained the situation, telling *Billboard*: "Brad is a muscular drummer with great feel and understands the groovy nature of their music – Rage Against The Machine is a groovy rock band, not a metal band – so it was worth a try. When they played together the first time, it was obvious he would do a great job in the seat Bill [Ward] left vacated."

Since then Morello has been the sole public voice of Rage Against The Machine. It's not that the other members are completely inaccessible, but when it comes to band matters, they leave it to their leader to take the public forum. In 2013 this included a show of support for Bradley Manning, the American soldier who leaked a large number of classified documents to the public and was rewarded for his (later her: he became Chelsea Manning after gender reassignment treatment) efforts with a 35-year stretch in prison. Morello also performed with Bruce Springsteen once more and guested on the debut album from Device, the new project by Disturbed singer David Draiman.

The case of sometime CIA employee Edward Snowden also attracted Morello's attention. Like Manning, Snowden had fallen foul of America's official secrets protocol by disclosing US surveillance tactics to the media and, unlike Manning, had become a fugitive. Morello was sympathetic to Snowden's plight, telling one interviewer: "I think Snowden should live a happy life in Ecuador [a country which had offered Snowden possible sanctuary]. That's what I think. I think he's a hero. He exposed the crimes of the government. [He revealed] that we're all being spied on, all the time by the Obama administration. If anybody deserves to be in jail, it's not Snowden... Today, I got an email from Obama's campaign, or whatever, asking me for money after they've been spying on me and their drones have been killing civilians. So I decided I'm gonna take whatever amount of money that I might have donated, which would have been not that much, and I'm gonna donate it to whatever airplane or flight is gonna get Snowden to Ecuador. Whatever fund that is, that's what I'm gonna donate that money to. I'd be happy to [do that], and that means I'm guilty of espionage as well, probably. But so are you for asking the question."

While Rage Against The Machine will surely be back in some form or other – they're too good at what they do to just vanish – there's nothing on the immediate horizon, and Morello spent a lot of time in the press round for *Rage Against The Machine: XX* looking back. After all, his band's career had encompassed many high points: as he once said, "We played many shows that have been great peaks, from European festival shows to surprise club shows to playing outside the Democratic National Convention, to rocking the Rosemont Horizon in Chicago where I went to see many shows as a kid. Every time we stepped on a stage, the interaction between fans and the audience is just something that can't even be described.

But beyond that, the fact that we've been able to weave our deep political convictions into our music and into our actions as a band... we've found that those convictions have resonated with an audience on a worldwide scale, and that's really a tremendous highlight."

He told Patrick Doyle of *Rolling Stone* that watching the old footage of his band was emotional. "In some ways, it's bittersweet," he said. "It's like, the very singular and combustible chemistry that made Rage Against The Machine the force of nature that it was, was the same thing that kept us from producing more. If it were up to me, I would've made two records a year. As it is, we have just three records of original material over 20 years. It's a testament to the strength of that material and to the mythos of the Rage live shows that there is an interest 20 years later in people looking at it. What this box set does is celebrate the exciting fusion of genres and politics that is Rage Against The Machine. It is something that is able to be a victory lap for fans of the band – and it's also a reminder for me of work left undone.

"Here's the thing: this is the first Rage Against The Machine release of any kind in 12 years. That to me is the more staggering number than 'It's been 20 years since the record came out'. The reason why we're doing this is very clear and simple: it's for our fans, which I believe are the single most dedicated, wild in concert, and patient fans maybe in the history of rock music. It was past due that we really did something that honoured their commitment to us over the course of 20 years."

Asked if the band had taken direction from the box set's compiler, the ubiquitous Rick Rubin, he remarked: "I don't know that there's much direction to go. There's no plans, no current direction of anything, so I guess the answer is no. It was my great hope that we'd celebrate the 20th anniversary with a five-continent world tour. But short of that, this box set that celebrates the 20-year span of Rage Against The Machine is something that will hopefully be very satisfying for longtime Rage fans as well as turn on new fans to what the band is all about."

Why is it so difficult to stage a Rage tour at this point, asked Doyle – a reasonable question after all this time. "We'd have to agree to go on one," was the answer. "Once a year, the band meets and very seriously discusses and turns down awesome offers to tour the world. That's part of the programme. I'm very grateful that we did agree to do this box set, which we're very, very proud of. Some of those early videos [show us] playing these clubs for 25 people. I remember that period very, very well. I had been in a lot of bands before Rage Against The Machine, bands that had tried hard to make it, and with that band, with Rage, it just spontaneously combusted. It immediately connected with something in the reptilian brain of fans of rock, hip-hop, punk, metal, activists in a way that was global right off the bat."

"Here's the thing," he added. "When Rage finally did break, and sort of created a genre of music, the audience that we created was then served by bands that may have had some of the sonic ingredients, but completely lacked the politics. They may have been artistically lacking in other ways, depending on your subjective point of view. You'd think that in the wake of Rage's success, in the course of the last 20 years, there'd be other examples of bands that were able to fuse genres with political content. And there hasn't been any. I think that really just speaks to the very, very unique musical and personal chemistry of the four guys in Rage Against The Machine. That band could've happened nowhere but Los Angeles, and it could've happened in no other way than with Zack, Tim, Brad and myself."

Asked about his relationship with Zack de la Rocha, the elephant in any room where discussion about Rage's future was taking place, Morello stated: "Oh, I mean, we communicate fairly regularly, and my relationship with those three guys is what it's been for some time. I love them. I consider them brothers and brothers-in-arms, and whether or not we ever play music again in any capacity is unknown. I'm grateful for the music we played together, and thank goodness the cameras were rolling at that first show at Cal State Northridge, and it's been very hard. For me, as a fan, not just as a member of the band, it's some of the most exciting stuff I've ever had the pleasure to hear, let alone to be a part of."

So what does all this activism mean, if at the end of the road a band as venomous and exciting as Rage Against The Machine can fade quietly away? Perhaps this – that their message, viral in its behaviour, lingers on long after the music itself has stopped. What Rage would no doubt tell you to do would be to stop reading, go out and *do* whatever you feel you need to do to make the world better. On which note, there's one more Noam Chomsky quote, as directed to Morello in that pivotal Radio Free LA interview, which we should revisit to ensure that this final point is hammered home.

Asked "What sort of society do you envision as one that would not be based on exploitation or domination, and how would we get there from here?" the great man replied: "I don't really understand the question. It's kind of interesting. I'm asked that question constantly in sort of privileged circles. I'm never asked it when I go to talk to poor people. They tell me what they're doing. Maybe they ask for a comment, but they don't ask how they do it. How you do it is very straightforward: you go out and do it. If you want a more free and democratic society, you go out and do it."

He elaborated: "The civil rights movement, the antiwar movement, the sharp critique and breakdown of illegitimate authority in all sorts of domains which took place since the sixties, the environmental movements, the feminist movement, the solidarity movements in the eighties – all of these things changed the society a lot. Well, how did they do it? Well, they just did it. People get together, they organise, they pressure, they try to learn, they try to help others to learn. That's the way things change. That's why we don't live under feudalism and slavery. That's why we have, by comparative standards, a very free society in the United States, with a lot of opportunities and options and very limited capacity on the part of the state for forced control. Well, that's been gained by struggle."

Chomsky continued: "People are now fighting to preserve workers' rights and Social Security and medical support and some sort of health programme, and so on. People are now fighting to preserve these things. Well, they were not there not long ago. They were achieved by plenty of popular struggle and there are no limits to this. There's no reason why corporate tyranny – which is a fairly recent development, its institutional form is from the early part of this century – there's no reason why that form of tyranny should not be dismantled, just as other kinds of totalitarianism were dismantled. Fascism and Stalinism, for example. And there are no particular limits to this.

"Any kind of illegitimate authority that exists, whatever it may be, from interpersonal relations up to huge states and transnational corporations, every such form of authority has to demonstrate legitimacy. They have the burden of proof, and we should understand that usually, very often, almost always that burden can't be met. When it can't be met, it should simply be dismantled. And that's the way to move more towards a free and just democratic society. I don't think there's any sphere of life where these questions don't arise. There's different answers in different places and that depends on the circumstances, but the mechanisms are always the same. It's engagement, education, organising, pressure, building new institutions. Those are the ways. In a country like ours they're much more available than in a place like Haiti or Colombia where you might get murdered for it. It won't happen here. But it's the same mechanism."

You take his point. Action is all that is necessary to make change happen: that and co-operation. Whether it's sending a song to number one at Christmas, or evicting a dictatorial leader from office, the approach is essentially the same: get together, form a plan and execute it. And while you're at it, play some inspirational music and turn up the volume. I'm sure you can think of the perfect band.

BOMBTRACK 4

The X Factor: David And Goliath

Let's finish with a chat with Jon Morter, the excellent chap who got Rage Against The Machine to number one back in 2009 – and while we're at it, since we're talking about the rapacious music industry, which chews up its offspring and spits them out, let's have a look at Tom Morello's plans to change it for the better.

What's wrong with the music business, then? Morello's response a while back, in an interview with *The Progressive*, was: "Today, if you sign a record deal with any of the majors or indies, this is what happens. They give a budget to make your record. Say it's $100,000, which they lend you. You make your album. You spend some of the money on guitars, and some of it on a recording engineer. Now your record contract says, for the sake of argument, you get 10 cents on the dollar – which is not an unusual amount – and the record company gets 90 cents on the dollar. Now that $100,000 they gave you to make that record, you owe them back. You pay them back with your 10 cents on the dollar. So they're in the black long before you've broken even. You might sell half a million records and be in debt to your record company. Unless you reach a certain threshold where you can increase that 10 cents, artists are just dicked all the way around. Prior to Rage Against The Machine I was in a band called Lock Up on Geffen Records. We had the exact same deal that I just told you about. I'd go back to Libertyville, and people would think I was a millionaire, and I could not afford [food]. I was on a $7-a-week food budget with my big record deal."

Of the issue of unionising the musicians across the rock and hip-hop communities, Morello explained: "There is a musicians' union, but it doesn't respond to the savage shafting that rock musicians and rap musicians get. If you play for the LA Philharmonic, they make sure you get your scale. But in our music, I could sign you today to a contract that says I get everything and you get nothing. There is no recourse. There's a cabal of record companies, management companies, entertainment firms, booking agencies, and concert promoters. They are the slumlords of the music industry. We artists rent a room. Sometimes you get the fleabag room, sometimes you get the penthouse suite. But all those people have been having dinner together and have been scratching each others' backs long before you put your band together, and they'll still be there long after they drop your band."

He added: "The structure is set, and it's not artist-friendly. What if you looked at the Billboard Top 200 and got the Dixie Chicks, Metallica, Audioslave, System Of A Down, Ja Rule, and DMX to say we're on strike. We're not going on tour. We're going to stop. We're going to take another seven percent of the already hurting music industry away by withholding our labour until we change the rules. What would happen then? I don't know, but I'd like to see."

This was the situation for most musicians, in most countries, even before the industry went into freefall around 2005, when iTunes took over from CD sales. Nowadays, things are much, much worse – which makes it all the more amazing that the Rage Factor campaign a) ever happened at all and b) was such a success. The power was back in the public's hands, albeit for a short time and by paying the great new god of commerce, Apple, to make it happen. But happen it did, and here's how.

The smiles, the sneers and the body art: Rage Against The Machine, more than the sum of their parts.
HOTOSHOT/DALLE

Tim Commerford climbed the set at the 2000 MTV Video Music Awards at Radio City in New York, July 2000. Security dragged him away, but his point was made. GETTY IMAGES

Brad Wilk, Rage Against The Machine's 'quiet one', photographed in May 2000. ANJA/DALLE

In August 2000, Zack took to the air during a concert next to Staples Center where the Democratic National Convention was taking place. A riot broke out afterwards. BRANIMIR KVARTUC/DAILY BREEZE/ZUMA/CORBIS

Meet the new band: Audioslave, featuring Soundgarden singer Chris Cornell, on the *Late Show With David Letterman* on November 25, 2002. CBS/PHOTOFEST

Chris Cornell (second from right) was a ferocious singer, despite the inner demons which haunted him at the time. JILL GREENBERG/CORBIS OUTLINE

One Day As A Lion, the short-lived project featuring Zack and sometime Mars Volta drummer Jon Theodore.
CR STECYK III

Flobots singer Jamie Laurie (left) joins Zack and Tom at the Iraq Veterans Against The War anti-war march on August 27, 2008 in Denver, Colorado. Their route went from the Denver Coliseum to the Pepsi Center, during the 2008 Democratic National Convention at which Barack Obama was officially nominated as the Democrats' candidate for US president. DOUG PENSINGER/GETTY IMAGES

Tim and Brad performing in 2007. While Zack and Tom provide the politics, these expert musicians supply the funk. TIM MOSENFELDER/GETTY IMAGES

Zack and Tom at Coachella in 2007: older, wiser and reformed – and with more to say than ever before.
EVIN WINTER/GETTY IMAGES

Making a point about just about everything in 2008. Censorship. War crimes. Foreign policy and militarism. Where does it end? KIKO HUESCA/EPA/CORBIS

Tom and Boots Riley of Street Sweeper Social Club perform on May 10, 2009 in Atlanta, Georgia. TAYLOR HILL/FILMMAGIC

Tom plays a concert in support of Occupy Wall Street in Foley Square on September 16, 2012 in New York City. He continues to lend his support to the Occupy and similar movements some years later.
ANDREW BURTON/GETTY IMAGES

Ultimately victorious. If Rage's mission was to open our eyes a little more, consider that mission fulfilled.
KEVIN WINTER/GETTY IMAGES

Zack de la Rocha celebrating a brief but sweet victory over the music industry at the Download Festival in 2010. The people spoke; the band responded; the Man lost. BRIAN RASIC/REX FEATURES

The X Factor: David And Goliath

Jon Morter, a marketing consultant and DJ who plays a huge role in this story, kindly consented to give me an interview for this biography – and what he says below will both leave you speechless, and form the perfect ending to this book.

How did the whole *X Factor* saga begin?
The whole idea of trying to find a chink in *The X Factor*'s armour came about in 2008. I like to keep my eye on the charts, and when the rules changed in around 2005 to include downloads I was interested in how that would work. I looked into it and it stated that any download is fair game, which I realised was a major game-changer, because instead of record companies telling us 'Here's your new Metallica song' or 'Here's a new Nirvana song for you', we can decide which song we want to be in the charts. We can say, 'Actually I prefer a different Nirvana song, so up yours! I don't care if you're releasing this one, I want that one'. In other words, any song could be a single. I hung on to that idea but I didn't do anything about it until 2008, when I'd been playing around on this thing called Facebook for a year or two.

What was the background to your first campaign?
One afternoon I was in the office, working in marketing at a hi-fi company, and on our lunch break the three of us who were there did what we called a Facebook race. The idea was that we each made a Facebook group about anything we liked, and the winner would be whoever got the most followers by the following Friday afternoon, and the rest of us would buy him a nice lunch. I made my group as vague as possible: it was about the county of Essex, because I live there and I've got loads of mates who live there, so about 20 people joined straight away. By the end of the week I had 7,000 people and I won the race, so I had my nice lunch. But this group kept on growing: it got to between 30,000 and 40,000 people, and I wasn't doing anything to encourage it either. It was all friends of friends who were joining it. I realised that I could instantly message them all, and lightbulbs went on in my head because I knew that it could be a very useful marketing tool.

So how did this become a reality?
Christmas 2008 came around, and the two ideas in my head collided. I realised that if I could get 1,000 people to join a Facebook group, and if I could get them all to spend £1 on a single, I could effectively make a hit single of my own, although I realised that I couldn't sing or dance and that I wasn't at all musically talented. That's why I'm a DJ, because I can play other people's stuff! At the time, everyone was doing that 'Rickrolling' thing where Rick Astley's 'Never Gonna Give You Up' was being played as a practical joke, and I wondered if we could Rickroll the charts – and in doing so, Rickroll the nation. I created a group and told the members, 'You'll have to buy 'Never Gonna Give You Up' on a particular date'. Three and a half weeks later we had 68,000 people. I was like, 'Let's do this!' The day came and the group members downloaded the song, and we were doing well on all the major download charts. Rick Astley's management got in touch and asked if there was anything they could do to help, so I told them to keep mentioning it. Then the Christmas Top 40 came out and the song was number 73. It had sold something like 4,000 copies, and I wondered what the hell was going on. Still, I only did it for a laugh, so I went off with my tail between my legs.

What happened next?
A few months later the Christmas 2008 campaign appeared on Rick Astley's Wikipedia page. The article read that the song had sold enough to get to number two or three on the charts, but that it hadn't gone that far because the sales figures had allegedly been lowered by its record company. I thought 'That's a bit strange' and checked the source of the data, which was a reputable search engine. It seemed that someone quite senior at Rick's record company had decided – again, allegedly – that the song was detracting from their new acts, or words to that effect. I thought 'You utter wanker!' It struck me then that a record company can influence the charts, which is a really bad thing. People had spent money on that song, after all. The Wikipedia entry was removed, although I took a screenshot of it first.

The X Factor: David And Goliath

So you had another go in 2009?
In late November 2009 [terrible reality-TV clowns] Jedward appeared on *The X Factor* and it looked like they were going to win it that year. I'm not the taste police and I won't wag my finger and say, 'You mustn't listen to that, it's shit', but I saw them on TV and I thought, 'Sorry, but this is just terrible. I'm going to have another go'. I had a year's experience this time, and also more experience of Facebook, which itself had grown a lot in the previous year – so I started again. Now, I want to make it clear that you can't do this now because it's not possible any more, but back in 2009, if you joined a group in a certain way and left and went back again, it would give you the option to be the new administrator of the group. Once you'd become an admin, you could message all the members – so if you were the admin of a group of 4,000 people, you could message them directly into their inbox. Not on their news feed: actually into their inbox.

Very handy.
It was brilliant. I kept noticing the same 20 or 30 names buzzing around of other people who had figured this out. We didn't snitch on each other: you just knew that the others had worked it out too! I also knew a certain Google search that would find these groups for me, so I'd spend five minutes at lunch time typing in 'no admins left' or whatever the search term was, and I'd think 'I'll have that one'. I was the admin of a really big Pearl Jam group, which is still growing to this day.

I bet a few people took the piss, didn't they?
Sure, the system was open to abuse, but back then Facebook were harsher on spammers than they are now: they'd block you for a week if they thought you were sending spam. If that happened to you, your admin rights were taken away, but when you went back, they were restored. So there was a window of opportunity there. I was a bit of a bastard and I took quite a few plum groups: a lot of regional ones, for example. I was finding all sorts of great stuff. Then I found a Rage Against The Machine group, which had something like 4,500 members, most of whom were American. I was a big Rage fan so

I took that right away. Of course, Rage didn't have their own official Facebook group back then: everything was done by fans.

How did you land on 'Killing In The Name'?
I knew I couldn't do Rick Astley again, so I wondered which song to choose. I wanted something a bit more like 'God Save The Queen' by The Sex Pistols: something a bit more 'fuck you'. I thought that would do the job. At the same time I knew it couldn't be too extreme, like a death metal song, because people wouldn't get it. It needed to cover a lot of bases, and Rage popped into my head because I knew that hip-hop, funk and rock fans would all love it. Also, for teenagers who didn't remember it the first time, it had 'fuck' repeated several times in it. It ticked all the boxes. So I made the 'Rage Against The Machine For Christmas Number One' group, added a quick logo which I made from the *Battle Of Los Angeles* cover – and off we went. That was on Saturday November 21, 2009, when *The X Factor* was on, so it got a few members straight away, maybe 30 or 40.

What was your strategy?
I wanted to be smart about this, so I went to work the following Monday and by the middle of the week the group had grown to 200 or 300. I knew it was still early days, but I also knew that people like to join big Facebook groups. They'll join a group just because it's big. I found an entire Excel spreadsheet on Google of media contacts, a fairly up-to-date one as well. It was the contact details of newsrooms and journalists, and it was a godsend. It's amazing what people leave lying around. I thought 'I'm having that!' and downloaded it. I emailed a few of the people from it, saying 'You might remember the Rick Astley campaign from last year: this one is gonna be huge!' and sent them the link to my Rage campaign. On the Friday I had three replies saying, 'Thanks, this doesn't look that great, but keep us posted'. Everyone else ignored me, and I thought 'Fine, no problem'.

What was next?
I went to the old Rage group with 4,500 members, and back in those days there was a back door where you could change the title of the

group, so I deleted all the content from the group – the cover picture, and every single post – and cloned the Rage group that I'd made, with 300 members, onto this old Rage group of 4,500 members, wrote a few posts and got some mates to comment on the page and make it look a bit lively. I hid the old group and sent the URL of the new group to the people I'd emailed the day before, and I said, 'Guys, look – this link that you didn't click on yesterday is up to almost 5,000 members now. It's seriously moving! Give me a shout if you're interested'. I knew it would only take one bit of press coverage and things would start to snowball. OK, I faked the beginning, but as long as the snowball gathered snow after that, I was happy.

Who bit first?
Sky News got in touch and asked me to come on their programme at 6pm on the following Monday, and I said I would. It was on a section called Buzz, and they were asking me questions like 'What has Simon Cowell done wrong?' and I answered them as fairly as I could. The last question they asked was 'Do you think this is going to work?' and I said 'It's definitely going to work. Trust me. Get behind me, and it will work'.

What was happening at Facebook?
So now British people were joining the group. Because the old Rage group was hidden, if you searched for Rage Against The Machine on Facebook, mine was the only one you could join. I emailed the BBC and a few others and told them that Sky had been onto it, and reminding them that I'd offered them the first option. BBC London then got in touch, asking if they could interview me. I was playing them off against each other, slightly, and now the wider media began to contact me. I said yes to all of them, although I was still doing a nine-to-five job – ironically, not in marketing any more because I had a new job.

Which were the next news organisations to get on board?
Local media from Northumberland and whatever were getting in touch, and so were international writers from Germany and Australia

and places like that. It was getting big now: we were building up a head of steam. Then the band got involved: Tom Morello tweeted about it. I hadn't got in touch with them beforehand because I'd assumed they wouldn't care about chart hits. Then John Lydon of The Sex Pistols sent me a Facebook message, which made me go 'Wow!' After that I thought 'I don't care if it works or not now. Job done...' I can't remember exactly what he said, but it was along the lines of 'Stick it up 'em, mate: it would be brilliant if Rage got to number one'. Then other people got in touch, like Lenny Henry, who said 'Good on you, man!' Then the guys from Muse sent me a message, and it kept coming. *The Wright Stuff* on Channel 5 did a whole thing on it, and Gail Porter was properly on board with it – she loved it. The numbers were just incredible. Fuck me, man, it was just amazing. It went to 10,000 and then it went to 100,000. Then we were looking at half a million by the time the actual buying week for the single came around.

What was the industry reaction when that happened?
Suddenly all these moles in the industry started contacting me. Someone who I can't identify for obvious reasons, who worked at a certain record company, contacted me to say, 'You know they're trying to derail this?' Certain people had allegedly been told to derail the whole thing.

As they'd tried to do the previous year with the Rick Astley campaign?
Absolutely. They didn't get away with it this time, though, because someone in that circle of workers was a big Rage fan and happened to agree with what I was doing, even though they worked for the enemy. In fact there were two people telling me this, neither of whom knew that the other one was in touch with me. I was so glad they did.

Did you go public with this?
No. I'm not sure it would have helped the cause. These are big companies we're talking about, and I knew they could probably cause the campaign major problems. Also, if I went public, they would have

known that I knew what they were up to. I was up for the fight anyway: I knew I could beat them.

Did anyone try to sabotage your efforts in any other way?
Wait till you hear this. My wife Tracy, who I'd asked to help me with the campaign, called me one night and said, 'The group's gone'. I said, 'What?' and she said 'The group's gone. It's not on Facebook any more'. I checked my email inbox and it was on fire. People were saying 'What's going on? Where's the group?' I knew we hadn't broken any Facebook rules, because I knew exactly what I could get away with, but I did know that if people report any piece of content like a group to Facebook enough times, that group automatically gets taken offline to be looked at. I knew instantly that there must have been some mass report of my Rage group, so I tried to get hold of Facebook.

How did you do that? They don't exactly publish a helpline.
I tried two things: I went through the usual channels, asking them where my group had gone, but I didn't get much back from that. They must get millions of queries through those channels. So I worked out where their physical offices in London were, walked in and left a note at reception: I didn't get an answer there either. That night, ITV News wanted me to go on and talk about the campaign, so I wrote on my personal Facebook profile, 'I hope the group comes back, because I'm going on national TV tonight and I'm going to have to tell them that Facebook have pulled my group'. I also renamed the Rick Astley group from the previous year 'Rage Against The Machine For Christmas Number One – Backup Group' because it still had 68,000 members. I told the media that a backup group had been started and that it had reached 68,000 members in two hours, and on the group I put a message in huge letters reading 'Facebook – Contact Us!'

What did Facebook do to resolve this?
Facebook's head of UK and European PR got hold of Tracy's number, phoned her and introduced herself. She told Tracy that they thought a bug in the location settings was responsible for the disappearance of the

main Rage group, which made us laugh. She was very nice, though. I told her, 'If you're going to bring the group back, I'll tell ITV News when I go on in a couple of hours' – and the group was back online shortly afterwards. So I didn't need to mention it on ITV. The group disappeared again a couple of days later, but by this time Facebook had given me my own personal manager, based in Ireland, who I could call if there were any problems. I'd realised by now that I had quite a bit of power in this situation, because Facebook might or might not want to be seen as in league with *The X Factor* if the group kept getting pulled.

Did you have a 'Rage Factor' website?
I didn't want a website. If we'd had our own site, it would have started to look a bit commercial, and I was doing this as an underground thing. All we needed was the Facebook group. Some guy in a digital agency did set up a website, though, and posted it on the group: I saw it and said, 'What the fuck is this?' I contacted him and he told me he just wanted to promote his agency, but I looked up the details of the person who had bought the website URL and it turned out that he was a former worker at a particular record company. That was all I needed to know. I wasn't having it. This guy's site had affiliate links on it, making money. This was my baby, so I told the fucker to get rid of it. He ended up making his own Facebook page and got 200,000 or 300,000 members. It was just stupid. And then other people figured out that this guy was a former record company worker and dismissed the whole campaign as a ruse by that company. I had all this to deal with.

At one point Simon Cowell spoke out about your campaign.
There was also an *X Factor* press conference around this time, and I asked a couple of journalist mates who were going along if they would ask Cowell about our campaign. One of them did, and Simon said 'Everyone's trying to stop us going to number one. This person is cynical and stupid'. I thought, 'Fucking gotcha!' The best thing Simon could have done for his own campaign would have been to say 'Fair play to Jon Morter, I wish him all the best with "Killing In The Name"'... but he did the opposite. Our group numbers were pretty high before

he said that about us being cynical and stupid, but after that, they went bang. It was stratospheric. I thought half a million was a lot of people, but effectively he'd told the whole world that I was annoying him, and everyone went and Googled our campaign as a result.

So what was the timeline in the last few weeks?
The announcement of the Christmas number one always happens on the Sunday before Christmas Day. In 2009, that Sunday was December 20. In the previous week, because *The X Factor* has a two-day final, finishing on Sunday 13 December, people started buying its winning single from midnight on that day. The official chart actually started on 23:59 on the night of Saturday 12, though, so I told the group to start buying it when they woke up on Sunday morning to give us a head start. That would mean that we would start Monday 14 in first place. At the end of Monday, they had 77,000 sales and we had 81,000, so the plan had worked. I knew the last remaining media who hadn't got involved yet would go for it now. They'd start saying 'How the hell is this nasty shouty, sweary song outselling *The X Factor*?' That's exactly what happened.

What happened then?
We were ahead on Monday 14 and Tuesday 15, and then it began to level out, because the *X Factor* CD single came out. It snowed really heavily, though, which was useful because retail always suffers in bad weather. By the way, Sony didn't want to know about issuing 'Killing In The Name' on CD. I didn't even bother to try and persuade them. By Thursday 17 *The X Factor* were slightly ahead, and I wondered if we were going to lose.

The band then came fully on board. How did that happen?
Zack was apparently in a bakery in Los Angeles and someone told him that 'Killing In The Name' was going to be a UK number one for Christmas, and understandably he said, 'What?' Then he and Tom talked about it and chatted to the other guys, and they promised to come over and do a free concert in the summer of 2010 if they got to number one. They'd done nothing in 2009, but they got together for a

live recording of the song for Radio 5 Live on Thursday December 17. They agreed to do a live linkup from LA, at 3am their time, solely for our campaign. They were in some kind of weird, carpeted warehouse.

What was it like?
Originally they were going to leave the swearing part out: I could hear them talking beforehand, because I was patched in to the studio. I had my first chat with the band, live on air too, right in front of the whole world. Tom said, 'We really appreciate what you've done for us, Jon, and we're going to play a song for you'. I was speechless. When they went ahead and started playing, I'm not sure the Radio 5 presenters really understood what was happening! Zack started to censor himself at the end, but then he started shouting the 'Fuck you' part in full, and the presenter immediately shouted 'Get rid of it!' After that they promised to come over and play a free show; they didn't know how, when or where, they just said they'd make it happen.

The X Factor winner, Joe McElderry, put his foot in his mouth at one point, didn't he?
At some time this week, Joe was in *The Sun* newspaper, saying 'It's dreadful and I hate it. It's just shouting' about 'Killing In The Name', and I had a feeling that *The Sun* was slightly supporting us. I could be wrong: it's just a feeling. They photographed him throwing darts at a dartboard which had Zack de la Rocha's face on it. I couldn't believe there was no-one at Sony who didn't say to Joe, 'Hang on, don't do that, it's just going to fan the flames!' You can imagine the reaction at our group, which by this time had got up to about 750,000 people. People said, 'What a tosser! If it means that much, we'll buy Rage's record'. The whole dartboard thing fell into our laps. Lots of little things like that happened: for example, Joe's song was terrible, but that was the one which they chose for him, so that helped us.

Did the media continue to give you support?
Yes. I'd been trying to get on Radio 1 for a while, and I finally managed it. I went on the Jo Whiley show and I was extra nice about Simon Cowell.

They were expecting me to have a go at him, because that was what I'd done on other radio stations, but this time I was super polite. Jo Whiley asked me what his reaction had been to all this, and I said, 'Well, I've been a bit disappointed in him, to be honest. He's a big lad, he's had numerous number ones, and we're just doing this for fun. He's got really narked about it and I'm just some idiot from Essex.' Then she says, 'To make it even, how about you introduce Joe McElderry's song on the show?' and so I did. I introduced it as the song that was going to be Christmas number two! After I got home, I started cooking dinner for my kids, and my mobile rang. I picked it up, and this voice said, 'Hi, it's Simon Cowell here'.

Blimey.
I said, 'Hello Simon, what an unexpected honour'. He replied, 'You probably didn't expect me to ring you?' and I said, 'Not really, no. How are you?' We talked and he said, 'I know I threw my toys out of the pram a bit back there' and I told him that I thought his words had helped us out a lot. He said that he'd worked that out pretty quickly, and he added: 'I've been pretty impressed with how you've managed to pull this off. People have been trying to knock me out of the music industry for years, and with all due respect, you're just some nobody who has turned up, and the numbers are neck and neck. You could actually do it.'

How was he to talk to?
He was very nice, actually, and I knew he was telling the truth about the numbers because I had contacts in the industry who had told me that. We had a good chat and I told him that I had nothing against *The X Factor* as a TV show, and that if that kind of music was what people liked, then that was absolutely fine with me. He then asked me to come and work for him, which I politely declined. He also invited me out for a beer, which I accepted, although that's yet to happen. I'll hold him to it. We wished each other the best of luck for the day after, and that was it.

How did the rest of it play out?
At 9pm on Saturday December 19, I told people to download the live version of the song, because I knew they would count towards the

main chart and that they would be more likely to buy another version of the song than buy the same verson twice. In the last three hours of the chart, we sold another 72,000 downloads. At midnight that was it. All over.

When did you hear the result?
I found out on Sunday, December 20 at about 2pm that the result was *The X Factor* 454,000, Rage Against The Machine 502,000. We won by 48,000 copies. A writer from *The Guardian* phoned me up and told me. If we hadn't told people to buy the live version the night before, we would have lost.

Can you describe the next few days?
I was on the front cover of every newspaper, and I bought them all, took them into the office and got on with some work. It was a relief to do something else for a change... The band got in touch the next day. They were in a British-style pub in LA, playing darts and drinking bitter. One of them was wearing a flat cap.

Any fond farewells from Simon Cowell?
Yes. He called and said, 'Well done. You pulled that off spectacularly'...

Discography

All releases on Epic unless indicated

Rage Against The Machine albums
Rage Against The Machine	1992
Evil Empire	1996
Live & Rare (Japan only)	1998
The Battle Of Los Angeles	1999
Renegades	2000
Live At The Grand Olympic Auditorium	2003

Rage Against The Machine singles
Killing In The Name	1992
Bullet In The Head	1993
Bombtrack	1993
Freedom	1994
Year Of Tha Boomerang (*Higher Learning* soundtrack)	1994
Darkness (*The Crow* soundtrack)	1996
Bulls On Parade	1996
Evil Empire	1996
People Of The Sun	1996

Down Rodeo	1996
Vietnow	1998
The Ghost Of Tom Joad	1998
No Shelter (*Godzilla* soundtrack)	1998
Guerrilla Radio	1999
Sleep Now In The Fire	2000
Testify	2000
Calm Like A Bomb	2000
Renegades Of Funk	2000
How I Could Just Kill A Man	2001
Killing In The Name (reissue, download only)	2009

Inside Out (featuring Zack de la Rocha)

No Spiritual Surrender EP (Revelation Records)	1990

Lock Up (featuring Tom Morello)

Something Bitchin' This Way Comes (Geffen)	1989

Audioslave albums

Audioslave	2002
Out Of Exile (Interscope)	2005
Revelations (Epic and Interscope)	2006

Audioslave singles

Cochise	2002
Like A Stone	2003
Show Me How To Live	2003
I Am The Highway	2004
What You Are	2004
Be Yourself	2005
Your Time Has Come	2005
Doesn't Remind Me	2005
Out Of Exile	2006
Original Fire	2006
Revelations	2006

Discography

Axis Of Justice album
Axis Of Justice Concert Series: Volume 1 (Columbia) 2004

The Nightwatchman albums
One Man Revolution 2007
The Fabled City 2008
World Wide Rebel Songs (New West) 2011

Street Sweeper Social Club album/EP
Street Sweeper Social Club (Warners) 2009
The Ghetto Blaster EP (Warners) 2010

One Day As A Lion EP
One Day As A Lion EP (Anti-) 2008

Other recordings featuring Zack de la Rocha (various labels)
The Unbound Allstars, Mumia 911 1999
Criminals In Action, Lyricist Lounge: Volume One 1999
Various Artists, Bamboozled Soundtrack 2000
Roni Size/Reprazent, In the Mode 2000
Blazing Arrow, Blackalicious 2002
DJ Shadow, You Can't Go Home Again 2002
Various Artists, Songs And Artists That Inspired Fahrenheit 9/11 2004
Saul Williams, Saul Williams 2004
Various Artists, Los Tigres del Norte 2011

Selected recordings featuring Tom Morello (various labels)
Run-DMC, Down With The King 1993
Various Artists, Kiss My Ass: Classic Kiss Regrooved 1994
KRS-One, Rappaz R. N. Dainja 1996
Snoop Dogg, Snoop Bounce (Roc N Roll Remix) 1996
The Prodigy, One Man Army 1997
Puff Daddy, Come With Me 1998
Indigo Girls, Shed Your Skin 1998

Joe Strummer, Chef Aid: The South Park Album	1998
Bone Thugs-N-Harmony, War	1998
Primus, Antipop	1999
Class Of '99, The Faculty Soundtrack	1999
Perry Farrell, Rev	1999
Atari Teenage Riot, Rage EP	1999
Wu-Tang Clan, Ain't Nothing Ta Fuck Wit	2000
Cypress Hill, (Rap) Superstar	2000
The Crystal Method, Tweekend	2001
Made Soundtrack, Katwalk (Morello Mix)	2001
Cypress Hill, Stash: This Is The Remix	2002
Macy Gray, Spider-Man Soundtrack	2002
Johnny Cash, Unearthed	2003
Anti-Flag, The Terror State	2003
The Coup, Pick A Bigger Weapon	2006
The Crystal Method, Drive	2006
Dave Matthews Band, Live Trax Vol. 10	2007
Tool, Live At Bonnaroo	2007
Puscifer, Cuntry Boner	2007
Various Artists, Iron Man Soundtrack	2008
Jason Heath & The Greedy Souls, The Vain Hope Of Horse	2008
Bruce Springsteen, Magic Tour Highlights	2008
Cypress Hill, Rise Up	2010
Travis Barker, Carry It	2011
Serj Tankian, Imperfect Remixes	2011
Various Artists, Note Of Hope: A Celebration Of Woody Guthrie	2011
Bruce Springsteen, Wrecking Ball	2012
Steve Jablonsky, Battleship	2012
Device, Opinion	2013
John Fogerty, Wrote A Song For Everyone	2013

Other recordings featuring Tim Commerford

Puscifer, V Is For Vagina (Warners)	2007
Various Artists, Sound City Movie Soundtrack (Roswell)	2013

Other recordings featuring Brad Wilk (various labels)

Various Artists, Kiss My Ass: Classic Kiss Regrooved	1994
Snoop Dogg, Snoop Bounce (Roc N Roll Remix)	1996
Cypress Hill, Skull And Bones	2000
Various Artists, The Dangerous Lives Of Altar Boys	2002
Puscifer, V Is For Vagina	2007
Various Artists, Sound City Movie Soundtrack	2013
Black Sabbath, 13	2013

Sources

All quotes are taken from interviews executed by the author except where stated. Quotes from Bob Gulla in *Guitar One* and from Ben Myers in *Kerrang!* reproduced with kind permission.

Chapter 1
"I was a mean-hearted" Launch Radio Networks
"Ever since I was..." *Modern Drummer*
"My mom trekked..." The Progressive
"I integrated the town..." The Progressive
"I had always been..." Steven Wells, *NME*, 13 February 1993
"Back in 1974..." Steven Wells, *NME*, 13 February 1993
"Living with Beto..." Propaganda
"I'd spend three..." RJ Smith, *Spin*, 1996
"I remember it..." Rob Tannenbaum
"I was a big fan..." The Progressive
"I was very influenced..." MTV.com, 4 December 2000
"I remember the..." Joe Bosso, Music Radar
"Now, you might not..." Neil Chrisley, Gibson
"Adam wasn't in..." *Guitar World*, 1994
"The second you have..." Rob Tannenbaum
"There was a..." The Progressive
"None of the..." Bob Gulla, *Guitar One*, February 2000
"I had the..." Jane Ganahl, Guitar.com
"I didn't even know..." Bob Gulla, *Guitar One*, February 2000

"I wasn't a..." Bob Gulla, *Guitar One*, February 2000
"When I was first..." Bob Gulla, *Guitar One*, February 2000

Bombtrack 1
"The problem is..." Charles M. Young, *Guitar World*

Chapter 2
"When I was..." David Weiss, *Drum Magazine*
"From the first..." Peter Atkinson
"Zack was like..." David Weiss, *Drum Magazine*
"We had no..." Kevin Martin
"I thought the politics..." Rob Tannenbaum
"One thing that..." Bob Gulla, *Guitar One*, February 2000
"It was shocking!..." Bob Gulla, *Guitar One*, February 2000
"We rehearsed for..." Ben Myers, *Kerrang!*, 16 October 1999
"The relationship that..." Bob Gulla, *Guitar One*, February 2000
"When Madonna kept..." Steven Wells, *NME*, 13 February 1993
"You don't treat..." Bob Gulla, *Guitar One*, February 2000
"Once we sat..." Kevin Martin
"I've come to..." Robert Hilburn, *Los Angeles Times*
"That sort of criticism..." MTV.com online chat, 4 December 2000
"You have two choices..." The Progressive
"We did that record..." Ultimate Guitar

Chapter 3
"It's very fashionable..." Charles M. Young, *Guitar World*
"Regarding the music..." Charles M. Young, *Guitar World*
"All American kids..." Steven Wells, *NME*, 13 February 1993
"The machine..." Steven Wells, *NME*, 13 February 1993
"You get your..." Steven Wells, *NME*, 13 February 1993
"I came up..." Simon Wooldridge, *Juice*, February 2000
"It's not just..." Simon Wooldridge, *Juice*, February 2000
"You labour..." Rachel Butera, *Music Monitor*, 2000

Chapter 4
"When we heard..." Steve Bloom and Steven Wishnia, *High Times*, 1999
"We became actively..." Steve Bloom and Steven Wishnia, *High Times*, 1999
"We were having..." Launch
"The tension for..." Matt O'Connell, *Rock Sound*
"We're four strong-willed..." Peter Atkinson
"I think it's..." Kevin Martin
"a musical path..." Joshua Sindell, *Kerrang!*, 29 January 2000

Sources

"It's just that..." Ben Myers, *Kerrang!*, 16 October 1999

Bombtrack 2
"We'd wake up..." RJ Smith, *Spin*
"This is the..." Jesus Ramirez Cuevas, Frontera, 7 July 1998
"The Zapatistas are..." Triple J radio, 1999
"I couldn't really..." RJ Smith, *Spin*, October 1996
"Inside I feel..." Propaganda

Chapter 5
"*Evil Empire* was..." David Weiss, *Drum*
"Three years ago..." RJ Smith, *Spin*
"It's not uncommon..." RJ Smith, *Spin*
"You should talk..." Propaganda
"It was the..." Ben Myers, *Kerrang!*, 16 October 1999
"I wish I..." RJ Smith, *Spin*, October 1996
"The Wu-Tang..." Ben Myers, *Kerrang!*, 16 October 1999
"I was first..." www.diabetes.org

Chapter 6
"When we came..." Matt O'Connell, *Rock Sound*
"I really want..." David Weiss, Drum
"We need to..." Dino Scatena, *Sydney Daily Telegraph*, October 28 1999
"Who would have..." Robert Hilburn, *New York Times*
"We share some..." Gary Graff
"Like everyone else..." MTV.com online chat, 4 December 2000
"Although our work..." Ben Myers, *Kerrang!*, 16 October 1999
"For every Nirvana..." Ben Myers, *Kerrang!*, 16 October 1999
"a show near..." Simon Wooldridge, *Juice*, February 2000
"They point out..." Rob Sheffield, *Rolling Stone*
'We wouldn't have..." Rich Kane
"shows up for..." Rob Tannenbaum
"After our early..." Ben Myers, *Kerrang!*, October 16 1999

Chapter 7
"The look on..." Tom Matlack, Huffington Post
"My job is..." Ben Myers, *Kerrang!*, October 16 1999
"That was just..." Ben Myers, *Kerrang!*, October 16 1999
"I'm mad..." Metal Sludge

Chapter 8
"There are many..." The Progressive

"Rage Against The..." The Progressive
"He was a..." Christopher John Farley
"It was spawned..." *Premier Guitar*
"I come from..." Teamster
"I think as..." Teamster
"The National Nurses..." Truth Out
"At Ozzfest a..." The Progressive
"I'm still really..." Pat Douglas, *Great Falls Tribune*
"I'm very proud..." *Grand Rapids Press*
"We went to..." *Grand Rapids Press*
"We both come..." *Grand Rapids Press*
"At the end..." *Grand Rapids Press*
"The three of..." Nuvo
"In Rage, we..." Launch
"It seems like..." *Grand Rapids Press*
Morello/Kenya story: Tom Matlack, Huffington Post
All non-attributed quotes supplied by the author

Bombtrack 3
All non-attributed quotes supplied by the author

Chapter 9
"In these political..." MTV
"We just try..." *Great Falls Tribune*
"So much has..." Ann Powers, *LA Times*
"I felt both..." Nicole Powers
"They [the cops]..." SuicideGirls.com
"I have to..." Greg Kot, *Chicago Tribune*
"I've known Jon..." Ann Powers, *LA Times*
"Now more than..." Ann Powers, *LA Times*
"I think people..." Nuvo
"We've had a..." *Billboard*

Chapter 10
"There is a..." Jason Leopold, Truth Out
"In some ways..." Consequence Of Sound
"In the studio..." The Pulse Of Radio
"I think [Snowden]..." TMZ.com

Bombtrack 4
"Today if you..." *The Progressive*

Index

All titles by Rage Against The Machine except where indicated.

120 Minutes (MTV programme), 74
13 (Black Sabbath album), 204
24-7 Spyz, 44
2 Live Crew, 72, 73
33 Revolutions Per Minute: A History Of Protest Songs (Dorian Lynskey book), 155, 156
60 Minutes (CBS TV programme), 139
9/11, see World Trade Center

A&M (record label), 152, 154
Abu-Jamal, Mumia, viii, ix, 56, 80, 81, 97, 106, 121, 122, 123, 124, 125, 126, 127, 128, 129, 133, 136, 144, 150
Accord On Fire And Building Safety, 110
AC/DC, 70, 115
Aerosmith, 43, 115
Aldi, 110
Alice Cooper (band), 7
All Shook Up (album featuring Electric Sheep), 9
America Votes Liberty Unity Fund, 200
American Civil Liberties Union, 144
American Composite (demo tape, aka *Rage Against The Machine*), 51, 52
American Idiot (Green Day album), 159
American Indian Movement, x
Amnesty International, 74, 80
Anthrax, 115
Anti-Flag, 186
Anti-Nazi League, 74
Appetite For Destruction (Guns N' Roses album), 43, 72
Arcade Fire, 159

Asda, 61, 70
'Ashes In The Fall', 133
Astley, Rick, 214, 216, 218, 219
Atkins, Martin, 21
Audioslave, 154, 162, 163, 164, 165, 166, 167, 168, 170, 171, 172, 173, 174, 175, 176, 177, 178, 179, 184, 212
Audioslave (British indie band), 163
Audioslave (Audioslave album), 163, 164, 177
Audioslave (Audioslave DVD), 166
'Autologic', 52
Axis Of Justice, 170, 171, 172, 174

Backstreet Boys, 119
Bad Animal Studios, 154
Bad Brains, 12
Baretto, Alex, 12, 13
Bark At The Moon (Ozzy Osbourne album), 70
Barker, Travis, 199
Barnes & Noble, 66
Barsamian, David, 180
Beastie Boys, 58, 77, 105, 115, 125, 144
Beatles, The, 203
'Beautiful World' (Devo song), 147
Beck, 106
Beethoven, Ludwig van, 203
Bell, Steffanie, 126
Bentham, Jeremy, 30, 32, 33
Berlin Wall, 89
Bettencourt, Nuno, 183
'Be Yourself' (Audioslave song), 175
Biafra, Jello, 113, 156

Biffy Clyro, 194
Billboard, 67, 103, 163, 192, 212
Black Panthers, 67, 79, 101, 159
Black Sabbath, 7, 8, 24, 70, 72, 105, 117, 153, 204, 205
Blink-182, 199
Blizzard Of Ozz (Ozzy Osbourne album), 9
Blood Sugar Sex Magik (Red Hot Chili Peppers album), 44, 57
Body Count (band), 72
'Bombtrack', 42, 51, 61, 66, 101, 102
Bonham, John, 40, 188
Bon Jovi, 43
'Born As Ghosts', 133
'Born Of A Broken Man', 133
'Born To Be Wild' (Steppenwolf song), 9
Boston Globe, 127
Bowling For Columbine (film), 139
Bradley, Tom, 45, 48
Bragg, Billy, 156, 167, 192-3
Bratton, Chris, 11, 13
'Break Stuff' (Limp Bizkit song), 141
B-Real (aka Louis Freese), 145
Brian Brain (band), 21
'Brick House' (Commodores song), 19
'Bring The Noise' (Anthrax/Chuck D song), 115
Briseno, Theodore, 45
Brokaw, Tom, 165
Brookes, Bruno, 60
Brown, James, 159
Browne, Malcolm, 64
'Bullet In The Head', 25, 51, 62, 66, 98, 158, 198
'Bulls On Parade', 98, 100, 168, 187, 194
'Burning Fight' (Inside Out song), 12
Burroughs, William, 104
Bush (band), 120
Bush, George H, 44, 48, 132, 180
Bush, George W, 75, 132, 134, 180, 181, 182, 190
Business Week (magazine), 28
Butler, Geezer, 204, 205

C&A, 111
California Music Awards, 150
'Calling Dr Love' (Kiss song), 79
'Calm Like A Bomb', 132
Cammarano, Pete, 125, 126
Cannon, Lou, 45
'Can't Stop The Bleeding' (Lock Up song), 24
Cardle, Matt, 194, 195, 196, 197
Carrefour, 110
'Carry It' (Tom Morello and Wu-Tang Clan song), 199
Carter, 'Hurricane', 121, 122
Carter, Jimmy, 180
Cash, Johnny, 170, 187
Castro, Fidel, 141, 173
Catfish (band), 44

Cheney, Dick, 173, 181, 182, 193
Chevolution (documentary), 201
Chicago (band), 10
Chomsky, Noam, vii, 26, 27, 28, 66, 102, 104, 106, 136, 138, 139, 161, 180, 209, 210
Christopher Commission (investigation), 46, 49
CIA, 101, 206
Civilian (band name), 151
'Clap For The Killers' (Street Sweeper Social Club song), 193
Clash, The, 7, 53, 89, 106, 115, 156, 160, 165
Clean Clothes: A Global Movement To End Sweatshops (Liesbeth Sluiter book), 109
Clean Clothes Campaign (CCC), 109, 110, 111
Clear Channel, 152
'Clear The Lane', 51
Clinton, Bill, 69, 106, 180, 182
Clufetos, Tommy, 205
Coachella (festival), 177
Coal Chamber, 116
Coalition Of Immolokee Workers, 169, 180
Cobain, Kurt, 44
'Cochise' (Audioslave song), 162
Codey, Senator Richard, 125
Cole Rehearsal Studios, 83
Columbus, Christopher, 133, 157
Commerford, Gerard, 2
Commerford, Tim, viii, 1, 2, 11, 39, 40, 42, 50, 51, 52, 61, 62, 64, 80, 81, 100, 117, 118, 134, 139, 140, 141, 142, 143, 145, 146, 147, 148, 149, 152, 153, 162, 172, 174, 176, 177, 183, 201, 204, 208
Commodores, 19
Continental Encounter For Humanity Against Neoliberalism, 93
Cooking Vinyl (record label), 199
'Cop Killer' (Body Count song), 72
Cornell, Chris, 150, 151, 152, 153, 154, 162, 163, 164, 165, 172, 173, 174, 177, 178, 179
Cotton, Randy, 10
Coulter, Ann, 180
Coup, The (band), 192
Covenant House, 166-7
Cowell, Simon, 194, 195, 196, 197, 198, 217, 220, 221, 222, 223, 224
Cranston, Senator Alan, 19, 20, 190
Crass (band), 161
'Crazy Train' (Ozzy Osbourne song), 8
'Cuntry Boner' (Puscifer song), 10
Cypress Hill, 57, 75, 77, 106, 143, 145, 147, 183

D, Chuck (aka Carlton Ridenhour), 94, 106, 115, 159
D, Mike (aka Michael Diamond), 144
Daddy, Puff (aka P-Diddy, Sean Combs), 118
Dalai Lama, 75
Dali, Salvador, 103

Index

D'Angelo, 142
Dan Reed Network, 116
Dark Horse Comics, 201
'Darkness Of Greed', 51
'Darling Nikki' (Prince song), 69
Dave Matthews Band, 183
Davis, Miles, 40, 103
Dead Kennedys, 20, 156
Def American (record label), 148
Def Leppard, 70
Degarmo & Key, 71
Dekker, Thomas, 30, 31, 37
De la Rocha, Roberto (aka Beto), 4, 5, 6, 133
De la Rocha, Zack, viii, 1, 10, 11, 12, 13, 14, 15, 39, 41, 42, 50, 53, 61, 62, 63, 64, 73, 74, 75, 79, 80, 81, 83, 91, 92, 93, 94, 95, 96, 97, 100, 101, 102, 103, 105, 106, 108, 113, 114, 115, 117, 119, 122, 123, 125, 127, 132, 133, 134, 135, 140, 141, 142, 143, 144, 145, 146, 147, 148, 149, 151, 155, 156, 157, 159, 160, 165, 166, 175, 178, 180, 181, 182, 188, 189, 193, 196, 198, 199, 208, 221
   childhood, 4–5, 6
   first experiences of racism, 7
   views on vegetarianism, 10–11
   joins Rage Against The Machine, 40
   leaves Rage Against The Machine, 144
Democratic National Convention (DNC), 143, 185, 206
Denver, John, 71
De Tocqueville, Alexis, 35
Device (band), 206
Devo, 7, 147
Dewy, John, 27
Diabolus In Musica (Slayer album), 116
'Diary Of A Madman' (Ozzy Osbourne song), 15
Diary Of A Madman (Ozzy Osbourne album), 9
DiCara, Vic, 11, 12, 13, 14, 15
Dick, Philip K, 9
Dickinson, Emily, 35
Diêm, Ngô Đình, 64
Disney, 178
Disturbed (band), 206
Dixie Chicks, 212
DJ Shadow, 165
DMX, 212
Do Androids Dream Of Electric Sheep? (novel), 9
Doobie Brothers, 18
'Do What I Tell Ya!' (Infectious Grooves song), 65, 73, 116
'Down Rodeo', 101
Doyle, Patrick, 207
Draiman, David, 206
Dre, Dr, 53
Duc, Thich Quang, 64
Durst, Fred, 141
Dylan, Bob, 4, 122, 147, 157, 183, 187

Earle, Steve, 167
Easton, Sheena, 70
Eazy-E (aka Eric Wright), 147
Eleanor Roosevelt Human Rights Award, 176
Electric Sheep, 9, 10
Engels, Friedrich, 103
'Epic' (Faith No More song), 115
Epic (record label), 54, 55, 56, 67, 78, 80, 95, 96, 97, 152, 154
EPMD, 147
Euphoria Morning (Chris Cornell album), 151
European Parliament, 75, 125
Evil Empire, 86, 100, 101, 103, 104, 105, 108, 113, 114, 132, 134
Extreme (band), 183
EZLN, see Zapatista Army Of National Liberation

'Facing Mount Kenya' (Nightwatchman song), 200
Fahrenheit 9/11 (film), 139
Faith No More, 22, 44, 79, 115, 116, 117
Farage, Nigel, 61
Farrell, Perry, 22, 113, 183
Faulkner, Maureen, 122
Fear Factory, 116
Firm, The (management company), 154
Fishbone, 44
'Fistful Of Steel', 63, 101
Flea (aka Michael Balzary), 106, 170
Fleetwood Mac, 10
FNV, 109
Foo Fighters, 204
Forbes, Steve, 99
Fox News, 180, 181
Frankie Goes To Hollywood, 147
Franti, Michael, 115, 186
Fraternal Order Of Police (FOP), 121, 122, 125, 126, 128, 144
Freeborn, Amy, 151, 154
'Freedom', 52, 64, 75
Freedom Fighter Orchestra, 184
Free Trade Area Of The Americas (FTAA), 150
Frehley, Ace, 7
Fricke, David, 145, 147
Fritts, Eddie, 69
'Fuck Tha Police' (NWA song), 108, 203
Fugazi, 56
Fugees, 105
Fukuyama, Francis, 133, 157
Funk-metal, 116
Fujimori, Alberto, 102

Gallegos, Gilbert, 121, 125
Gang Of Four, 147
Gandhi, Mahatma, 14
Gap (clothing brand), 110

237

Gap Band, The, 147, 153
'Gasoline' (Audioslave song), 163, 164
Gates, Daryl, 47, 49
Geffen (record label), 22, 23, 54, 212
General Electric, 99
George, Chris, 10
Gersh, Gary, 144
G-Funk, 72
Gibson Explorer (guitar), 18
'Girls, Girls, Girls' (Mötley Crüe song), 72
Gittins, Ian, 198
'God Save The Queen' (Sex Pistols song), 216
Godsmack, 116
Godzilla (film), 126, 127
Goldstone, Michael, 54, 55, 80
Gordon Childe, Vere, 32
Gore, Al, 69, 134
Gore, Tipper, 68, 69, 70, 73
Gorilla Biscuits, 11
Gorky, Maxim, 34, 35
Gould, Billy, 79
GQ (magazine), 155
Grammy (awards and ceremony), 101, 126, 150, 170
Green Day, 157, 159
Greta (band), 40
Grillo, Brian, 20, 21, 22, 23, 24
Grohl, Dave, 196, 204
Guano Apes, 44
Guardian (newspaper), 155, 198, 224
'Guerilla Radio', 131, 134, 150
Guess (clothing manufacturer), 108
Guevara, Che, 104, 201
Guitarmy, 170
Guitar Hero III: Legends Of Rock (video game), 187
Guitar One (magazine), 52
Gulla, Bob, 52
Guns N' Roses, 23, 43, 72, 171
Guthrie, Woody, 187
Guzman, Abimael, 62
GWAR, 72

'Half Man Half Beast' (Lock Up song), 24
Hampton, Fred, 101
Hardstance, 11
Harper, Ben, 179
Harrelson, Woody, 113
Harvard (university), 16, 17, 19, 26, 191, 192
Hayworth, Mark, 11
'Heartbreaker' (Led Zeppelin song), 7
Hendrix, Jimi, 183
Henry, Lenny, 218
Herman, Maureen, 141
Higher Learning (film), 79
High Times (magazine), 123
Hilburn, Robert, 54, 67

Hill, Joe, 167
Hirschman, Alfred O, 35
Hmong tribe (Laos), 101
Hole, 44
House Of Pain, 57, 73
'How I Could Just Kill A Man' (Cypress Hill song), 147
'How Long, Not Long' (Martin Luther King speech), 63
Huffington Post, 140
Humanitarian Law Project, 127

Ice Cube, 57, 79
Ice-T, 72, 73
Ill Manors (Plan B album), 159
'Imagine' (John Lennon song), 153
'I'm Housin'' (EPMD song), 147
Industrial Workers Of The World, 169
Infectious Grooves, 44, 65, 116
'In My Eyes' (Minor Threat song), 147
Inside Out (band), 11, 12, 13, 14, 15, 39, 41
International Concerned Friends And Family Of Mumia Abu-Jamal, 80, 120
International Monetary Fund, 138, 139
Interscope (record label), 154
In Utero (Nirvana album), 72
Iommi, Tony, 117, 204
Iraq Veterans Against The War, 185
Iron Maiden, 116, 201
Iron Maiden: Flight 666 (film), 201
Iron Man (film), 183

Jabberjaw (club), 50
Jackson, Reverend Jesse, 75
Jane's Addiction, 22, 54, 71, 106, 113, 119, 193
Jay-Z, 118
Jedward (novelty act), 215
Johnson, Geoff, 10
Johnson, Lyndon, 180
Jones, Adam, 9, 10, 62, 63
Jones, Elvin, 40, 181
Joyce, James, 104
Judas Priest, 70
Juice (magazine), 127, 148
Jurassic 5, 170
Juvenile Expression, 11

'Kashmir' (Led Zeppelin song), 63
Keenan, Maynard James, 10, 21, 62, 63, 79, 170, 183
Kennedy Memorial Center For Human Rights, 75
Kenyatta, Jomo, 3, 16
Kerrang!, 134
Khasnabish, Alex, 84, 85, 86, 87, 88, 89, 90, 91, 101
Kid A (Radiohead album), 156
Kiedis, Anthony, 117

Index

'Killing In The Name', 52, 59, 60, 61, 62, 65, 100, 129, 157, 158, 197, 198, 216, 220, 221, 222
Killing Joke, 21
King Blues, 160
King, Kerry, 115
King, Martin Luther, 63, 159
King, Rodney, 45, 49, 66, 132
Kiss, 40, 79, 106
Kiss My Ass: Classic Kiss Regrooved (covers album), 79
Klein, Naomi, 156
K-Mart, 72
Knox, Jon, 39
'Know Your Enemy', 51, 62, 63
Koestler, Arthur, 104
Koon, Stacey, 45
Korn, 114, 116, 118, 130
KPFK, 171
Kramer, Wayne, 170, 200
Kropotkin, Petr, 32
KROQ, 165
KRS-One, 115
Ku Klux Klan, 121

L7, 23
Labour Behind The Label, 111
Landless Workers' Movement (Brazil), 199
Late Night With Conan O'Brien (NBC TV programme), 125, 185
Late Night With David Letterman (CBS TV programme), 134, 165
Late Night With Jimmy Fallon (NBC TV programme), 193
La Tercera (newspaper), 199
Latinpalooza, 78
Launch (magazine), 153, 176
Lauper, Cyndi, 70
Led Zeppelin, 7, 12, 57, 63, 117, 149, 162, 203
Lee, Michael, 20
Lennon, John, 152
Leonard Peltier Defense Fund, 77, 78
Leopold, Jason, 200
Let Fury Have The Hour (documentary), 201
'Like A Stone' (Audioslave song), 166, 170
Limp Bizkit, 116, 117, 118, 129, 141, 142
Linkin Park, 116
Live 8, 174
Live Aid, 105
Live And Rare, 108
Live At The Grand Olympic Auditorium, 166
Live From Death Row (Mumia Abu-Jamal book), 128
Living Colour, 44, 116
Livingston, Mike, 20
Local 47 (union), 169
Lock Up, 20, 21, 22, 23, 24, 38, 41, 52, 54, 55, 108, 212

Lollapalooza (festival), 57, 58, 67, 73, 120, 166, 171
Lopez, Fidel, 47
Lopez, Jennifer, 142
Los Angeles Times, 54, 67
Los Four (collective), 5
Love At First Sting (Scorpions album), 70
Lovesexy (Prince album), 72
Luther, Martin, 14
Lutz, Mike, 126
Lydon, John, 196, 218
Lynskey, Dorian, 155, 156, 157, 158, 159, 160, 161

Madball, 44
Madonna, 51, 70
'Maggie's Farm' (Bob Dylan song), 147
Mandela, Nelson, 74, 125
Manifesto (record label), 108
Man Makes Himself (V. Gordon Childe book), 32
Manning, Bradley (later Chelsea), 205, 206
Manson, Charles, 203
'Many Of Horror' (Biffy Clyro song), 194
Mao, aka Chairman Mao, Mao Zedong, 5, 40
March Of Conscience, 108
'March Of Death' (DJ Shadow song), 165
Marcos, Subcomandante, 85, 94, 103, 106, 150
'Maria', 133
Marilyn Manson (band), 116, 122
Marley, Bob, 78, 103, 115, 132, 133
Marr, Johnny, 160
Marshall (amplifiers), 7
Mars Volta, The, 188
Martin, Dean, 68
Marx, Karl, 103
Mary Jane Girls, 70
Mau Mau uprising (Kenya), 3
Mau Maus (band), 20
Maverick (record label), 51
MC5, 78, 170, 200
McCartney, Paul, 196
McElderry, Joe, 195, 196, 197, 198, 222, 223
Mercury (record label), 40
Mercyful Fate, 70
Metallica, 43, 116, 117, 129, 187, 212, 213
Metallica (Metallica album), 43
'Mic Check', 132
Milarepa Fund, 105
Miller, Henry, 104
Mills, Mike, 167
'Mindset's A Threat', 51
Minor Threat, 10, 147
Mojo (magazine), 155
Moon, Keith, 40
Moore, Michael, 106, 134, 137, 139, 141, 142, 156
Morello, Mary, 3, 7, 68, 73

239

Morello, Tom, viii, ix, x, 1, 6, 8, 9, 10, 15, 16, 18, 21, 23, 24, 25, 26, 27, 39, 40, 41, 42, 50, 51, 52, 53, 54, 55, 56, 57, 59, 62, 63, 64, 65, 66, 67, 68, 70, 73, 74, 75, 76, 77, 78, 79, 80, 81, 94, 98, 99, 100, 101, 102, 104, 105, 106, 107, 108, 115, 117, 118, 119, 120, 121, 122, 123, 124, 125, 128, 130, 131, 132, 134, 135, 136, 137, 138, 139, 140, 141, 142, 145, 147, 148, 149, 150, 151, 152, 153, 154, 155, 159, 160, 162, 164, 165, 166, 167, 168, 169, 170, 171, 172, 173, 175, 176, 178, 179, 180, 183, 184, 185, 186, 187, 188, 189, 190, 191, 192, 193, 194, 195, 199, 200, 201, 202, 203, 205, 206, 208, 209, 211, 212, 218, 221, 222
  on democracy, vii
  childhood, 3
  first experiences of racism, 3
  early music, 7
  attends Harvard, 16, 17
  works as stripper, 19
  works for Senator Alan Cranston, 19
  joins Lock Up, 20
  as guitarist, 52
  builds ties with family in Kenya, 175
Morrison, James, 196
Morrissey, Stephen, 160
Morter, Jon, 195, 197, 198, 211, 213, 214, 215, 216, 217, 218, 219, 220, 221, 222, 223, 224
Morter, Tracy, 195, 197, 198, 219
Mother (Maxim Gorky book), 35
Mother Tongue, 77
Mötley Crüe, 14, 57, 70, 72, 116
Motörhead, 116
'Mr Brownstone' (Guns N'Roses song), 72
Mr Bungle, 44
'Mr Crowley' (Ozzy Osbourne song), 16
Mumford & Sons, 161
Muse (band), 218
Music Connection (magazine), 40
Mutual Aid: A Factor In Evolution (Petr Kropotkin book), 32
'My Country Boner' (Electric Sheep song), 10
Myers, Ben, 134, 146

Nader, Ralph, 189
National Association Of Black Journalists, 128
National Association Of Broadcasters, 69
Navarro, Dave, 22
Nazism (also neo-Nazism), 56, 74, 79, 126, 171
Nebula (band), 7
'Never Gonna Give You Up' (Rick Astley song), 214
Never Mind The Bollocks... Here's The Sex Pistols (Sex Pistols album), 7
'New Millennium Homes', 133
New York Stock Exchange, 137, 138, 139, 140
New York Times, 121, 130, 178

Nightwatchman, The, 166, 167, 168, 170, 172, 179, 183, 189, 191, 192, 199
Nine Inch Nails, 119, 120, 170, 193
Nirvana, viii, 44, 50, 54, 72, 120, 213
Nixon, Richard, 180
Njoroge, Stephen Ngethe, 3, 176
Nkrumah, Kwame, 16
NME, x, 51, 66, 68, 163, 199
No Logo (Naomi Klein book), 156
'Nookie' (Limp Bizkit song), 119
'No One Left', 170
North American Free Trade Agreement, 85, 92, 93, 94, 95, 103, 134
'No Shelter', 126, 127
'No Spiritual Surrender' (Inside Out song), 12
No Spiritual Surrender (Inside Out EP), 12
'Nothing New' (Lock Up song), 22
Nothing's Shocking (Jane's Addiction album), 72
Nu-metal, 114, 115, 116, 117
Nutini, Paolo, 197
NWA, 72, 108, 203

Obama, Barack, 189, 190, 191, 203, 204, 206
O'Brien, Brendan, 83
Observer (newspaper), 155
Occupy movement, 36, 91, 158, 170, 199, 200, 201
Ochs, Phil, 187
O'Connor, Christopher, 125, 126
Official Negligence: How Rodney King And The Riots Changed Los Angeles And The LAPD (Lou Cannon book), 45
OK Computer (Radiohead album), 156
Olade (beverage), 193
Omnibus Press, 63
One Day As A Lion (band), 188, 189
One Day As A Lion (EP), 188
One Man Revolution (Nightwatchman album), 179, 183, 184
Orchid (comics series), 201
'Original Fire' (Audioslave song), 177
Orwell, George, 133
Osbourne, Ozzy, 8, 9, 70, 71, 153, 171, 204, 205
Osbourne, Sharon, 153
Out Of Exile (Audioslave album), 174
Ozzfest, 153, 171

Page, Jimmy, 8, 149
Pantera, 117
'Paradise City' (Guns N'Roses song), 43
Para Los Niños, 78
Parents For Rock And Rap, 73
Parents' Music Resource Center (PMRC), 68, 69, 70, 71, 72, 73, 74
Patton, Mike, 117
Pearl Jam, 44, 55, 57, 83, 120, 134, 215
Peligro, DH, 20

Index

Peltier, Leonard, viii, ix, 56, 74, 76, 77, 80, 106, 136, 204
'People Of The Sun', 97, 100
Perkins, Stephen, 106
'Pigs In Zen' (Jane's Addiction song), 22
Pitchshifter, 116
Plan B, 159
Plant, Robert, 7
Plato, 30, 32
Poison (band), 119
Police, The, 10
Polygram, 70
Popmart (U2 tour), 107
Popper, Karl, 32
Porno For Pyros, 58, 113
Porter, Gail, 218
Powell, Larry, 45
Presley, Elvis, 68
Price, Christopher, 163
Primus, 44, 116
Prince, 68, 70, 72
Prodigy, The, 196
Propaganda (magazine), 96
Public Enemy, 24, 53, 78, 94, 106, 115, 117, 134, 156, 157, 159, 193
Public Image Ltd (aka PIL), 21
'Punch Drunk' (Lock Up song), 24
Purple Rain (Prince album), 68
Puscifer, 183

Q (magazine), 155, 161
Quayle, Dan, 44
Questlove, 166
Quicksand (band), 77

Radio Free LA, viii, 106, 138, 180, 209
Radiohead, 156, 159
Raekwon, 199
Rage Against The Machine, 13, 24, 25, 33, 43, 44, 47, 49, 50, 53, 54, 55, 56, 57, 58, 61, 62, 63, 64, 66, 67, 68, 73, 74, 75, 77, 78, 79, 80, 81, 83, 84, 86, 87, 88, 89, 90, 91, 92, 95, 96, 97, 98, 99, 100, 101, 102, 104, 105, 106, 107, 108, 113, 114, 115, 116, 117, 118, 119, 120, 121, 123, 124, 125, 126, 127, 128, 129, 131, 132, 134, 135, 136, 137, 139, 140, 142, 143, 144, 145, 146, 147, 149, 150, 151, 152, 153, 155, 156, 157, 158, 159, 160, 162, 163, 164, 165, 166, 167, 169, 171, 172, 173, 174, 175, 178, 179, 180, 181, 182, 183, 184, 185, 187, 189, 193, 194, 196, 197, 198, 199, 200, 201, 202, 203, 204, 205, 206, 207, 208, 209, 212, 215, 216, 217, 218, 219, 220, 222, 224
  formation, 39, 40
  early shows, 50
  signing to Epic, 53
  internal dissent, 80, 105

anti-sweatshop stance, 108
influence on nu-metal, 115
split, 144
songs banned after 9/11, 152
reformation, 177
'Rage Against The Machine' (Inside Out song), 15, 42
Rage Against The Machine (demo tape, aka *American Composite*), 51, 52, 56
Rage Against The Machine (album), 56, 59, 61, 64, 67, 78, 100, 103, 108, 132
Rage Against The Machine (DVD), 108
Rage Against The Machine: XX (box set), 201, 202, 206
'Rape Me' (Nirvana song), 72
Reagan, Ronald, 69, 103, 118, 180
Real World (MTV programme), 80
Recording Industry Association of America (RIAA), 69
'Redemption' (Inside Out song), 12
Red Hot Chili Peppers, 20, 22, 44, 57, 105, 106, 116, 117, 170
Reinhardt, Django, 184
R.E.M., 167
Renegades, 145, 147, 148
Republican National Convention, 186
Revelation (record label), 12
Revelations (Audioslave album), 176
'Revolver', 101
Reynolds, Michael, 37
Reznor, Trent, 170
Rhoads, Randy, 8, 9, 15, 70
Richardson, Garth, 56, 57, 202
Riley, Boots, 192, 193
Riot Grrrl, 156, 161
Ripston, Ramona, 45
Robin Hood Tax, 169, 170
Rock And Roll Hall Of Fame, 165
Rock For Choice, 74
'Rock For Light' (Bad Brains song), 12
Rock, Kid, 118
Rolling Stone (magazine), 70, 129, 141, 145, 201, 203, 207
Rolling Stones, 18, 147
'Roll Right', 103
Roots, The, 166
Rubin, Rick, 147, 148, 149, 151, 202, 205, 207
Rule, Ja, 212
Run-DMC, 15, 115, 156
Rush, 147
'Ruthless Villain' (Eazy-E song), 147
Ryan, Paul, 202, 203, 204
RZA, 199

'Sacrifice' (Inside Out song), 12
Sai Choi, Choi, 47

241

'Salvador Death Squad Blues' (Electric Sheep song), 10
Salvation Army, 73
Samerjan, John, 126
San Andres Accords, 93
Sandinista! (Clash album), 165
Sands, Bobby, 16
Sartre, Jean-Paul, 79
Satanism, 70, 107
Satterwhite, Pamela, 28-38
Saturday Night Live (NBC TV show), 98, 99
'Say It Loud, I'm Black And I'm Proud' (James Brown song), 159
SB1070 (Arizona anti-immigration law), 198
Schneider, Dave, 130
Scorpions (band), 70
Screaming Trees, 44
Season Of The Snow Bitch (Electric Sheep film soundtrack album), 10
Seeger, Pete, 187
Sen Dog (aka Senen Reyes), 183
'Settle For Nothing', 62
Seuss, Dr, 104
Seven Year Bitch, 146
Sex Pistols, viii, 7, 11, 83, 216, 218
Sexytime (Brazilian TV programme), 199
Shandi's Addiction, 79
Sheffield, Rob, 129, 130
Shining Path (aka Sendero Luminoso), 62, 90, 101, 102, 103
'Show Me How To Live' (Audioslave song), 166
Silva, John, 144
Simmons, Gene, 79
Singleton, John, 79
'Six, Six, Six' (Degarmo & Key song), 71
Size, Roni (also Reprazent), 143
Ski School (movie), 24
Slash (aka Saul Hudson), 171
Slayer, 115, 116
'Sleep Now In The Fire', 133, 137, 139, 140, 141, 144, 156, 157
Slipknot, 116, 171
Sluiter, Liesbeth, 109, 110, 111
Smashing Pumpkins, 44, 58, 105, 119
Smith, Senator Ed, 45
Smith, RJ, 6, 67, 102
'Snakecharmer', 101
Snider, Dee, 71
Snowden, Edward, 206
Something Bitchin' This Way Comes (Lock Up album), 21, 22, 108
Somewhere Back In Time (Iron Maiden tour), 201
Son De Madera, 175
Songs And Artists That Inspired Fahrenheit 9/11 (soundtrack), 170
Sony (record label), 54, 55, 96, 97, 134, 196, 197, 222

Sony Playstation, 119, 142
Sound City (studio), 56
Sound City Movie (film and soundtrack), 204
Soundgarden, 44, 57, 150, 151, 164, 173
South Central Farmers, 175
Spandau Ballet, 161
Speak Of The Devil (Ozzy Osbourne album), 70
Spider-Man (film), 183
Spin (magazine), 70, 96, 102, 105, 155
Spitfire Tour, 113
Springsteen, Bruce, 108, 187, 201, 206
'Stairway To Heaven' (Led Zeppelin song), 7
Stanford Prison Experiment (band), 77
Star Trek: Insurrection (film), 183
Star Wars (film series), 178
Steinbeck, John, 104
Steppenwolf, 9
Stern, Howard, 121, 122
Stone Sour, 171
Stone Temple Pilots, 57, 83
'Street Fighting Man' (Rolling Stones song), 147
Street Sweeper Social Club, 192, 199
Street Sweeper Social Club (album), 193
Strummer, Joe, 159, 165
'Subterranean Homesick Blues' (Bob Dylan song), 4
Suicidal Tendencies, 73, 116
'Suicide Solution' (Ozzy Osbourne song), 71
Sunbirth Studio, 51
'Sweet Child O' Mine' (Guns N' Roses song), 43
Sweet Content (Thomas Dekker poem), 30-31
System Of A Down, 116, 170, 171, 212

'Take The Power Back', 42, 51, 62, 63
Talladega Nights (film), 183
Tankian, Serj, 170, 183, 188
Tannenbaum, Rob, 16, 134, 140
Taylor, Corey, 171
Tell Us The Truth tour, 167, 193
'Testify', 132, 134
Thatcher, Margaret, 89
The A-Team (film), 183
The Awful Truth (Bravo TV programme), 139
The Axis Of Justice Concert Series Volume 1 (Axis Of Justice album), 171
The Battle Of Los Angeles, 131, 132, 133, 134, 135, 144, 151, 164, 216
The Battle Of Mexico City, 149, 150
The Chomsky Reader, 104, 180
The Chronic (Dr Dre album), 53
The Daily News, 75
The Dangerous Lives Of Altar Boys (film and soundtrack), 153
The Decline Of Western Civilization, Part II: The Heavy Metal Years, 18
The Electric Sheep Video, 10

Index

The Fabled City (Nightwatchman album), 183, 200
'The Fabled City' (Nightwatchman song), 191
The Ghetto Blaster EP (Street Sweeper Social Club EP), 199
'The Ghost Of Tom Joad' (Bruce Springsteen song), 108, 187
The Late Late Show With Craig Ferguson (CBS TV programme), 184
'The Lights Are On In Spidertown' (Nightwatchman song), 184
The Lorax (Dr Seuss book), 104
The Most Terrifying Thing (band), 163
'The Narrows', 52
The Nation (magazine), 24
Theodore, Jon, 188
The Open Society And Its Enemies: The Spell Of Plato (Karl Popper book), 32
The Passions And The Interests (Alfred O. Hirschman book), 35
The Progressive (magazine), 152, 211
The Rage Factor (single campaign and subsequent live show), 196, 197, 212, 220
'The Twist' (Hank Ballard & The Midnighters song), 68
The Wright Stuff (TV programme), 218
The X Factor (TV show), ix, 194, 195, 196, 197, 211, 213, 215, 220, 221, 222, 223, 224
'The Whirlwind' (Nightwatchman song), 200
Tibetan Freedom Concert, 105, 129
Timbaland, 178
'Tire Me', 101
Todd Whitman, Governor Christine, 121, 123, 125, 126
Tone Loc, 115
Tool, 10, 21, 50, 58, 62, 63, 79, 119, 120, 170
'Township Rebellion', 51, 63, 100
Travolta, John, 7
Trudell, John, 34
Truman, Harry, 180
Truth Out (magazine), 200, 201
Turner, Frank, 161
Tutu, Archbishop Desmond, 75
Twisted Sister, 70, 71
'Two Tribes' (Frankie Goes To Hollywood song), 147

U2, 57, 107
UK Independence Party (UKIP), 61
Union Of Needletrades Industrial And Textile Employees (UNITE), 107, 108
United Farm Workers, 5, 78
United Nations Commissioner For Human Rights (also International Commission For Human Rights), 74, 127
United Nations Millennium Conference, 141
United States Flag Code, 98

Union Town (Nightwatchman EP), 200
Unleashed: The Story Of Tool (Joel McIver book), 63
Urban League, 73
Urungus, Oderus, 72
Use Your Illusion I/II (Guns N' Roses albums), 43

Vai, Steve, 24
Van Halen, Eddie, 8, 24
Van Halen (band), 40
Vanity (singer), 70
Velvet Revolver, 171
Venom, 70
Viet Cong, 4
Vietnam War, 3, 133, 158, 159
'Vietnow', 101
'Voice Of The Voiceless', 133

'Wake Up', 63, 181
Waking Up: Freeing Ourselves From Work (Pamela Satterwhite book), 28, 31, 34
Walker, JJ, 7
'Walk This Way' (Run-DMC/Aerosmith song), 115
Wallace, Matt, 22
Wallerstein, Immanuel, 38
Wal-Mart, 61, 70, 72, 110
Ward, Bill, 204, 205
Warhol, Andy, 104
'War Within A Breath', 97, 133
Washington Times, 45
WASP (band), 70
Weathermen (protest group), 3
Webster, William, 49
Weinglass, Leonard, 122, 128
Weister, William, 107
Wells, Steven, x, 161
'We Want It All' (Zack de la Rocha and Trent Reznor song), 170
Wham!, 161
'Wham Bam, Thank You Ma'am' (Dean Martin song), 68
'What We All Want' (Gang Of Four song), 147
'When The Levee Breaks' (Led Zeppelin song), 12
'When We Collide' (Matt Cardle song), 194
Whiley, Jo, 222, 223
White, Timothy, 67
Who Is Mumia Abu-Jamal? (leaflet), 123
Who, The (band), 40
'Wild Thing' (Tone Loc song), 115
Wilk, Brad, viii, ix, 1, 2, 39, 40, 41, 42, 50, 52, 64, 74, 79, 100, 104, 105, 111, 112, 113, 117, 118, 134, 142, 143, 145, 146, 147, 149, 152, 153, 162, 172, 173, 174, 183, 190, 191, 193, 204, 205, 208
Wilk, Selene, 146

Williams, Willie, 49
Wilson, Ward, 10
'Wind Below', 97, 103
Wind, Timothy, 45
Winfrey, Oprah, 73
'Without A Face', 97, 101
Women Alive, 107
Woodstock (festivals), 129, 130, 131, 144
Wool (band), 11
'Working Man' (Rush song), 147
World Trade Center, 138, 152, 153
World Trade Organisation, 156
World Wide Rebel Songs (Nightwatchman album), 199, 200
Wu-Tang Clan, 107, 199

X (band), 77
X, Malcolm, 103
X, Terminator (aka Norman Rogers), 117

Xtra Fancy, 24

Yardbirds, 149
'Year Of The Boomerang' (also 'Year Of Tha Boomerang'), 78, 79, 103
'You Dropped A Bomb On Me' (Gap Band song), 147, 153
'(You Gotta) Fight For Your Right (To Party)' (Beastie Boys song), 115
'Your Time Has Come' (Audioslave song), 175

Zapatismo Beyond Borders (Alex Khasnabish book), 88
Zapatista Army Of National Liberation (aka EZLN or Zapatistas), 75, 83, 84, 85, 86, 87, 88, 89, 90, 91, 92, 93, 94, 96, 97, 100, 102, 103, 106, 107, 133, 134, 136, 150, 204
Zappa, Frank, 71
Zeigler, Troy, 188